MINIATURE SHRUBS

MINIATURE SHRUBS

ROYTON E. HEATH
F.L.S. F.R.I.H. (N.Z.)

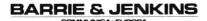
BARRIE & JENKINS
COMMUNICA-EUROPA

© Royton E. Heath 1978

First published in 1978 by
Barrie and Jenkins Ltd.
24 Highbury Crescent, London N5 1RX

ISBN 0214 20477 4

Printed litho in Great Britain
by W & J Mackay Ltd, Chatham

Contents

Introduction

Miniature shrubs have until recently been greatly neglected in the garden and often relegated to a few lines in books dealing almost exclusively with rock plants. That they have a character all of their own and that they are eminently suitable not only for the rock garden but also in a mixed shrub border or even in a border of their own is apparent to cultivators who have grown a really comprehensive collection of these delightful small shrubs.

This becomes even more important today with the ever rising spiral of land prices, resulting in the decrease of available garden space. Not confined to the cities and towns the spread of smaller gardens has encroached on suburbia as well. These little plots if given a backcloth of dwarf shrubs which will not outgrow their allotted space even in a decade, will over the whole year give both form and grace, enhanced in due season with flowers, followed often with decorative fruits and in many instances autumn coloration of leaves.

If both evergreen and deciduous shrubs are grown in conjunction with each other they present a picture even during the dull winter months with their grace of form often enhanced with berries. These backed by foliage in the evergreen forms which seem to be more attractive at this period of the year freed from floral competition, provide delightful scenic pictures. Shrubs such as the *Gaultherias, Pernettyas, Rhododendrons, Skimmia* and ground covers like *Schizocodon* and *Shortia* to name but a few come into their own and provide a picturesque focal point in winter. *Shortias* and *Schizocodons* are of particular interest in that their persistent colourful foliage in rich reds merging to lustrous browns is retained throughout winter. These coupled with the berried species of shrubs are exceedingly attractive.

The careful placing of the deciduous species by using a backcloth of evergreen shrubs allows their natural structural formation to be seen to the best advantage. This is more so in small shrubs where the scenic balance is maintained seldom marred by injudicious pruning and their many shapes, prostrate, pendulous and erect are at their best at this period of the year. The branch and twig formation are just as delightful in the smaller editions of the taller species and are not only in keeping with the small garden but also appear less artificial.

Another point to remember is that a shrub border once planted needs very little after care, just a light forking over once a year and then a topdressing in late spring to retain moisture of either peat or some other form of organic material to which has been added a little general fertiliser. If no underplanting is carried out weeds can be controlled by the application of one of the proprietary weedkillers which kill these and is itself neutralised as soon as it comes in contact with the soil.

In the rock garden shrubs serve a threefold purpose, first they can be considered the backbone of a collection with their diverse shapes providing the necessary scenic picture which would be dull and uninteresting if confined to prostrate herbaceous perennials and evergreen cushion plants. Secondly they give shelter to the many rare alpine plants from searing dry winds or the extremely harmful midday sun, this mode of shelter being more decorative than rocks. Lastly and most important, as I have already said, they usually provide a grand floral display often enhanced in late summer and autumn with brightly coloured fruits thus giving at least nine months of useful service.

If the main object is to use these shrubs for the rock garden a little forethought will repay the planter for these will be permanent tenants, many are bad transplanters once they have settled down and resent disturbance. Shelter or shade according to their needs can be achieved by the use of rocks and with the exception of such sun loving genera amongst which *Cytisus, Genista* and *Helianthemum* are prominent, the midday sun can sometimes do more harm than good. As plants for the front of the border or as beds on their own, the natural association with other plants will provide shelter to those requiring it, especially root shade where the plants are surface rooting. Far more plants are lost through failure to provide this than is generally realised. The prostrate rock-hugging species and varieties should be used in the higher reaches of the rock garden while the columnar and fastigiate forms are best kept to the middle heights. The position is changed in the small shrub border; here the prostrate mat-forming species are best accommodated in the front whilst the larger will provide the backcloth. Care should be taken that a uniform grouping is broken up by the judicious placing of dot plants otherwise the whole border will appear like a regiment of soldiers graded to size.

The majority of suitable shrubs fall into three categories. There are the natural species from all over the world and these range from completely prostrate hard-wooded plants which in nature mould themselves to rocks over which they clamber. They can be used in the small garden as a cover for the more erect growing shrubs which in themselves are still small subjects rarely above 50 cm. high. The second category is of the many improved forms and cultivars which have been bred from the natural species, these sometimes producing dwarf forms which by vegetative increase are induced to become permanent inhabitants in our gardens.

The third category is of the unusual and often bizarre forms which nature produces either from dwarf seedlings of normal sized trees or 'witches' brooms'. To date no satisfactory explanation has yet been given as to why normal arborescent trees capable of growing over 40 m. high can produce seed from which dwarf trees will grow that are less than 60 cm. high when twenty to thirty years old. It is only on rare occasions that the dwarf characteristics are fixed for the next generation of seedlings. If seed is produced at all it will normally revert once again to forest trees. 'Witches' brooms' are abnormal shoots which occur on the branches of trees resembling birds' nests with a congested

viii

mass of dwarf branchlets. There have been several theories put forward as to why they appear. The best known are: some abnormal constriction of the sap; deformity set up by infection from insect attack; or bud mutation or fungus infection. Whatever the cause it will be found that they invariably come true if propagated by cuttings and to a lesser degree by grafts, although with the latter they often tend to bear abnormal shoots similar to the type of tree from which they originated. Conifers are prone to 'witches' brooms' and it is always worthwhile to study stands of arborescent conifers in the chance of discovering whether there are any 'witches' brooms' present. Birch, willows and wild cherries are amongst trees which often bear 'witches' brooms'.

Within the confines of a small garden it is possible to specialise in different types of gardens. Space could be arranged to have a collection of stone or artificial troughs in which different species of small shrubs suitably underplanted could be used. Beds for shade-loving shrubs are ideal in a peat garden. Raised scree beds too, can be constructed to grow a representative number of the rarer shrubs suitably underplanted with the mat-forming shrubs from high altitudes. There are others such as collections of the dwarf forms of roses, or complete beds of heathers dotted with one or two of the columner growing small conifers such as *Chamaecyparis lawsoniana* 'Ellwoodii' and *Juniperis communis* 'Compressa' to give a scenic balance to the whole.

These different aspects which can be successfully adapted in a small garden are explained in more detail in the chapter on Types of Gardens.

In a small work of this nature it is not possible to give more than a condensed list of miniature shrubs for the rock or small garden. There are over a thousand species and varieties which come within this category, all being suitable although not all suited to one individual garden, with every type of soil, aspect and climatic conditions to take into account. The plants have been chosen so that there are types for both calcareous and neutral mediums also shade- and sun-lovers thus providing a good number of dwarf shrubs which can be successfully grown whatever the conditions offered. Types of soil are legion, often varying from garden to garden in the same district so that specific instructions cannot normally be given for individual plants. Where special conditions are required these have been noted when dealing with the plants in question. No instructions mean that the plants will grow in any ordinary well drained medium. Size too must be a consideration for the great majority of gardens being limited in area today the need for small plants was never more apparent. Nothing lends itself so well for this type of gardening as a planting of really dwarf conifers so I have included a selction of these plants, keeping them together for ease of reference.

With few exceptions all plants noted here can be relied upon not to exceed 12 to 80 cm. in stature over a period of years although the spread may be greater, but this can be constrained by careful pruning or in the case of soft-wooded specimens these can be trimmed back to the required size. In relation to size I am writing about the drier side of the country, here in West Kent the rainfall is similar to that generally experienced on the eastern seaboard therefore many of these plants will grow more luxuriously in the moister warmer climatic conditions of the west. This should be taken into account when studying the list of suitable plants.

I have given a great deal of thought to the illustrations for this work as this can be difficult. Because of their size, when the complete plant or say, a group of plants is photographed the result far too often is a meaningless jumble rarely portraying the shrub to its best advantage. Accordingly, I have tried to take, where possible pictures, often in close-up, that give a better view of the shrub, even if it is only a part of the plant in question.

1. Types of Gardens

SHRUB BORDERS

If the object is a labour-saving garden then underplanting of miniature shrubs with dwarf bulbs or corms is the answer. With a careful choice from a widely available selection it is possible to create a colourful carpet of flowers from dwarf bulbs or corms over a period of nine months so that, even when the shrubs have finished flowering, colour is still maintained. The majority can be left to multiply over a number of years with only a minimum of attention, consisting of a yearly dressing of coarse bone meal and humus in the form of peat or leaf-mould in early spring. Roughly a handful of bone meal to a pailful of humus will be sufficient. Their foliage also acts as a deterrent to weeds so that labour is reduced to a minimum.

There is a large selection of suitable bulbs or corms to choose from and these include the following. The 'onions' *Alliums*, summer flowering plants; *Anemones* mostly early spring, forming wide carpets of dainty flowers; 'Glory of the Snow' *Chionodoxas*, March, April; *Crocus* the garden or Dutch forms are well known for a colourful display in early spring, but the species are far superior, normally flowering at a time of the year when colour is at a premium. They are divided into autumn-flowering (August to November), winter flowering (December to February) and spring (February to late March) and these, if left undisturbed, will seed themselves quickly, filling any bare patches of soil, especially under deciduous shrubs. Where partial shade can be given the small *Cyclamen* species are ideal corms which once planted can be left to increase by seeding themselves under small deciduous and evergreen shrubs. Both in and out of flower they are charming, for all have extremely decorative foliage and it is possible to have them in flower from mid August until mid May. Like the *Crocus* species they benefit from a mulch of humus to which bone meal has been added during the dormant season.

The winter aconites *Eranthis* will give a good display in early spring and will readily increase if left undisturbed, they are ideal for planting beneath small rhododendrons. Snowdrops too provide a grand display in late February–March and are useful in sun or part shade. Where a sunny position can be provided the dwarf bulbous *Iris* make welcome clumps in early spring and can flower from late February through

1

March. In a warm sheltered spot *Lapeyrousia cruenta* can be relied upon to flower throughout the summer months with their charming scarlet-crimson flowers. The 'grape hyacinths', *Muscari*, can be had in a variety of species and forms and all make a grand display in different shades of blue during spring. There are a number of dwarf daffodils up to 15 cm. high that can be used under deciduous shrubs for a range of shapes and colour from a pale lemon to a golden-yellow in the months from February to April. The 'squills', *Scilla*, can also be naturalised in a small shrub garden and these will give a good display in early spring. One or two varieties of montbretias, *Crocosmia*, will spread quite rapidly in a dry warm spot and provide a colourful display during late summer. The small Tulip species are not recommended as they rarely get enough sun to ripen their bulbs in this country.

RAISED SCREE BEDS

Another form of gardening which has come to the fore in recent years is the raised scree bed and this type of gardening is ideal where space is at a premium. Modern architecture too has a tendency to be box-like or square in outline and the raised scree bed fits into this type of building as if designed for it.

Basically the raised scree bed consists of a shell in the form of a box-like structure and can be of any length to suit the site where it is to be built. The actual width will naturally depend on the available space but to be really effective should not be less than 50 cm. across. The outer casing can be built from several types of materials; for instance natural walling stone or broken paving slabs, which are cheaper and easily obtainable from local council yards. The natural stone is expensive unless there is a source of supply locally or manufactured concrete slabs that can be obtained in a variety of shapes and sizes. For cheapness the broken slabs are useful as these come in a uniform thickness of 5 cm. are quite easy to lay with a spirit level, producing a neat worthwhile job. Size is of no importance, but the slabs should not be too wide for as much space as possible is needed between the two walls for planting.

If the beds are to be built as an edging to a lawn or flower border it will be necessary to provide a firm base, consisting of a fillet of cement and ballast in the proportion of one part cement to four parts ballast, laid 7 cm. deep along the sides and ends of the site. The slabs or natural stone are best laid in a cement mix of three parts builder's or soft sand to one part cement with the rough or broken edges facing the front of the bed. Use a spirit level to ensure that the courses of slabs are horizontal, and lay subsequent layers until the desired height is reached. The height is of some importance and will depend on what the basal medium is. On a stone or concrete base such as one finds on a terrace the minimum should be about 30 cm. or five courses of slabs and cement; this will allow enough depth for the drainage and compost. When constructing the raised scree bed drainage holes must be left at intervals along the base of the whole length of the structure, the gaps having pieces of perforated zinc cemented over them to prevent ingress by snails, slugs, woodlice and other pests.

On heavy clay soils the height of 30 cm. is also a minimum height, for the base soil must not be used as a drainage base, otherwise after

2

heavy or prolonged rainfall this will act as a sump with disastrous results to the plants. On walls built in this type of soil ample drainage holes must be left in the first course of stone or paving slabs and the same precautions regarding pests taken. On light loams or sandy soils the minimum can be cut to 15 cm. or about three courses of slabs for the soil base with the addition of broken rubble or over similar coarse material to provide the drainage.

The method of filling and planting these raised scree beds, whatever the length or depth is as for troughs or other containers, bearing in mind whether lime-loving or -hating shrubs are to be grown. If there is any doubt it is far better to use a lime-free medium for although lime-loving plants can grow in a lime-free medium, lime haters will not thrive in a compost containing lime. For the rarer and less easy shrubs a different compost is required, these plants are noted in the List of Plants as being suitable for the scree. Over good drainage the medium should consist of 75% coarse sand to 25% flaked leaf-mould, peat must not be used as it contains no food elements at all. The shrubs can be planted in this and prostrate cushion alpine plants used as a surface cover. If the whole is then surfaced with chippings, limestone chippings must not be used if the occupants are lime haters, and dressed with small pieces of rockstone suitably placed, a living picture will be created which will show a constant changing face over the whole of the year.

Possibly one of the greatest assets of this type of gardening is that once satisfactorily planted, upkeep is minimal and the whole bed becomes a garden in miniature lasting and improving over a good number of years. All that is required in the way of feeding is a fort-nightly watering with a diluted liquid manure, one containing trace elements is ideal, during the growing and flowering season.

PEAT BEDS

With the building density that is the outcome of the existing land shortage today, shade is often a problem. The majority of plants require a good deal of light and this includes sun to give of their best. There is one group of shrubs which do better in half or even full shade and these are the members of the large *Ericaceae* and other kindred families. Many dislike full sun, especially in the southern counties, where coupled with a dry atmosphere they soon show signs of distress or even collapse.

There is a type of garden which is an ideal home for these plants and for want of a better name is called the 'Peat Garden'. The chosen position should be marked out in any desired shape to suit available space, even the smallest can grow a representative collection, while a larger area will enable one to cultivate some of the small fastigiate rhododendrons. If the natural soil is neutral, or on the acid side, the top 15 cm. should be well broken up and if on the heavy side drainage in the form of rubble, broken bricks etc. incorporated.

It is possible to grow lime-hating plants on a chalky soil by leaving the surface of the soil firm and spreading an 8 cm. layer of really rough bracken over this before laying the compost on top.

Peat blocks are readily available today, at least one well-known firm sells them already cut to a uniform size and bagged for delivery. They

3

are approximately 30 cm. in length by 10 cm. deep and wide. One important thing to do before starting to build is to see that the blocks are well moistened, for once in position it will be found that it is almost impossible for them to absorb sufficient water. If for some reason or other they are dry it will be necessary to soak them for at least twenty-four hours before use. This is best carried out by immersing them in a container filled with water. Watering with a hose or can is useless, this will just run off without the peat blocks absorbing any of it.

To build the peat bed the blocks should be laid as in building a brick wall. Each layer of blocks being bonded, these should have a slight inward tilt as each layer is laid. At the same time a soil mixture comprising four parts of leaf-soil or horticultural peat, one part fibrous neutral loam and one of coarse sand should be worked in amongst the joints as one would use mortar; fill the bed as building continues. It is not necessary to build high, 30 cm. being ample, especially in districts where the annual rainfall is low as there may be a tendency for the soil to dry out if there is a prolonged dry spell. This means that three courses of peat blocks will be needed. In districts where birds, who have a tendency to pull off the top layer of blocks, are plentiful, it will pay to peg the blocks down by driving through the centre of each block thin iron rods. The large metal meat skewers are ideal and these will effectively pin and make the structure secure. When filled with the prepared compost a light treading is needed to consolidate the soil and a period allowed to elapse before planting is started, making good any depressions which may occur during the interim period. If built in late autumn or early winter the bed will have settled by the following spring.

The best period for planting is in early April if pot-grown plants are used and September if planting from the open ground. The plants should be well firmed in and watered, a mulching of peat being placed over the roots afterwards to conserve moisture and keep them cool. Great care must be taken the first summer after planting to ensure they do not suffer from drought, as this is the critical time for the complete re-establishment of the plants. There is a wide choice of shrubs which will thrive in this type of garden, from the dwarf creeping species only a few centimetres high to the more upright plants of up to 45 cm.

HEATHER GARDENS

In a small garden space can often be found to grow a fair number of the dwarf species and varieties of this family together in a collection that will give colour either of flower or foliage over the whole year. Contained in the heaths are all the *Ericas* and *Daboecias* and all their forms while the Heathers belong to that monotypic genus *Calluna* and its many forms but here I use the heading 'Heather Gardens' to include all species and forms of the three genera.

Their main requirement is an open porous medium, not rich, for this can result in foliage but fewer flowers. They require sun to flower well, so the part of the garden chosen should have either a south or south-west aspect. The majority of heathers demand a lime-free soil and the only exception to this is the varieties of *Erica herbacea (carnea)* which will tolerate some kind of lime in some places. Even here it will be necessary to add plenty of peat to the soil in which they are to be grown.

4

Where possible planting should be in groups of at least three, six is better if room is available and the varieties chosen should be carefully mixed so that there is colour either of foliage or flower over the whole year. Planting distance is from 15 cm. for the real dwarfs to 46 cm. for the taller growing varieties and this should be carried out so that the smaller plants are mixed with the taller, thus the overall effect is of undulating hillocks. Small conifers such as *Chamaecyparis lawsoniana* 'Ellwoodii' and *C. pisifera* 'Filifera' can be used as dot plants to break up the formal outline. The varieties which have an added attraction with their brightly coloured foliage must be in a position facing south or south-west for they need sun to show this to best advantage.

ROCK GARDENS

The small garden is an ideal situation in which to construct a rock garden and here the dwarf shrubs mingle well with the small cushion-like rock plants giving both colour and form throughout the year.

I do not believe in giving plans for a rock garden but just a few basic rules as no two sites are the same and no two gardeners think alike. Each must build to his own choice and although some may find difficulty in achieving a rock garden *par excellence*, the majority will get great satisfaction from creating a landscape in miniature. There are many good books on rock gardens and they can be studied to give ideas to suit ones particular needs.

An open site is best and this should be away from large trees, although in a small garden it is doubtful if there will be any present. A light well-drained soil is needed, and should the natural soil be of clay or heavy loam the rock garden is best built above the surrounding level to ensure that the drainage is perfect. If this is not possible then raised scree beds may be the answer for success depends on the drainage being faultless. The addition of a really coarse washed sand will help, but on no account should builders' sand be used as this is too soft and will only bind the soil together forming a hard pan almost like concrete.

It is not necessary to provide special soils if the normal type of dwarf shrubs are being grown as most are adaptable. For plants which require more specialised conditions either the scree or peat beds can be utilised.

It is difficult to give precise instructions on the actual building of a rock garden, so much depends on the available space and type of rock to be used. It should be remembered that the ultimate aim is to grow plants not rocks. It is always possible to grow plants without rocks but a garden of rocks without plants is neither required nor desired. The best rock to use is that which can be obtained locally, for this could be cheaper as the further it has to come the greater the transport costs.

When laying the rocks the most important thing to remember is that a firm steady base is essential and enough rock should be buried to ensure this. If the stone has a natural stratum this must be parallel to the surface on which the rocks lie and not mixed, some with horizontal strata and some vertical; nothing looks more artificial than this. I have always been of the opinion that a simple outcrop is fundamentally the best, and much easier both to construct and plant, also from the aesthetic point of view it is the nearest approach to Nature that one can achieve in a limited space.

CONTAINERS FOR SHRUBS

With the advent of small gardens the use of containers to hold plants have come into their own. Until a decade or so ago these were confined in the main to the natural stone sinks or troughs. In the early days it was possible to obtain the real article for a small sum but as they became popular and the number being limited, the cost has risen to an almost prohibitive figure. There are many stone substitutes on the market and the local garden centres are now making a feature of these artificial containers. They can be obtained in moulded plastic which are very durable, artificial stoneware, or even troughs made up from natural stone. The average amateur can also make up containers to suit the existing surroundings. Broken walling or paving stone can be used if a natural effect is required or the container can be constructed from the many artificial ornamental bricks that are available.

Whatever type of container is used it should be as large as possible. A small one less than 60 cm. by 45 cm. and 30 cm. deep is not suitable, the reason being that during hot dry spells watering becomes a problem and if left unattended for a few days will result in the death of many plants. It must have drainage holes in the base for without these the plants will become waterlogged in wet spells and here again the results are just as fatal.

Over faultless drainage a good compost should be placed, John Innes No. 3 is suitable provided the shrubs to be grown are lime-tolerant. If the plants are lime-haters such as rhododendrons, dwarf heathers etc. a special soil must be used. A good mixture is equal parts of a good medium-heavy loam from a lime-free source and leafmould or peat to one part sharp sand. If peat has to be used, this being a sterile medium devoid of food a quarter part of well-rotted manure or hop manure should be added. Whatever the mixture, it should be allowed to settle for a week or so then be topped up to within an inch of the top and watered, after which the container is ready for planting.

There are many uses to which these troughs or containers can be put, such as a collection of dwarf roses which will give colour from June to when the frosts appear in autumn. A display of the smaller conifers makes a fine scenic picture and if these are underplanted with the cobweb houseleek *Sempervivum arachnoideum* the combination is extremely effective throughout the year. Another idea is in a semi-shady position a plantation of the dwarf willows. *Salix* species will in spring present a dainty display of the different coloured catkins which over a period of weeks will present a charming scene of changing colour.

There are many other combinations of the smaller almost cushion-like shrubs including dwarf heathers, prostrate rhododendrons and the many charming miniature ericaceous shrubs which are made to measure for this type of gardening. If obtainable locally an added refinement is the use of small pieces of natural rockstone. These can be arranged to suit the shrub being grown and it is surprising how easy it is to build up an artistic scene with the judicious use of this stone. A top dressing with small stone chipping will then complete the picture.

2. Propagation

SEED DIVISION LAYERING CUTTINGS FRAMES

A general knowledge of the art of propagation is essential to keen amateurs who desire to increase their stock of plants. It is a fascinating side of the cultivation of dwarf shrubs and conifers and is well worth the time and trouble spent in carrying out the simple but necessary rules.

There are five main methods of reproduction. These are: by seed, cuttings, layering, division and grafting. Of these a knowledge of the first four is all that will be required, for grafting is a method of propagation which should be avoided at all costs when reproducing dwarf plants that have occurred either as sports or 'witches' brooms' from a normal sized plant or from seedlings which have produced a number of dwarf forms.

Seed is Nature's method of reproduction of the species and should be employed wherever practicable. There is no doubt that a plant raised from seed is more healthy and less liable to disease than anything reproduced by vegetative means. The raising of plants by this method is not however, always a practical means of increase, for a large number of flowering shrubs, especially the more prostrate types, do not readily set viable seed in this country. If the specimen from which the seed is collected is only a small form of a naturally tall-growing species the chances of the resultant plants being dwarf will be very remote although in a batch of seedlings there may be an outstanding new dwarf variety.

Propagation by cuttings is the most likely method that amateurs will employ for there is a certainty that the resultant plants will be in all aspects identical with the specimens from which they are taken and they are easier to deal with from the time of taking the cuttings until they are rooted ready to be planted out or potted up.

It is also possible to increase certain shrubs by division and this is an easy means of increase where this method can be employed.

Layering should be attempted with the low-growing plants which have trailing or flexible stems and do not readily root by any other means.

SEED

Seed is best sown when ripe where there is any doubt as to the length of time it will remain viable; in this connexion it may be mentioned that generally the smaller the seed the shorter the time it will remain good. All other seeds are best sown at the end of February, or when otherwise noted.

7

Compost

It is not possible to give more than a general idea of compost best suited to the majority of flowering shrub seeds but the following three should cover all plants dealt with here.

1. For the majority of seeds which require normal conditions outside in the rock or small garden the John Innes seed compost has proved successful.

2. For the rarer, sun-loving shrubs and more difficult plants the following is a good compost.

One part of heavy loam and leaf-mould, sieved through a $\frac{1}{16}$ in. (1.5 mm.) sieve to two parts of coarse sand.

3. Ericaceous plants, including rhododendrons and all woodland and shade-loving plants, do well in a compost containing equal parts of leaf-mould, Sorbex peat and coarse sand.

Sowing

The seed should be sown on the surface and covered with a topdressing of coarse sand. The amount of coverage should be in ratio to the size of the seed. A good working rule is the same depth of sand as the width of the seed. With minute seeds I have found that before sowing, a fine layer of sifted coarse sand should be placed over the compost and the seed sown direct on to this not covered at all. To facilitate the sowing of fine seed evenly it should be mixed with equal quantities of dry sand. All seed should be sown thinly and where possible, as with large seeds, individual placing will allow the resulting seedlings to grow healthily and strongly without being overcrowded. Seeds of rhododendrons and other ericaceous subjects and of woodland plants, are best sown direct onto a layer of sphagnum moss which has been finely chopped up and made firm on top of the compost; no further covering is needed.

The pans should be placed by immersing the pan in water until the surface of the compost darkens. Overhead watering must not be employed, for this will cause the seeds to be washed out of the soil, generally to one corner of the pan.

Pricking out

More plants are lost during their first move than at any other time of their lives, great care is necessary when removing the young seedlings as soon as they have formed their first true leaves.

Damage to the roots must be avoided at all costs otherwise there is a likelihood of spoiling the young plant, if not killing it. Before attempting to remove the seedlings from the seed pan the pan should be well watered so that it will be possible to lift out the plant without damage to its roots. A very handy tool for this purpose can be made out of a strong piece of wood, oak for preference, shaped like a wedge at one end and notched at the other, roughly 6 in. (15 cm.) in length by $\frac{3}{8}$ in. (1 cm.) wide, this will allow the removal of the seedlings from the seed pan to the potting bench without damaging or bruising the delicate plant.

The young plants should be potted up in small 'thumbs' or 2 in. (5 cm.) pots, using the appropriate soil mixture (see seed composts) over good drainage, to which has been added an extra part of heavy loam.

These pots should then be placed in a closed frame in a shaded spot for a few days, afterwards admitting a little air until they have settled in the new compost. From this potting the young plants can be placed out in their final quarters in the garden.

DIVISION

Many woody plants can be pulled to pieces, each part with a number of roots attached, and carefully placed in a nursery bed for a few weeks until they have become established, then they may be planted out in their permanent quarters. Spring is the ideal time for division and it is preferable to remove all flower buds if these are present to conserve the energy of the plant while it is recovering from the shock of division. Delicate or rare shrubs which have only a few wiry roots should be treated as cuttings and placed in the cutting frame until re-established.

LAYERING

To increase the stock by this method it is necessary for the amateur to choose the low growing dwarf mat-forming shrubs which readily lend themselves to propagation by this means owing to their natural tendency to root where the prostrate branchlets are in contact with the soil. The small rhododendrons and ericaceous plants are also good subjects for rooting by layering and other plants can be increased in this way.

Method

Spring is the best time of the year to carry out this operation and the method is as follows; all surfacing material such as chippings should be removed from round the base and extending to the diameter of the plant. A compost of equal parts leaf-mould and coarse sand is then spread over this area to a depth of 8 cm. this being retained by a banking of small stones so that the rooting medium will not be washed away during heavy rainfalls. The depth of compost will allow the branches to be bent down into position without any undue strain or fear of snapping.

Laterals and foliage where the layer is in contact with the soil must be removed. A slit is made in the branchlets and the shoots pinned down firmly. This is essential, for any looseness at this point will prevent the shoot from rooting. At no time must the rooting compost be allowed to dry out, and a constant watch is necessary during the hot summer months to see that does not occur. A layer of small stones placed over the shoots will do much to conserve and maintain a steady moisture content of the soil. The period necessary before rooting takes place will depend to a large extent on the type of shrub being propagated. Some difficult plants may take up to two years by this method but even if it is a slow process it is almost a certainty and very often the only means of increasing the stock. No attempt should be made to disturb the branches for at least six months even for the easy species. After this period has elapsed the compost should be gently scraped away and if rooting has taken place the layer should be severed from the parent plant. Allow the rooted plant to remain for a further period to recover from this shock, then it may be potted up or transplanted to its permanent position.

CUTTINGS

Of all the methods of propagation this is the one most commonly employed to increase stock. For the perpetuation of a good form, hybrid or a sport this is the only method for amateurs, although grafting is very often used in commercial houses where the need of a mature plant in the shortest possible time is the deciding factor. The drawback of propagation by this means has already been stressed early on in this chapter; too often a dwarf plant loses all its dwarf characteristics when grafted.

Type of cutting

When dealing with cuttings the greatest difficulty to be overcome is knowing when and what type of cutting is suitable. There are two distinct kinds, green cuttings and cuttings taken from well-ripened wood, or soft-wood and hard-wood cuttings respectively. The first is generally used for all evergreen shrubs and cuttings that are struck with the aid of bottom heat. The second week in June and up to the third week in August is the normal time to take this type of cutting but a great deal will depend on the current season's weather. A cold spring can mean that the date of taking the wood for the use of cuttings may have to be retarded for a period of up to two weeks. All the times of the year quoted here are applicable for gardens in the south of England where normally ripening will take place approximately two weeks earlier than in the north. Due allowance should be made for this, but as with all other gardening operations it is impossible to lay down hard and fast rules as to the best period.

The ability to know when the wood is ripe enough can only be obtained with experience and it is recommended that cuttings be taken over a period until proficiency is attained. A general idea of when a shoot is ready can be given, the tip or growing shoot should be firm but not hard and a good test is to bend a shoot. If this shoot cracks or breaks readily it is ideal for the purpose, but if it only bends the cutting is not yet sufficiently ripe. Side shoots should be used in preference to leading shoots and these may be up to 8 cm. in length.

The second type of cutting in which the shoot is well ripened is generally used for deciduous shrubs, taken at the end of October and allowed to stay in the cutting frame until the following spring when rooting should start to take place.

How to make cuttings

A side shoot with a heel of old wood attached is torn away from the parent plant with a sharp downward pull. It is now prepared for the cutting frame by neatly trimming the heel, taking care not to cut into the hard core of the wood, and removing all leaves, where evergreens are concerned, from the base to one third of the length. There is on the market a synthetic rooting hormone in powder form in two grades which are suitable for shrubs. They are 'B' for semi-hard cuttings and 'C' for hard-wood. All that is necessary is to prepare the shoot in the usual way, then dip 1 cm. of the prepared end in water, afterwards placing it in the correct grade of powder. Shake the cutting free of all loose powder and it is then ready to be inserted in the compost.

Inserting the cuttings

A hole large enough to take the cutting is made with a dibber so that when it rests on the bottom, the leaves are just above the surface of the compost. Next place the dibber in the soil round the cutting and firm the compost by an inward-pressing movement towards the shoot. All cuttings should be neatly set in rows, close to but not touching each other, then when all are inserted an overhead watering with a fine rose watering-can should be given. This will settle the compost round the cuttings.

Labels with the name of the plant and date written on them should be inserted in the compost at the front of each batch of cuttings.

Striking the cuttings

There are three methods widely in use by which cuttings are rooted. They are; first a closed frame situated in a cool position facing north for preference where the large majority of cuttings can be successfully rooted. A frame in this position is almost essential for the rooting of plants which need a shady situation. This is an ideal method where the garden has to be left all day, for a frame of this description only needs attention in the morning and evening and possibly not even that often. A great deal depends on the weather. Naturally during hot dry spells more attention will be needed than when the weather is less settled or the humidity is high.

Second, a small frame in which bottom heat can be employed. This is used to root the more delicate, difficult or rare plants, many of which would not strike by the first method.

Last, the method used a great deal by professionals; that is, frames situated in a sunny spot where green cuttings are inserted in sand and kept moist. This means that a constant watch must be maintained, for at no time must the cuttings be allowed to flag, and watering has to be carried out continually throughout the day.

Of these three methods I shall describe only the first two in detail for the third is not a practical one for the ordinary amateur, for the time needed in watering alone during the hot summer months would be excessive.

FRAMES

The closed frame

A useful size for a cutting frame for a small garden, to be placed in a position facing north, is 1 m. by 75 cm., the body being constructed of brickwork, 1 m. at the rear and 84 cm. at the front. A brick built frame has several advantages over a wooden one; it is rot proof, practically everlasting, temperature fluctuations are not so great (this is an important item in a cutting frame) and the moisture content is more constant so reducing the need for frequent watering. The frame light should be a good fit for a close atmosphere is necessary for striking cuttings.

The propagating frame is filled to half its depth with broken bricks or clinker, followed by a fine layer of peat or leaf roughage to prevent the drainage from becoming blocked up. The remainder is filled to within 15 cm. of the top with 2 parts of sharp sand and 1 part of fine peat. The frame is then well watered with rainwater to which 2 tsp.

potassium permanganate for each gallon (4.546 l.) of water has been added, making sure that all compost is well saturated. Afterwards a good watering with clear water is given and the frame closed for twenty-four hours to obtain an even temperature; it is then ready to receive the cuttings.

The heated frame

There are two methods by which bottom heat can be applied to frames for the purpose of striking cuttings. The first is by installing one of the mains-voltage soil heaters which are obtainable commercially and may be used in a similar type of frame to that just described. The mains-voltage element, which is a length of resistance wire, should be spread out evenly on top of a 5 cm. depth of sharp sand over the drainage. The maker's instructions should be followed exactly and there should be no danger or risk of shock in using this system.

This method is fairly economical to run. 12.20 m. of resistance wire consumes only 150 watts of electricity and covers an area of approximately 7 sq. m. and if a thermostat is installed the cost of heating, if the rooting compost is maintained at about 15°C. (60°F.), is extremely low over a normal season. There is no doubt that this is best, where it can be employed, for not only can a greater number of plants be increased with the use of bottom heat, but also cuttings can be rooted during periods when it is not possible by other means.

The other, where a greenhouse is available, is to purchase one of the propagating frames which abound in different sizes on the market today. These can be obtained with or without heat and here again used according to the maker's instructions.

Management of frame

The outdoor frame must be kept closed and watered every day during spring, summer and early autumn. It is a good plan to keep a small maximum and minimum thermometer in this cutting frame so that a record can be kept of any fluctuation of temperature as this must be avoided as much as possible, for a steady temperature facilitates rooting. A temperature of 21°C. (70°F.) during the day, falling to 18°C. (65°F.) at night is ideal.

Once a fortnight a watering of potassium permanganate, 1 tsp. to a gallon (4.546 l.) of rainwater, should be substituted for plain water. This has a twofold action, it keeps in check the growth of moss which always accompanies overhead watering and also acts as a mild stimulant. A watch should be kept for any rotting tissues or dead leaves and these should be removed at once. If left they are liable to set up stem rot disease among all the cuttings.

During winter it will only be necessary to give enough water to keep the compost from drying out and it is a good plan to wipe any moisture off the inside of the frame light, at the same time admitting a little air when the weather is fine. During damp, foggy or frosty weather withhold water entirely.

When well rooted the cuttings are potted on into a compost consisting of 2 parts sand, 1 part loam and 1 part of leaf-mould and removed to a shaded frame which should be kept closed until the roots have taken a hold of the compost and new growth has commenced. They can then be gradually hardened off by admitting air in increasing quantities. Once well established the plants can be planted in the garden.

3. Transplanting

PLANTING PRUNING

Evergreens

There are several do's and dont's to be observed when transplanting shrubs in the open ground. Evergreens are best moved from early September to the middle of October and the last two weeks of April to the first two weeks in May. It does not necessarily follow that they cannot be planted at other times of the year but unless constant attention can be given there is a chance that they will fail. Naturally, warm moist weather is ideal for moving evergreens but in any case it is advisable to spray these plants with water both morning and evening until root action has taken place once more. This will do much to prevent excessive loss of moisture through transpiration which is not easily replaced until the roots are again working properly.

To prevent undue check to these plants, including conifers, which are normally bad transplanters, I have used the following method over many years with success.

For a period of up to two months before the plant is lifted a spade is thrust periodically, vertically into the soil to its full depth; this being repeated until a circle equal to the spread of the branches has been cut. This has, to a certain extent, the effect of root pruning but unlike bodily transplanting a plant at once it allows the remaining roots contained in the ball of soil within the circle to function quite normally, thus minimising to a great degree the extent of the check sustained by the plant. During the following two weeks the soil must be kept well watered and if warm, dry or windy weather ensues during this period it will be of great assistance to the plant if it is protected by erecting a shelter on the sunny or leeward side. This may take the form of sacking suspended on stakes.

Provided that the total bulk is not too unwieldy or heavy, and this should not be so where evergreen shrubs or conifers are being transplanted, all soil within the circle should be retained. The position in which the specimen is to be replanted should have been well prepared and hole made which will allow the ball of soil containing the roots of the plant to be accommodated comfortably without any undue squeezing. A quantity of fine compost comprising equal parts of leaf-mould, loam and coarse sand should be forked in and round the edges of the soil and roots of the plant, making the whole firm. Until well established once more plenty of water should be given and it will be of great assistance to the plant if daily syringing of the foliage with water is carried out during this period of rehabilitation.

14

Deciduous shrubs

Deciduous plants are normally easier subjects to move, due, in a large measure, to the fact that transplanting is done during the dormant season when the shrub is devoid of foliage, thus the need for activity by the roots is lessened. There is at this period no loss of water due to transpiration, therefore the root system can devote all its energy to the re-establishment of the plant. It is still essential that every care is taken in transplanting deciduous shrubs and a careful watch should be maintained during the first growing season to ensure that the plant does not suffer from drought.

The period of the year when deciduous shrubs may be moved is from early November to March in the south and up to two weeks earlier and later in the north during open weather. No attempt must be made either to transplant or replant any shrub during frosty weather. They are best heeled in, in a vacant plot or kept in a frost-proof shed during the cold spell. For difficult or bad transplanters the last week of March and the first in April are advised, for at this period of the year root action has started once more and provided a careful watch is maintained to ensure plenty of moisture at the roots satisfactory results should be achieved. This time can be safely advanced by two weeks in the north of the country.

This is only a general guide, for no gardener can work to a calendar but must take all the changes of the weather in his stride and an ounce of practical common sense applied at the right time is worth a ton of theory.

PLANTING

Planting of new stock, which is usually pot grown, or larger specimens that are obtainable in containers from garden centres, can be carried out at any time of the year, except during frosty weather, and provided the plant is shaded and kept moist for a few days it will soon settle down in its new quarters. It is better to remove a little of the old soil ball so that a few of the roots are loose, then after placing in position the soil can be worked in among these roots thus allowing them to take hold of the fresh compost.

Often the early death of a plant can be traced to failure in this respect, due to the roots having remained within the old compost, and the specimen slowly starving to death.

When planting, the soil should be removed to the depth of the roots of the plant and the hole should be made wide enough for all loose roots to be spread out, not bunched together, then a mixture of equal parts of leaf-mould, loam and coarse sand can be worked in among these roots, firming the compost well. The top 2 cm. should be left in the shape of a saucer so that any watering required will reach the part of the plant where it is most needed, at the roots. After a week the depression may be filled up with either fresh compost or surfaced with chippings. It is important that the shrubs should be planted at the same depth as before.

PRUNING

Very little pruning should be necessary when growing a collection of dwarf shrubs. Sometimes these miniatures will throw an abnormal shoot and a watch must be kept for this type of growth. When noticed the branch or lateral should be cut right back to the base. Where there is a tendency for a plant to outgrow its position either in the rock garden or shrub border, a pinching back of the new growth will not only keep the plant in check but also help to retain a symmetrical balance.

4. Pests and Diseases

Unfortunately the temperate weather of these isles is conducive to the breeding of a number of pests and to the diseases to which dwarf shrubs grown in the open are prone, but a little wise planning together with common sense will do much to minimise the effect of an attack. Prevention is better than cure should be the maxim of all good gardeners. A regular routine of spraying and dusting will possibly stop an attack before it can get a good foothold, necessitating more drastic measures, so that a little time spent regularly in carrying out these operations will save a lot of heartache later on. A systematic approach should be made to the problem and a regular routine will minimise, if not completely eliminate all traces of these pests and diseases.

PESTS

There are on the market today a good number of insecticides which are effective in giving a large amount of control over a wide range of pests and a choice should be made from those available. It is not necessary to have a large supply of equipment and for the average small garden all that is needed is one sprayer with an approximate capacity of 4 pts. (2.273 1.). This will be sufficient for effective control over any infestation in a small garden.

For ease of control there is at least one combined insecticide and fungicide available which can be safely used to eliminate both pests and diseases. The active ingredients of this control are lindane, derris and thiram and these are effective against such pests and diseases as greenfly, blackfly, caterpillars, weevils, capsids, cuckoo spit, sawflies, leaf miners, red spider, ants and earwigs as well as rust, black spot, downy mildew, scab, leaf moulds and many other pests and diseases. There are only a small number of plants against which it is inadvisable to use this combined control, but as the only possible ornamental shrub is hydrangea which is in itself rarely prone to attack, only one combined insecticide and fungicide need be purchased to give maximum freedom from both pests and diseases.

DISEASES

There is now a systemic fungicide based on Benomyl which is extremely effective against most diseases, giving a good control over a long period.

5. Dwarf Conifers

The beauty of rock and small gardens is greatly enhanced by the inclusion of suitably placed dwarf conifers. Their different shapes both prostrate and fastigate allow them to be utilised to great advantage either at the base of rock work or on the higher reaches where they add a certain completeness to the whole scenic effect. Another method of cultivation of these dwarf trees is to plant them in a bed of their own. This can be prepared by cutting out an irregular shape either in the corner of a lawn or on one of the edges and arranging the conifers to suit one's own taste, there with their fantastic shapes and different coloured hues an attractive picture during the whole year can be achieved. They can also be used in the small shrub border, either as dot plants or to relieve the bareness among deciduous shrubs.

Care is necessary in choosing these delightful miniatures for a number of them offered are far from dwarf and if planted will soon outgrow their allotted position proving a nuisance on rock work, where it may even be necessary to remake a part of the rock garden. If possible, plants grown on their own roots are preferable to grafted specimens which are often quicker growing due to a vigorous rootstock but they often throw abnormal shoots, these if allowed to develop will in time dominate the whole plant. If either through scarcity or cost it is necessary to have plants which will normally outgrow their position in a short period of time, it is possible to delay this by planting the specimens *in situ* without removing them from the pots in which they are growing. A hole is made large enough to accommodate the pot and when resting on the bottom, the rim should be 2 cm. below the surface of the soil. The soil is then packed around the sides of the pot up to the rim and after firming, the last 2 cm. should be topdressed with coarse granite chippings, or a mulch of peat if being grown in the shrub border. The root restriction caused by the pot will retard growth considerably, even up to one third of the normal annual amount. A word of warning before planting, the pot should be completely immersed in water and left for at least an hour, until the compost is thoroughly moist. Failure to do this will if the soil is at all dry result in the loss of the plant.

Nomenclature of these miniatures is extremely involved in a mass of synonyms, doing duty for what are only variants from the same plants which often bear three different types of foliage, juvenile, intermediate and adult together. When it is understood that by taking basal, intermediate and top cuttings from the same plant three different resultant specimens are produced it is no wonder that so much confusion in the naming of these plants abounds. Far too many so called dwarfs are sold under names which are invalid and it will certainly be wise to deal with a reputable nurseryman who specialises in this type of conifer. A small tip which I have used with success over a large number of years is when buying these plants (the best time is late August, by then the annual growth is completed) a quick look at the amount of new wood made will give a general idea of ultimate size over a given number of years. A visit to the botanical gardens at Kew and Edinburgh and the Royal Horticultural Gardens at Wisley where there are good collections growing correctly named should be helpful in assessing true specimens.

The cultivation of these plants is simple; all need an open compost enriched with leaf-mould or peat. Lime is not essential but all will grow well in a limy medium provided there is an ample amount of humus in the soil. The bun and close branched types are best sited in a position where the base of the plant is protected from hot sunshine, a shadow thrown by an adjacent rock is ideal or dwarf carpeting plants may be used if grown in the shrub border. An annual topdressing should be given in early spring of equal parts of coarse leaf-mould and sharp sand, to which should be added bonemeal approximately 2 oz. (57 g.) to a bushel.

Space does not allow of more than a selection of dwarf conifers but the following are representative of the whole family and all can be planted with full confidence that they will not outgrow their station in ten years.

THE PLANTS

Abies (Pinaceae)

The number of species of this genus that have produced real dwarf conifers are few and there are not many of these in cultivation today.

A. balsamea var. *hudsonia* (E). (Syns. *A. hudsonia; Picea fraseri hudsonia*)
A native of N.E. America the Balsam Fir, *A. balsamea*, has produced a few dwarf forms but there are only two that are suitable for our purpose. This is a sterile form from the White Mountains, New Hampshire, growing at high altitudes. It has medium thin branchlets growing at an angle of 60°. The leaves are straight at right angles to the laterals, deep bright green above, the undersides have two sunken blue lines. The leaf margins and mibrib are dark deep green. Annual growth is from 1 to 2 cm.

A. balsamea 'Nana' (E). (Syns. *A.b.* 'Globosa'; *A.b.* 'Globosa Nana')
A form which in the past has been confused with *A.b.* var. *hudsonia* and in some cases has done duty for it. There is a great difference between them, 'Nana' forms a rounded flat topped bushlet with slender branches growing at an angle of 45°. The leaves are not straight but in the form of an arc and bright green above. Underneath there are two sunken white bands divided by a raised yellow-green median rib the whole surrounded by an edge of pale yellow. Annual growth is about 1 cm.

A. lasiocarpa 'Compacta' (E). (Syn. *A. subalpina* 'Compacta')
A closely knitted globular bushlet with small, thickish, stiff downy branchlets. Leaves small in irregular ray formation round the stem, crowded at apex, thick, slightly curved; linear, apex obtuse, bright glaucous blue-green. A slightly faster growing form with annual growth in the region of 3 cm.

Cedrus brevifolia

Cedrus (Pinaceae)

The cedars have produced a few forms which are quite suitable for culture in the garden. Unfortunately they will in the course of time become too large although such a situation may take up to twenty years depending on aspect and cultivation, so this should be borne in mind when choosing a suitable spot in the small garden.

C. brevifolia (E). (Syn. *C.libani* var. *brevifolia*)

This tree has now been accorded specific status and is a native of Cyprus where it makes a tall specimen after many years growth. Due possibly to climatic conditions here it is a dwarfer and very slow growing plant. It forms an erect tree with a stout bole, branches are borne at right angles to the trunk with a slight pendular drop at the tips. Leaves crowded linear, stout roundish up to 1 cm. in length, slightly incurved, same width along whole length, terminating in an acute sinewy tip; dark green in colour. Growth 2 to 5 cm. yearly, while young, later faster.

C. brevifolia 'Hillier Compact' (E)
A remarkable dwarf form introduced by Mr W. Archer, a well-known grower of dwarf conifers. It forms a close compact shrub of dense glaucous roundish linear leaves crowded on short branches. Very slow growing, less than 2 cm. annually.

C. libani 'Comte de Dijon' (E). (Syn. *C.* 'Comte de Dijon'; *C. libanotica* 'Comte de Dijon')
This is the rarest of the dwarf forms of the cedars of Lebanon and when offered by the trade *C. brevifolia* is often sent out for it although the form is quite distinct. It makes a very dense pyramidal bush seldom with a bole, although this is almost certain to be present on grafted forms or sometimes due to starvation when young. Branches are slightly ascending, slender and downy. Leaves crowded 1 cm. long linear, tapering to base and a sharp acute sinewy point at apex, straight not incurved, dark green. In cultivation annual growth is about 2 cm.

C. libani 'Nana' (E). (Syn. *C. libanitica* 'Nana')
A form which is near to 'Comte de Dijon' but is more spreading than upright and not so dense. Leaves larger up to 2 cm. long, similar in shape but slightly convex, tapering to both base and apex, crowded. The annual growth is approximately 5 cm. and the whole plant is coarse when compared with 'Comte de Dijon'.

C. libani 'Sargentii' (E). (Syn. *C. libani* 'Pendula Sargentii')
Sargent's Cedar is a cultivar named after Professor Sargent of the Arnold Arboretum. It should be sited carefully because it will outgrow a small garden in about fifteen to twenty years. It is a fine dwarf conifer and readily obtainable. It makes a small stout bole with radiating slender branches, horizontal at first then pendulous. Leaves crowded linear up to 5 cm. long, deep green. Annual growth in the region of 5 cm.

Chamaecyparis (Cupressaceae)

Over a great number of years this genus has been included in *Cupressus* and even today a large number of nurserymen still retain the name when selling forms. Botanically the main differences between the genera *Chamaecyparis*, the false cypress and *Cupressus*, the true cypress, is that the former have flattened branches and small cones while the latter have more rounded branches and larger cones. Also included in *Chamaecyparis* today are the many varieties once under the generic name *Retinospora*. These are nothing more than forms of *Chamaecyparis obtusa* and *C. pisifera*, but the name is invalid, although here again a number of the older generation and even some of the younger retain it on their labels.

Of all the different genera which have produced species and forms of dwarf conifers it can be said that *Chamaecyparis* is far, far ahead of all others. These alone could fill a collection of worthwhile plants that would provide a display over many years without the slightest fear of them outgrowing their allotted space. Some of the *C. obtusa* forms are among the smallest and slowest growing of all, their annual rate of growth being almost negligible.

C. lawsoniana 'Aurea Densa' (E)
This is a close compact pyramidal form, wide at the base then roundish, terminating in an acute point. Branches erect, branchlets curved and congested, leaves glaucous golden yellow. Annual growth less than 2 cm.

C. lawsoniana 'Ellwoodii' (E). (Syn. *Cupressus 1.* 'Ellwoodii')
This plant has been included because it is easily obtainable and will make a fine specimen provided it is remembered that it will grow into quite a large conifer in ten years depending on soil and situation. This can be overcome to a certain extent by planting it in a pot.

It originated from a seedling at Swanmore, Bishops Waltham, and was named after the gardener there Mr Ellwood. All plants in cultivation today are from the original seedling and these are numerous so it can be seen that it is easy to propagate and cultivate. It forms an upright column thickening from the base to the middle then tapering to apex rather abruptly. Branches erect, splayed, recurving; leaves grey-green recurved, crowded, inner leaves very pale in colour. The plant differs from *C.1.* 'Fletcheri' which it is sometimes called upon to do duty for, in that 'Fletcheri' is quicker growing, branches are upright to their tips. Leaves in opposite pairs, less crowded, blue grey-green on the outside growth but dark green towards the centre of the plant.

C. lawsoniana 'Ericoides' (E). (Syn. *Cupressus l.* 'Ericoides')
This is a form that has retained its juvenile foliage under cultivation and makes an attractive dwarf conifer for the rock or small garden. Branches erect, wiry, crimson-brown, branchlets congested columnar, colour ranging from green through to brown. Leaves very minute 2 to 4 mm. in opposite pairs, scale like but not appressed, almost horizontal to branchlets, linear with acute apex; upper surface concave with glaucous sunken median rib, below convex, keeled, glaucous. General colour bright green. Annual growth about 2 to 3 cm.

C. lawsoniana 'Filiformis Compacta' (E). (Syns. *C.l.* 'Filiformis Globosa'; *C.l.* 'Globosa Filiformis')
A good form but unfortunately will outgrow its position in the garden after a time; planting in a pot is recommended. This makes a rounded globular bush with crowded spreading crimson-brown branches. Branchlets drooping, leaves narrow ovate, appressed to stem with the exception of their tips, the whole have the appearance of whipcord, small, deep glaucous green. Annual growth in the region of 6 cm. under normal conditions.

C. lawsoniana 'Fletcheri Nana' (e)
The origin of this dwarf form is a mystery but by its appearance it would appear to have come into being by a cutting taken from the base of a plant of 'Fletcheri' with juvenile foliage. It is very compact making rounded cushions of congested feathery leaves, glaucous green in colour, the clue to its parentage is that the inner leaves have the characteristic dark green colour. The plant is never columnar in habit, always being wider at the base than in height and it retains its juvenile foliage. Annual growth in the region of 2 cm.

C. lawsoniana 'Forsteckensis' (E). (Syn. *C. forsteckiana*)
A good form which has unfortunately got itself a bad name due to grafting or the propagation of strong growing shoots. If increased only from basal cuttings it forms a slow growing compact plant. It makes a tight congested mass with abnormal contorted tasselled mossy branches, fan shaped when young. Leaves glaucous green, densely crowded on the twisted 5 to 8 cm. sprays when adult. The true dwarf forms do not exceed an annual growth of more than 3 cm.

C. lawsoniana 'Gimbornii' (E)
Another rare form not often seen but in cultivation which originated from a seedling on the Von Gimborn Estate, Doorn, Holland and is slow growing. It forms a flattish topped roundish bushlet with stout branches that have a tendency to be upright, purple tinged at apex. Laterals in the form of a fan, less flat than in 'Minima', having a distinctive twist. Foliage linear, crowded, deep bluish green. Annual growth about 2 cm.

C. lawsoniana 'Minima' (E). (Syn. *Cupressus l.* 'Minima')
This is a rare conifer in its true colour form making a slow growing roundish bushlet of stiff crowded branches. The branchlets are ascending and twisted so that the sprays appear sideways, the colour being a distinctive bluish yellow-green. Annual growth 3 cm. and although slow growing it will make a large plant in time.

C. lawsoniana 'Minima Aurea' (E). (Syns. *Cupressus l.* 'Minima Aurea'; *Cupressus l.* 'Minima Aurea Rogersii')
This is similar to the type with the twisted sideways sprays but the colour is a distinctive golden-yellow. Annual growth 3 cm. This form was raised at W. H. Roger's Red Lodge Nursery.

C. lawsoniana 'Minima Glauca' (E)
This plant will make a large growing specimen in time and should be planted in its pot to restrict growth and so keep it dwarf for rock or small garden. It makes a wide roundish specimen with very compact numerous branchlets. Leaves minute linear, apex obtuse, closely appressed to the laterals, bright glaucous blue in colour. Annual growth in the region of 5 cm.

C. lawsoniana 'Pygmaea Argentea' (E). (Syn. *C. l.* 'Pygmaea Backhouse Silver')
The plant bearing this name has been under a cloud for a number of years as it varies from the original plant grown in Holland, but it has been found to be caused by climatic conditions rather than any other reason. It forms a slow spreading half-rounded bushlet with congested semi-horizontal slender branches with sprays of dark glaucous green, linear acute foliage, which is white tipped in the juvenile state. If grown under shady conditions the white tips will persist but if exposed they will darken to a light green. Annual growth 3 cm.

C. obtusa (E). (Syn. *Cupressus obtusa*)
The species *C. obtusa* is a native of Japan and was introduced into Europe in 1861 by that eminent Victorian nurseryman J. V. Veitch who was responsible for many noted plants finding their way into cultivation. The Japanese have cultivated a number of abnormal forms of this species and since its introduction here there have been still more, in fact it is safe to say that *C. obtusa* has been responsible for producing more of the slow-growing conifers than any other arborescent conifer in cultivation. Although not all these forms are suitable for the smaller

garden they consist of juvenile, adult, compact, abnormal and small bun-shaped plants thus providing in this species enough material to satisfy all but the most avid collector of dwarf conifers.

C. obtusa 'Caespitosa' (E)
This is one of the three best bun forms which came from seedlings of *C. obtusa* 'Nana Graclis' grown in the Red Bank Nurseries of W. H. Rogers Ltd. With *C.o.* 'Juniperoides' and 'Minima' it must be considered the slowest growing of all dwarf conifers in cultivation today. It forms a roundish bun of congested tufts of small branches on which the minute bright green scale-like obtuse leaves are appressed to the laterals, these being so placed that they have the appearance of doll's saucers. Annual growth in the region of 8 mm.

C. obtusa 'Compacta' (E)
A very slow-growing plant and although rare in cultivation the true plant is available as I have propagated it over the last twenty-five years and distributed it to a number of keen growers of these miniatures. It forms a low, compact bushlet more high with radiating almost horizontal branches. Laterals densely covered with the minute stout appressed dark green obtuse leaves, these forming small fan-shaped upright saucers. This is to all intents and purposes a miniature *C.o.* 'Nana'. Annual growth approximately 8 mm.

C. obtusa 'Coralliformis' (E). (Syn. *C.o.* 'Lycopodioides Coralliformis')
A rare form with abnormal branches making a tight congested bushlet. The laterals are roundish, slender, twisted, almost contorted forming coral-like knobs. Leaves crowded, minute, obtuse, appressed to the stems, brownish with paler dots. Annual growth between 2 and 3 cm. This form will in time outgrow its position but will take a good number of years to reach this stature.

C. obtusa 'Ericoides' (E). (Syns. *Juniperus sanderi*; *Retinospora sanderi*; *C. obtusa* 'Sanderi')
This is a delightful miniature which originated in Japan and was introduced in the late nineties, although it has never been common here possibly because it dislikes cold searing winds and requires careful placing in the garden to avoid these. It is a form which retains its juvenile foliage with thick stout branches and slightly ascending thickish laterals borne at right angles to the branches. Leaves in threes, small 1–1½ cm. long, thickish, not appressed but at an angle to the stem, congested, apex obtuse to rounded, flat on top, convex below. The whole forms a tightly congested roundish bush tending to become flat on top. An attractive plant owing to the colour of the foliage, this is a glossy blue-green in spring and summer turning to purple-red in winter. It requires a little more sun than most *obtusa* forms but still needs wind protection. Annual growth in the region of 1 cm.

C. obtusa 'Flabelliformis' (E)
A fine distinct form of close compact nearer horizontal than ascending branches making a mound more like a deep upturned saucer than a bun. The laterals are crowded with the small minute appressed deep green obtuse foliage, each branch representing a fan, quite flat not saucer shaped like many of the *obtusa* forms; the varietal name is well applied to this form. Annual growth less than 2 cm.

C. obtusa 'Juniperoides' (E)
Another dwarf form but less compact than 'Ericoides' which it resembles. The main difference is its more open habit and slightly decurved,

not ascending narrow fan-shaped branches. Leaves minute almost needle-shaped and born away from the laterals, not appressed, the tips being free and incurved. Colour bright green. Annual growth approximately 1 cm.

C. obtusa 'Juniperoides Compacta' (E)
This is a difficult plant to place correctly unless one has both forms together. If only *C.o.* 'Juniperoides' is grown, it will often, if the conditions are a poor sparse, growing medium, produce a close compact form like the variety. It is smaller in all its parts and more compact. Possibly originated either as a seedling or a basal cutting from the type plant in Messrs Roger's nursery. Annual growth around 1 cm.

C. obtusa 'Lycopodioides' (E). (Syns. *Retinispora lycopodioides*; *R. monstrosa*)
An unusual type of dwarf conifer and provided it is realised that it will in time outgrow its station it should be included. It forms a crowded uneven pyramid of spreading thinnish branches. Laterals uneven and sparse towards base of branch, crowded towards apex and flattened, similar to a cockscomb. Leaves congested round stem, basal appressed oval, overlapping in pairs, keeled on reverse; terminal leaves rounded, blunt needle-shaped, keeled, arranged in spirals; shining dark blue-green. Annual growth 2 to 5 cm.

C. obtusa 'Lycopodioides Aurea' (E)
This colour form is in cultivation and obtainable but whether it is superior to the type is open to question for the only difference is that the foliage is a bright yellow-green.

C. obtusa 'Mariesii' (E). (Syn. *C.o.* 'Nana Albo-Variegata')
This is one of the compact forms making a pyramidal conifer spreading slightly at base, rather flat topped with horizontal branches and thinnish fan-shaped laterals. Leaves slender appressed blunt at apex less crowded than in *obtusa* 'Nana'. Colour is whitish green in spring and summer turning to yellow-green in winter. Needs placing with care as the foliage is quickly browned if sited in a cold draughty spot. Annual growth 2 cm.

C. obtusa 'Minima' (E). (Syns. *C.o.* 'Tetragona Minima'; *C.o.* 'Pygmaea'; *C.o.* 'Minima Densa')
As its varietal name implies it is a tight congested ball composed of 2 cm. semi-erect tetragonal branches; the minute recurved branchlets radiate in a brush-like cluster at the top half of the branches. Leaves arranged in fours round the stems, bright glossy green, minute oval, not obtuse but slightly pointed at apex, incurving and not appressed to stem but at narrow angle. This is one of the smallest of all the dwarf conifers and the annual growth rarely exceeds 8 mm.

C. obtusa 'Nana' (E). (Syn. *C.o.* 'Nana Densa')
No dwarf conifer is more delightful than this form of the species if obtained true to name. Unfortunately, too often *C.o.* 'Nana Gracilis' has to do duty for this as the plant is rare. 'Nana Gracilis' is a much quicker and more vigorous form and makes a large specimen in a short period. Grafted plants too seem to lose a number of the dwarf characteristics of the form so that it is essential to obtain this on its own roots. There is one great difference between the plants in that the foliage of 'Nana' is of a deep sombre green while that of 'Nana Gracilis' is bright deep green. Branches are horizontal, not so crowded as in other forms with distinctive dense branchlets forming a deepish saucer

shaped spray of the small appressed thickish obtuse leaves. Annual growth less than 2 cm.

C. obtusa 'Nana Aurea' (E)
Here again is a colour form which is desirable, but unfortunately it is more vigorous and quicker growing, making a large plant in a number of years. If this is remembered there is no reason why it should not be included. It is stouter in all its parts with the saucer shaped sprays on open almost horizontal branches, so that it is flatter on the top than 'Nana'. The colour which is constant is of a golden-yellow. Annual growth between 3 and 5 cm.

C. obtusa 'Nana Kosteri' (E)
Yet another form that is as slow growing as *C.o.* 'Nana' which originated in Holland in the nurseries of M. Koster & Sons, Boskoop. It differs in that it is much more compact, and the congested appressed obtuse leaves have a distinct tinge of brownish green. Annual growth less than 2 cm.

C. obtusa 'Nana Pyramidalis' (E)
A seedling from 'Nana Gracilis' which was raised by Messrs H. den Ouden & Sons of Boskoop, Holland, was responsible for this charming form. It differs from 'Nana' in that instead of forming a low flattish-topped bushlet it is quite conical, tapering to the apex with congested branchlet more ascending than horizontal, otherwise foliage and colour is the same as 'Nana'. Very slow in growth, not more than 2 cm. annually.

C. obtusa 'Pygmaea' (E)
Care must be taken not to confuse this form with the variety 'Pygmaea' of the trade which is a dwarf, prostrate, spreading, open fan-shaped plant covering a great deal of ground in a short period. The true plant which is rare in cultivation is intermediate between 'Nana' and 'Nana Kosteri' forming a low bush with horizontal fan shaped branches, lateral fairly widely spaced almost at right angles to the branch, not saucer shaped but slightly inverted; leaves almost appressed, small obtuse, not incurved, colour shining brown-green. There are two magnificent specimens of the true plant in the alpine house at Kew and Wisley respectively. Annual growth less than 2 cm.

C. obtusa 'Pygmaea Aureo-Variegata' (E)
A slightly faster growing form which originated in the nurseries of K. Wezelenburg & Son, Hazerswoude, Holland, is similar to the type in that it makes a low rounded bushlet with bronze-gold leaves, that are at their best in winter. Annual growth between 2 and 3 cm.

C. pisifera (E). (Syns. *Cupressus pisifera*; *Retinospora pisifera*)
The Sawara Cypress a native of Japan was introduced into cultivation by J. G. Veitch in 1861 and it has produced a number of dwarf forms which are suitable for the small garden, provided the true dwarfs are obtained and grown, of these the juvenile forms are amongst the best.

C. pisifera 'Aurea Nana' (E). (Syn. *C. pisifera* 'Aurea Nana Fretsii')
A rare form of *C.p.* 'Aurea' which is a good dwarf conifer. It makes a roundish slightly higher than wide bush with tightly congested branches and laterals densely clothed with the small juvenile linear foliage of a bright yellow. Annual growth 2 to 3 cm. This is definitely a form to buy after it has made its annual growth for with the best will in the world 98% of plants sold under this name are nothing more than young plants of *C.p.* 'Aurea'.

C. pisifera 'Compacta Variegata' (E)
A small conifer which is often confused with *C.p.* Nana 'Aureo-Variegata', a rarer and much more compact plant. It forms a more or less open much branched flat-topped bush. Foliage crowded, light green, covered with specks and splotches of pale yellowish white, giving the appearance of a bush of changing colour in the wind. Annual growth in the region of 3 cm.

C. pisifera 'Ericoides' (E)
An extremely rare form with persistent juvenile foliage. It makes a close compact conifer, widely pyramidal in shape. Branches thick, semi-erect crowded. Laterals very dense, red-brown. Foliage in threes, narrow deltoid, abrupt at apex, recurved, light bright green, turning dull red-brown in winter, glaucous beneath, midrib raised on both sides, underneath two recessed bands. Annual growth in the region of 2 cm. This being a rare, slow-growing conifer, *C. thyoides* 'Ericoides' often does duty for it, but it can be distinguished in that it is not so dense, laterals more horizontal, slender, leaves much greener in summer, linear, flat, not so abrupt to apex with two stomatic bands below, turning to purple-brown in winter, very aromatic.

C. pisifera 'Filifera Aurea' (E)
The green original type is rather too quick-growing for the average small garden, although it is often seen planted as young specimens. If due note is taken of this, it can be tried and the only difference is that the colour of the foliage is bright green, glaucous below. The golden form makes a lax open bushlet of pendulous thin, undivided, thread-like branches, the whole forming a roundish mound, wider than high. Laterals slender, short, flattened, tufted at apex, clothed with ovate needle tipped, loosely overlapping leaves, keeled on reverse, bright golden-yellow. This plant requires sunshine to bring out the best of its foliage coloration. Annual growth about 3 cm.

C. pisifera 'Nana' (E)
The smallest of all the bun forms of *C. pisifera* this is an extremely slow-growing plant. It makes a congested roundish bun-shaped specimen of fan-like branches, decurving at apex, branchlets and laterals also fan shaped. Leaves crowded, tufted, slightly incurving, of a deep blue-green. Annual growth in the region of 1–2 cm.

C. pisifera 'Nana Aureo-Variegata' (E). (Syn. *Retinospora pisifera* 'Nana Aureo-Variegata')
Similar to the type but not quite so slow growing, unfortunately when ordered this plant is seldom received, *C.p.* 'Compacta Variegata' doing duty for it. The golden form is not so flat but more rounded, almost ball shaped with similar congested fan like branches and branchlets. The leaves are variegated, yellow-green and gold and the whole has the appearance of molten gold. Annual growth about 2 cm.

C. pisifera 'Plumosa Compressa' (E). (Syns. *Cupressus pisifera*; *C.p.* 'Squarrosa Nana'; *C.p.* 'Squarrosa Pygmaea')
The 'Plumosa' forms were introduced from Japan by J. G. Veitch, and these bear both juvenile and intermediate foliage or sometimes only intermediate, this is one of the reasons why it is often offered under one or the other of its synonyms. A slow growing form which is still rare in cultivation, making small hummocks of tight congested ascending branches, densely clothed with the almost appressed foliage; narrow linear to an acute apex, concave, green on outside, convex, white on

inside normally but this varies often standing clear of the laterals and much flatter. General appearance a ball of moss rich glaucous green in colour. Annual growth less than 2 cm.

C. pisifera 'Plumosa Nana Aurea' (E). (Syn. *C.p.* 'Plumosa Aurea Nana')
The type plant *C. pisifera* 'Plumosa Nana' seems to have disappeared from cultivation today and was a rare, desirable, extremely slow-growing specimen. The 'Aurea' form is not so slow in growth but still suitable for the small garden. It makes a compact sub-globose specimen with slender branches and needle shaped rounded, minute, intermediate, light golden-yellow leaves, growing at right angles to the laterals. The whole a delightful mound of light gold. Annual growth about 2 cm.

C. pisifera 'Plumosa Rogersii' (E). (Syns. *C.p.* 'Plumosa Nana Aurea Rogersii'; *C.p.* 'Plumosa Aurea Compacta')
Another of Messrs Rogers' fine introductions, this makes a small broad columnar bushlet which is the main difference between the last plant and this. It is not so coarse, the foliage being more lax and finer and is at an angle of 45° to the laterals rather than at right angles as in 'Plumosa Nana Aurea'. Colour light golden-yellow which is retained throughout the year. Annual growth in the region of 2 cm.

C. pisifera 'Squarrosa Intermedia' (E). (Syn. *C.p.* 'Plumosa Pygmaea')
There are really only two dwarf forms of *pisifera* 'Squarrosa' which are suitable, and both of these are extremely rare, although in cultivation. They are recorded here because the type plant is often sent out when either is ordered. *C. pisifera* 'Squarrosa Intermedia' is a fascinating shaped plant best described as a small inverted cup ending in a point bearing both juvenile and intermediate foliage, the latter being present almost exclusively on the upper part of the plant, including the spire. The juvenile foliage, small oblong, is tightly packed on the laterals in whorls of threes at right angles, or slightly ascending, apex incurved, terminating in an acute point. The intermediate foliage almost lanceolate and incurved is about half the size, borne in opposite pairs, just as crowded as the juvenile, ascending at a narrow angle, incurved, colour pale grass-green. Annual growth about 2 cm.

C. pisifera 'Squarrosa Minima' (E)
This is a rare, slow growing conifer with almost horizontal branches from which the ascending branchlets are tightly packed, bearing recurving leaves in whorls of three, broad tapering to a point, the last third almost at right angles; glaucous green, margins dark green, midrib wide, green, this being separated by two sunken white lines; underneath two broad white lines and a narrow keel. Annual growth about $1\frac{1}{2}$ cm.

C. thyoides 'Andelyensis Nana' (E)
This has an interesting history and also helps to prove my remarks concerning propagating from different parts of dwarf conifers which produce forms differing from the parent plant. Hornibrook found this plant in Angers at the nurseries of Chas. De'triché but the origin was unknown and then Grootendorst of the Dutch nursery of Grootendorst & Sons, Boskoop, told him that he had similar forms which were propagated from the side branches of *C.t.* 'Andelyensis'. This makes a low, spreading, inverted, saucer shaped mound of congested semi-ascending branches. The branchlets are very crowded towards apex,

fan shaped, flat. Leaves juvenile in whorls of three, flat linear incurved. Adult wider, imbricated in opposite pairs flat with pronounced median resin pit. Colour towards base glaucous green, apical green with reddish bands. Annual growth in the region of 2 cm.

CRYPTOMERIA (*Taxodiaceae*)

The type plant *C. japonica* was introduced into Europe from Japan in 1884 where it became known as the Japanese Cedar. It has produced a number of dwarf forms but with the exception of one, as far as it is known, all these originated in Japan. They need care in placing in the garden, requiring a sheltered position, for they are very susceptible to cold and drying winds. Planting them in the lee of rock boulders giving protection from the north and east will help in exposed areas, but they are really only suitable for the warmer gardens.

C. japonica 'Bandai-Sugi' (E)
A fine form of *japonica* making a wide conical plant as it has a tendency to spread sideways rather than upwards, with semi-compact branches and congested irregular sizes branchlets. On the majority of these laterals are borne the long narrow linear leaves at an angle of 45°; on the others, which are shorter, the leaves are small thick and closely congested. The whole is a bluish green with tips that turn reddish brown in winter. Annual growth about 2 cm.

C. japonica 'Knaptonensis' (E)
This is a dwarf form which owes its origin to being a 'witches' broom' from another dwarf *C.j.* 'Alba-variegata' growing in Isola Madre, Lago Maggiore, Italy. It is a slow growing congested plant making an open bun-shaped bushlet with a mixed conglomeration of different sized branchlets, both pendant and ascending, densely covered with the very fine linear foliage of dazzling white when young, turning to a light green as it matures. A word of warning here, propagation can only be carried out by using adult foliage with a good percentage of green colouring, otherwise the material will not root. Annual growth approximately $1\frac{1}{2}$ cm.

C. japonica 'Pygmaea' (E). (Syns. *C.j.* 'Nana'; *C. nana*; *C.j.* 'Lobbi Nana')
As the number of synonyms signify this has had a varied career with its multiplicity of names, for it is the oldest form in Europe. Although it will in time outgrow the small garden, it can be used for a number of years before this stature is reached. It forms an irregular bush wider than it is high with short, crowded, stiff twisted and erect branches. The laterals are also congested like a cockscomb and these are densely clothed with the linear appressed foliage, the apex of which are free and recurved, deep green. Annual growth in the region of 3–5 cm.

C. japonica 'Spiralis' (E). (Syns. *C.j.* 'Spiralter Falcata'; *C.j.* 'Kusari-Sugi')
Another variable form that has a tendency to throw normal shoots of the species *C. japonica*, which, if not removed, will soon dominate the plant and the result will be a forest tree instead of a dwarf. It makes an irregular globose specimen with stout almost pendulous branches. Branchlets whip-like slender pendulous crowded with the almost appressed linear leaves twisted round the stems in the form of a spiral, mid-green. Annual growth about 2 cm.

Cryptomeria japonica 'Spiralis'

C. japonica 'Vilmoriniana' (E)
An outstanding plant which was introduced to this country in 1923 by Murray Hornibrook from Les Verriers, France and named after M. Philippe de Vilmorin who had introduced it from Japan about thirty-five years previously. It is absolutely essential to obtain this plant on its own roots to ensure its dwarf characteristics. Grafted plants will in the course of a year or so throw abnormal shoots completely out of character from different parts of the plant. Unfortunately, too often *C. japonica* 'Compacta', a much taller growing form, is sold under this name. The true plant is slow growing, semi-erect with ascending branches. These are slightly incurving and well clothed with stout linear foliage with an acute point, deep green, shading to dark copper in autumn. Annual growth 2 cm.

CUPRESSUS (Cupressaceae)

There is only one dwarf form of the true cypress which is in cultivation today and this is the small edition of the well known 'Monterey Cypress'; *C. macrocarpa,* that is used extensively, not always with success, for quick growing hedges.

C. macrocarpa 'Pygmaea' (E)
An extremely rare and slow growing dwarf conifer of compact habit
with widely spreading branches both horizontal and ascending. The
laterals are clothed with two different kinds of foliage, lower in four
tiers, wide linear, tapering to apex, apical appressed, scale like, colour
grey-green. Annual growth about 2 cm.

DACRYDIUM (*Podocarpaceae*)

A small genus of about twenty species of conifers related to the Yew,
these are confined to the southern hemisphere, unfortunately not too
hardy here but there is one charming dwarf species which, given a
warm sheltered position, will add distinction to the small garden.
D. laxifolium (E)
This dwarf, often monoecious conifer, is a New Zealand endemic found
in both the North and South Islands. It makes a prostrate shrublet
which will climb over a rock face if planted at its base. Branches normally radiating and horizontal, very slender and wavy. Leaves variable
in the juvenile state, subulate to narrow-linear, acute, flat often curved.
Adult oblong-ovate, appressed, imbricated, obtuse with keel, colour a
deep glossy green. Annual growth 2 cm.

JUNIPERUS (*Cupressaceae*)

A large race of conifers containing a great number of semi-dwarf forms
which have been given names and synonyms creating great confusion
among gardeners. There are only a few plants which can be classified
as being suitable for our purpose. Of these the 'Noah's Ark' juniper *J.
communis* 'Compressa' known under many varietal names will seldom
become too large.
J. chinensis 'Echiniformis' (E). (Syn. *J. communis* 'Echiniformis')
This is certainly one of the best of all dwarf conifers, rare and slow
growing, and not as unobtainable as it was a few years ago. I have
found that it strikes quite well from cuttings of semi-ripened wood
taken in August. If given bottom heat this will root by the following
spring. It makes a small rounded bush of slightly ascending short stout
branches with small laterals densely packed with the spine-like foliage,
sharp to the touch, colour deep bright green. It is a form which needs
protection from cold winds and should be sited accordingly. Annual
growth about 1 cm.
J. communis 'Compressa' (E). (Syns. *J. communis* 'Hibernica
Compressa'; *J. compressa*; *J. communis* 'Hispanica'; *J. hispanica*; *J. hibernica* 'Compressa')
Despite the numerous synonyms, this plant is more recognisable by its
common name 'Noah's Ark' juniper. It forms an upright perfectly
symmetrical column of closely congested erect branches with acutely
ascending triangular laterals white in the juvenile state, red-brown
when adult; densely clothed with the small linear foliage in whorls of
three, glaucous green above with sunken narrow green midrib, below
bright green and convex. This form needs a sunny position to give of its
best. Annual growth approximately 3 cm.
J. communis 'Echiniformis', see *J. chinensis* 'Echiniformis' *J. communis*
'Effusa' (E)
A form from the nurseries of Messrs H. den Ouden & Son, Boskoop, it

is a dwarf slow growing more spreading than erect bushlet with both horizontal and semi-ascending branches. Laterals crowded with the almost appressed slender linear foliage tapering to an acute point, light green with 2 white and green bands. Annual growth about 3 cm.

J. communis var. *hemisphaerica* (E). (Syns. *J. hemisphaerica*; *J. nana* 'Hemisphaerica')

This is another rare variety which makes a semi-globular bush of congested tufted roundish branches, grey in colour. Leaves minute, wide, linear, grey-green, below white with raised keel. Requires care in placing as this form seems to detest cold biting winds. Annual growth about 1 cm. A native of S. Europe.

J. communis 'Hornibrookii' (E). (Syn. *J. communis* 'Prostrata')

A form found by the late Mr Hornibrook in Co. Galway, W. Ireland, which can be used with discretion in the larger rock gardens, if it is remembered that it will spread over a wide area if not restrained, although rarely above 12 cm. in height. It forms a low growing mat, shaping itself to the contours of a large flattish rock which it will readily clothe with its horizontal spreading branches. Branches long light brownish green in the juvenile state, deep black-brown when mature. Leaves small slender needle shaped in threes and crowded on the laterals, glaucous green above with wide white median band, below convex deep dull green. Annual growth 2–5 cm. according to site.

J. communis 'Minima' (E). (Syns. *J. nana*; *J. communis* 'Nana'; *J. prostrata*; *J. nana* 'Prostrata')

Another form which has had a chequered career as far as nomenclature is concerned, being pushed from pillar to post and I doubt if the last word has been said on this. It makes a more or less dwarf compact mat of small horizontal or slightly ascending branches. Leaves densely crowded small thickish, tapering to apex, concave and glaucous blue median band, underneath convex, keeled, colour grey-green. Annual growth about 3 cm.

J. communis 'Nutans' (E)

A form which will in time become too large for the small garden but as it is slow growing it can be included in this list. Introduced into this country by Messrs H. den Ouden & Son, Boskoop, Holland, it forms an upright crowded bushlet of erect branches. Laterals at apex of bush are semi-pendant, grey-white when young, ageing to red-brown. Leaves slender linear, tapered to a sharp apical point, smaller on the side laterals, the whole a delightful colour of blue-green. Annual growth about 2 cm.

J. communis 'Prostrata' (E)

A much stronger form quite dwarf with a bending main stem from which radiates the long flexible branches a few cm. from the ground, it will in time spread over a good area but being slow growing will take a long period before this happens. Laterals greeny white with brown shading in the juvenile state turning to red-brown when mature. Leaves crowded, small flexible slender, narrow linear, apex acute, upper surface light green with wide glaucous white median. Annual growth 2 to 3 cm.

J. squamata 'Prostrata' (E)

Another more spreading than erect dwarf conifer with radiating horizontal green branches turning to red-brown when mature. Branches straight, forward facing; densely covered with narrow linear

32

Microcachrys tetragona

leaves, tapered to apex in whorls of three. Above narrow median band, glaucous blue-white, rest bright green, below keeled, green. Annual growth about 2–3 cm.

MICROCACHRYS (*Podocarpaceae*)

This is a monotypic genus containing one species confined to the summits of the Western Range and Mount Lapeyrouse in Tasmania and is a most interesting dwarf conifer especially when in fruit.

M. tetragona (E)

A completely prostrate dwarf conifer spreading more horizontally than in height being only a few cm. high, with lax roundish red branches. Laterals alternate at regular intervals. Leaves small linear imbricated, appressed not free, mid-green in colour. It is monoecious, the flowers of both sexes are borne at apex of the shoots. The delightful miniature cones are only $\frac{1}{2}$ cm. in length, deep orange in colour and profusely borne on a well established plant. Annual growth about 2 cm.

PICEA (*Pinaceae*)

The spruces have produced a surprising number of dwarf forms, though many would be unsuitable for the average small garden as they will over the course of years become too large. The Norway spruce, *P. abies*, alone has over sixty dwarf forms. Unfortunately there is a great deal of confusion in their naming and care has to be exercised when buying for many are practically indistinguishable when young.

P. abiea 'Abbeyleixensis' (E)

A fine form found by Hornibrook at Abbeyleix, Ireland, in a stand of common spruce. It forms a prostrate inverted cup shaped compact shrublet with radiating curved semi-pendulous branches and laterals, the latter being quite distinctly feathered. The foliage is long, thin, fine and arranged on the branchlets like a comb, blue-grey in colour. Annual growth 1 cm.

P. abies 'Capitata' (E). (Syns. *P. excelsa* 'Capitata'; *P. excelsa* 'Dumosa')

A plant which over the course of time will become too large but if planted with its pot will remain suitable for a good number of years. It forms an unequal sized pyramid with light yellow glabrous irregular branches and congested ascending terminal laterals, creamy in the juvenile state. Buds broadly conical, blunt, brown, non-resinous. Leaves appressed pointing forward, incurved stout, wide at base, tapered to blunt apex, keeled slightly convex, bright yellow-green. Annual growth 2–3 cm.

P. abies 'Clanbrassiliana' (E). (Syns. *Abies clanbrassiliana*; *Abies excelsa* 'Clanbrassiliana'; *P. excelsa* 'Clanbrassiliana')

Another form which will in time outgrow its station and also there are plants sent out under this name which are much faster growing due possibly to being propagated from strong leading branches. It makes a low more or less flat topped compact bushlet wider than tall with congested fine wiry, short glabrous bright white branches and crowded laterals. Buds quite small, conical, acute, red-brown. Leaves very crowded, arranged comb shaped at angle of 45°, sometimes radially, pointing forward, flat narrow lanceolate, tapered to apex, bright green. Annual growth about 2 cm. There are a number of forms of this plant mostly larger growing.

P. abies 'Crippsii' (E). (Syns. *Abies excelsa* 'Brevifolia'; *P. excelsa* 'Remonti'; *P. excelsa* 'Brevifolia'; *P. abies* 'Brevifolia')

It makes a broad conical shrub which in time will grow to 1 m. high and about 2 m. across, but for many years it will remain a small compact plant. The branches are wide spreading and slightly ascending. Branchlets irregular pointing forward, closely congested, very fine, wiry, pale yellow turning to grey-yellow when adult. Leaves small fine, tapered, arranged radially, below almost appressed, yellow-green. Buds small conical, acute, pale brown. Annual growth about 2 cm.

P. abies 'Echiniformis' (E). (Syns. *Abies excelsa* 'Echiniformis'; *P. excelsa* 'Echiniformis')

This is a dwarf form rare in cultivation making a low hummock more or less flat on top of congested glabrous, brown branches, with slightly ascending branchlets. Buds small roundish non-resinous, light brown and darker outer scales. Leaves linear, thin rounded, long almost 2 cm. in length, sparsely set at right angles to the stem, pale yellow-green in colour. Annual growth about 2 cm.

P. abies 'Gregoryana' (E). (Syns. *Abies excelsa* 'Gregoryana'; *P. excelsa* 'Gregoryana')

A charming dwarf making a close congested mound of individual hummocks with small densely packed branches. Laterals thin, grey-brown, congested at a slight angle to the branches, descending at the apex. Buds small roundish or oval, light brown, darker on the outer scales, terminal buds having ring of deep brown, long pointed scales. Leaves linear with abrupt apex, pale grey-green, arranged radially on all the laterals, irregularly angled, some even at right angles to the stem. Annual growth less than 1 cm. Of all the dwarf *Picea,* this is possibly the plant which is seldom found true, many other forms of *P. abiea* doing duty for it. There are other forms of *P.a.* 'Gregoryana' but these without exception are not as slow growing or as desirable. There is one infallible test for the type plant and that is that the leaves are always radially all over the plant and the emphasis is on the word all.

P. abies 'Humilis' (E). (Syns. *Abies excelsa* 'Humilis; *P. excelsa* 'Humilis'). Another extremely slow-growing plant which is still rare in cultivation making a bushlet that has a greater spread than height of crowded horizontal branches densely packed with the fine white ascending laterals. Buds minute roundish, apex obtuse, light brown with ring of deep brown outer scales. Leaves linear, rounded, slightly tapering to apex, congested, radial, less than $\frac{1}{2}$ cm., twisted or recurved, semi-right angle to the stem pointing forward, deep glaucous green. Annual growth about 1 cm.

P. abies 'Knaptonensis' (E). (Syn. *P. excelsa* 'Knaptonensis')
A semi-globular form more or less wider at the base with extremely congested, slightly ascending stout horizontal spreading branches. Laterals reddish-orange, glabrous, slightly descending, crowded near the apex of branches these super-imposed by even smaller congested laterals at right angles to the others. Buds roundish, small, acute, of a pleasing bright red. Leaves almost spatulate with acute obtuse apex, small, slightly incurved, radial, glaucous pale yellow-green. Annual growth under 2 cm.

P. abies 'Maxwellii' (E). (Syns. *Abies excelsa* 'Maxwellii'; *P. excelsa* 'Maxwellii')
A rare form which originated in the Maxwell Nurseries, Geneva, New York, making a semi-prostrate roundish dwarf conifer with smallish thick branches. Branchlets crowded especially towards apex of branches, short, stout, slightly ascending, white ageing to whitish brown. Buds oval, deep brown, centres lighter, scales rounded at tips, appressed. Leaves radial pointing forward and out, round thickish rigid, slightly curved, acute towards apex ending in an extended wiry hair like point, sometimes hooked; bright green. Annual growth about 1 cm. This is a rare plant in cultivation and is often confused with *P. abies* 'Pseudo-Maxwellii' which very often does duty for it. In the latter the buds are conical light brown and the leaves are smaller with appressed bases and rarely have the long extended wiry hair like point.

P. abies 'Minutifolia' (E)
A form introduced into this country by Herman J. Grootendorst of Boskoop, Holland, which is quite distinct although near to 'Crippsii' in shape being broadly conical with slight wiry rigid ascending branches. Laterals densely congested in narrow sprays short and fine, borne at an angle of 30°, light pale yellow. Buds pronounced, very small, broadly ovate, light reddish-brown. Leaves radially minute, pointing forward at an angle of 15° abrupt to apex, obtuse. Deep bright green, annual growth about 2 cm.

Picea abiea 'Pygmaea'

P. abies 'Nana' (E). (Syns. *P. excelsa* 'Nana'; *P. excelsa* 'Brevifolia')
A rare form making a roundish bush more wide than high of very congested ascending branches and clustered stout stiff irregular shaped bright deep yellow laterals. Buds globose flattish at apex, orange-brown. Leaves not congested, narrow lanceolate like the laterals, they vary in shape often thick rigid, tapered to abrupt point, sometimes appressed and arranged radially; bright shiny green. Annual growth not more than 1 cm.

P. abies 'Nidiformis' (E). (Syn. *P. excelsa* 'Nidiformis')
Reputed to have originated near Hamburg, Germany, this is an outstanding dwarf conifer. It forms a very close compact, narrow, conical bush with congested ascending branches. Laterals crowded, pointing forward at an acute angle, some ascending with decurving tips, light white-brown. Buds small cone shaped, deep brown. Leaves flat, thin linear, abrupt to apex with slightly incurved gristley point, borne at right angles, deep dark green. Annual growth 2–3 cm.

P. abies 'Procumbens' (E). (Syns. *P. excelsa* 'Procumbens'; *P. excelsa* 'Prostrata')
This forms a low-spreading bush much wider than high with horizontal spreading branches. Laterals thinnish, rigid, pointing forward, light

36

yellow. Buds small, conical, acute, deep brown. Leaves arranged comb like slightly forward, flat wide linear, thin with incurved apex; yellow-green. Will outgrow its station in time but as it is easy to obtain can be used over a period of years. Annual growth 3–5 cm.

P. abies 'Pygmaea' (E). (Syns. *Abies excelsa* 'Pygmaea': *Abies parvula*; *P. excelsa* 'Pygmaea'; *P. excelsa* 'Gregoryana')

A charming dwarf with crowded irregular branches more ascending than horizontal, almost narrow, conical. Laterals glabrous, white, irregular in size but always semi-erect, so that the bushlet is more conical and erect than *P.a.* 'Gregoryana' which it closely resembles. Other differences are, in 'Pygmaea' the size of the branches and laterals are irregular and often fasciated whereas in 'Gregoryana' they are more or less constant and the leaves are much thicker. Buds globose, stout, dark brown. Leaves short stout, flattish not rounded, arranged radially, pointing out and forward, deep yellow-green, acute to apex from underneath. Annual growth 1–2 cm.

P. mariana 'Nana' (E). (Syn. *P. nigra* 'Nana')

A dwarf rounded form with congested thin branches, leaves arranged radially, incurved and pointing forward at an acute angle, light blue-green. Annual growth about 1 cm.

PINUS (*Pinaceae*)

This is a large family of trees with over fifty species but unfortunately few of these have produced dwarf forms and although a number of the species and forms can be and are grown as specimens on the rock garden for a number of years without becoming too large, it is as well to bear this limitation in mind.

P. cembra 'Pygmaea' (E). (Syns. *P. cembra* 'Pumila'; *P. pygmaea*)

An extremely slow growing form which originated from a seedling of the Arolla Pine making a small conifer of close spreading pendulous branches. Buds small, oval, resinous with long pointed scales, light brown. Leaves in fives, lanceolate, irregular, small fine, curved, grey-green in colour. Annual growth is about 2 cm.

P. cembroides 'Blandsfortiana' (E)

An extremely rare form making an erect compact shrublet with stout congested pliable branches, green-brown in the juvenile state ageing to grey, the whole covered with pale brown downy hairs. Buds small ovate with few imbricated scales, green margined brown. Leaves crowded towards apex of shoots mostly in twos or fives, awl-shaped recurved at tip, sometimes serrulate, three sided, two of which have stomatic lines, light green in colour. Annual growth between 1 and 2 cm.

P. nigra 'Pygmaea' (E). (Syns. *P. laricio* 'Pygmaea'; *P. laricio* 'Nana')

A dwarf slow-growing rounded plant which will in time become too large but only after a period of years, with crowded glabrous branches and laterals of dark brown. Buds cone shaped, tapered to apex, small scales appressed, brown. Leaves in pairs very congested, linear-lanceolate, twisted, apex sharp pointed, margins serrulate, flat on upper surface convex below, bright green. Annual growth about 2 cm.

P. pinaster 'Nana' (E)

A very tight-growing form of the Maritime Pine making a half-rounded bush slightly flat on top with thick ascending brown branches and laterals. Buds from two to five, ovoid, small, bright red-brown. Leaves stout, appressed, congested, recurved, light green. Annual growth about 2 cm.

P. pumila (E). (Syn. *P. cembra* 'Pumila')
The smallest of all the species and in its natural habitat it is quite prostrate spreading over large areas, rooting as it goes but seldom raising itself off the ground or contours of the rocks. Even when introduced to the lowlands in cultivation it is rarely above 30 cm. in height. The majority of the plants seen in cultivation are far from typical, often being grafted which gives them a bole and the appearance of a top heavy tree which, in its native habitat, would be broken in two by the first gust of a gale. In nature and on its own roots in cultivation the main stem is always prostrate or slightly ascending, never upright. It is a native of Japan and Siberia and is considered a true species, although it has been treated as only a dwarf form of *P. cembra*, even Hornibrook called it the Japanese and Siberian form of *P. cembra*. That there are several differences besides ultimate size is apparent by making a comparison between the two plants. The following will assist in identification.

Pinus pumila	*Pinus cembra*
Leaves 3 cm., crowded in bundles of five. Slender curved, margins serrulate right to apex, two marginal resin canals.	Leaves 5–6 cm., crowded in bundles of five. Slender curved margins partly serrulate, never to apex, resin canal median.
Buds ovoid, obtuse, resinous scales.	Buds ovoid, acuminate, resinous scales.
Cones hairless, small.	Cones slightly hairy, larger.
Habit prostrate or slightly ascending even in the lowlands.	Habit upright.
Annual growth from 2–5 cm. horizontally.	

P. strobus 'Pumila' (E). (Syn. *P. strobus* 'Minima')
This dwarf form of the Weymouth Pine is a real gem, slow growing and making a roundish bush of compact habit and slender branches and laterals. Buds ovoid, acuminate, small, light brown, scales not appressed. Leaves slightly incurved, narrow to a pointed apex, twisted; bright silvery green. Annual growth about 3 cm.

Pinus strobus 'Radiata' (E). (Syn. *P. strobus* 'Nana')
A plant which in the course of many years becomes too large for a small garden. It forms a more or less globular bush of slender brownish congested branches. Buds dark brown, ovoid tapered to fine point, scales appressed. Leaves crowded in tufts of five at end of branches erect or horizontal not drooping, variable in length, slender, triangular; upper deep green, two under glaucous blue-white, sharp at apex, margins serrulate. Annual growth approximately 5 cm.

P. sylvestris 'Beauvronensis' (E)
The Scots pine, a native of these Isles, has produced a number of dwarf forms, all are rare but there are at least two in cultivation. This dwarf form of the Scots pine is believed to have originated from a 'witches' broom' and the general appearance bears this out. It makes a dense congested mass of branches, smooth shining green, with crowded right-angled laterals. Buds small ovoid, acuminate, resinous, brown-red,

Pinus strobus 'Radiata'

scales often free at apex. Leaves crowded in twos, 1 cm., slightly toothed and twisted glaucous grey-green in colour. The annual growth is about 2 cm.

P. sylvestris 'Pygmaea' (E). (Syn. *P.s.* 'Globosa Nana')
Another small form which is slow growing but will after many years be over 1 m. high. It makes a roundish bush of congested branches and shiny red glabrous laterals. Buds ovoid acuminate, resinous red; tips of scales not appressed but free. Leaves in pairs, stout, thick, twisted, grey-green with serrulate margins. Annual growth about 2 cm.

TAXUS (*Taxaceae*)

The yews have a reputation for longevity and slowness of growth as anybody knows who has tried to establish a hedge in a short time. Somehow strangely enough they have produced very few forms which can be considered for the average small garden, but the five mentioned here are suitable.

T. baccata 'Compacta' (E)
A small form making a rounded bushlet slightly higher than wide of close congested ascending branches and laterals. Leaves wide linear slightly recurving arranged radially round the laterals, deep shining green. Annual growth about 2 cm.

T. baccata 'Nana' (E). (Syns. *T. foxii*; *T. baccata* 'Foxii')
A slow-growing conifer which is not so crowded and congested but more open in growth of ascending stiff irregular branches less in number than other forms and making a narrow topped bushlet. Leaves small narrow ovate to narrow linear, curved, deep shiny green, often reddish brown at apex. Annual growth 1 cm.

T. baccata 'Paulina' (E). (Syns. *T.b.* 'Nana'; *T.b.* 'Cheshuntensis')
Another dwarf conifer which although sometimes confused with *T.b.* 'Nana' is a much more close and compact conical bushlet with ascending stout irregular branches and laterals. Leaves mostly arranged radially on the laterals, thick linear slightly recurved, deep shining green, sometimes tipped deep reddish brown. Originated in Paul's Nurseries, Cheshunt. Annual growth about 1 cm.

T. baccata 'Pumila Aurea' (E)
An extremely rare and slow-growing form which retains its coloured foliage throughout the year. It makes a low almost bun shaped bushlet of semi-ascending congested branches and laterals. Leaves radially around the stems, wide linear, crowded recurved, of a bright golden-yellow colour. Annual growth about 1 cm.

T. baccata 'Pygmaea' (E)
Another very slow-growing yew which came originally from the Dutch nurseries of Messrs den Ouden of Boskoop, Holland. It forms a shallow, almost oval bushlet of densely crowded semi-erect branches and laterals, red-brown in the juvenile state ageing to a deeper colour. Leaves crowded, narrow ovate, thick recurving, deep shining green. Annual growth is about 1 cm.

THUJA (Cupressaceae)

There are two species from which dwarf forms have originated which are quoted here, these being the American Arbor-Vitae *T. occidentalis* and the Chinese Arbor-Vitae, *T. orientalis*. Of the two the former is much hardier whereas the latter which was introduced into Europe during the eighteenth century is less hardy and needs careful placing in bleak gardens for cold winds or extensive frosts can cause damage to their foliage.

T. occidentalis 'Caespitosa' (E)
A small dwarf compact form making a tight rounded bun, flattish on top, of very stout small branches and laterals, the sprays being almost as long as they are wide. Leaves minute linear, thin quite flat, dull green with a tendency to turn brown in winter. Annual growth 1 cm.

T. occidentalis 'Ericoides' (E). (Syns. *T. ericoides*; *T. orientalis* 'Ericoides'; *Retinospora dubia*; *R. ericoides*; *R. juniperoides*)
This has had a chequered career as its many synonyms testify, even being confused with the Chinese Arbor-Vitae, *T. orientalis*, and possibly the last words have not yet been written about this form. It makes a close compact pyramid of erect much divided branches and many congested slender, erect laterals. Leaves linear in opposite pairs quite juvenile, apex acute slightly incurved, upper surface flat, below rounded, yellow-green, blackish brown in winter. Annual growth about 1 cm. but this plant will extend to 1 m. after many years, planting in a pot will help it to retain a dwarf stature.

T. occidentalis 'Ohlendorfii' (E). (Syn. *T. spaethii*)
A small form which bears both adult and juvenile foliage, so care must be taken when propagating this conifer. If a dwarf form is required basal laterals bearing juvenile foliage should be selected. It makes a semi-globular bushlet with large almost straight branches and crowded laterals borne at the upper third. Leaves clustered minute in opposite pairs, awl shaped slightly recurved with incurving apex; adult scale-like almost appressed giving the laterals the appearance of being four-sided, light green turning grey-brown in winter. Annual growth about 3 cm., this will make a largish bush in time and it is best planted in its pot to restrict growth.

T. orientalis 'Meldensis' (E). (Syns. *Biota meldensis*; *B. orientalis* 'Melden-sis')
A small flat topped roundish compact shrublet with numerous semi-erect or spreading branches and crowded laterals and sprays. Leaves linear, opposite, pointed, intermediate, glaucous green turning to reddish purple in winter. Annual growth in the region of 2 cm.

T. orientalis 'Minima Glauca' (E). (Syn. *Biota orientalis* 'Minima Glauca')
This is smaller in all its parts than 'Meldensis', which it resembles, but it is more rounded with ascending flexible congested branches and laterals densely clothed with fine needle shaped juvenile glaucous green foliage turning to yellow in winter. An extremely slow growing form its annual rate being about 1 cm.

6. List of Shrubs

ACANTHOLIMON (Plumbaginaceae)

This genus contains a number of suitable plants for the rock or small garden, making spiny cushions of almost indestructible foliage and everlasting flowers. All being avid sun lovers, coming as they do from Asia Minor, Persia and India they cannot get too much sun in this country. They add a touch of colour to the garden in winter with their persistent cup like bracts.

Cultivation. Provided they can be given a hot, dry, well-drained spot in full sun they are quite hardy; all resent an excess of moisture at the roots and will quickly show their dislike of such conditions by rotting away. To keep them close and compact a topdressing of two parts coarse sand to one part leaf-mould should be worked in amongst the rosettes in early spring. They do well in a limy medium.

Propagation. Unfortunately they rarely set viable seed in this country and the majority also show reluctance to root from cuttings; a batch will only give a small percentage of strikes. The best method is to use one of the hormone rooting powders such as the grade recommended for half-ripened cuttings used in conjunction with a heated propagating frame. The first two weeks in August is the best period.

A. glumaceum (E)

This is an easy species from Armenia making rather loose cushions more wide than high, rarely up to 15 cm. of individual rosettes of dark green linear foliage ending in a sharp spine, these are not as spiny as other members of the genus. Flowers on 15 cm. stems in sprays, open chalices of rosy pink and persisting calyces. June.

A. olivieri (E)

Similar in appearance to *A. venustum* but with larger less-congested rosettes of stout, fleshy, linear, crowded mid grey-green spiny leaves, the whole up to 15 cm. wide. Flowers on graceful 8 cm. arching stems, up to six, bright pink, saucer shaped, backed with the everlasting light buff calyces. June. A native of Asia Minor. Best in scree.

A. venustum (E)

There is no doubt that given the right position in the garden, this should be planted with its back to a rock ledge, in the sunniest position that can be found, this species is the most desirable of the genus in cultivation today. A native of Asia Minor it makes lax 15 cm. wide cushions of rosettes each made up of linear shaped foliage, wider at the base narrowing to a spine at the apex, thick fleshy recurving margins, light grey-green owing to the dense covering of minute whitish glands. Flowers up to nine on 15 cm. arching stems, open saucer shaped, deep rose, backed by white papery bracts, which persist throughout the winter months. June.

Acantholimon venustum

ACER (*Aceraceae*)

From such a large genus there is no species which is really suitable for the small garden, but one often sees cultivars of *A. palmatum*, the Japanese Maple used with effect in gardens. Provided it is realised that these will in time outgrow their station they add both a decorative and delicate charm with their outstanding shapes and foliage coloration.

Cultivation. They like a good moist soil, this must be well drained, and also protection from cold biting winds is essential, for these will quickly destroy the delicate foliage.

Propagation. The cultivars of *A. palmatum* have to be grafted and for the trouble involved, the same stock of the species as the scion has to be used, the amateur is advised to buy fresh plants.

A. palmatum (D)

A native of Japan, the type plant will in time make a rounded shaped tree up to 5 m. high of slender glabrous shoots. The leaves are up to 8 cm. long, palmate, five-lobed, deeply ovate-lanceolate, bi-toothed, light green in colour turning scarlet in winter.

The following are cultivars which provide an interesting range of shape and colour:

'Atropurpureum'. A good colour form with bronzy crimson leaves.

43

'Crippsi'. A much dwarfer and slower growing plant with finely cut foliage of bronze-red.
'Dissectum'. Leaves cut into seven to eleven segments of a bright green, quite a dwarf growing cultivar retaining this stature over a number of years.
'D. Aureum'. A good golden-yellow form.
'D. Atropurpureum'. With almost finely cut crimson foliage.
'D. Flavescens'. A cultivar with bright green foliage flushed cream and yellow.

There are many more so it is best to visit any of the large nurseries which specialise in this type of shrub and select one's own.

AËTHIONEMA (Cruciferae)

A genus which contains a number of delightful plants for the small, rock and scree gardens. The majority are easy good natured plants which will give a fine display of flowers in their season. Some are suspect as to their hardiness but provided they are in a well-drained soil in full sun, it would take an exceptionally hard winter to kill them off.
Cultivation. A sunny spot over good drainage will suit these plants but where other positions in the garden are best these will be given when describing the plant.
Propagation. Is by seed sown in March for the species, or green cuttings of the cultivars in June.
A. armenum (E)
A native of Armenia this is a densely tufted plant making small compact bushlets less than 10 cm. high but 30 cm. across of congested, narrow, pointed glaucous grey foliage. Flowers in terminal racemes, four petalled, pink with deeper veinings. June.
A. armenum 'Warley Rose' (E)
A form which originated in the garden of Miss Willmott at Warley, which is superior to the type, making a bushlet of blue-grey leaves closely packed on erect much divided 15 cm. stems with many terminal racemes of deep pink flowers. This will spread to 45 cm. in time but can be kept cut back. May–July. A good wall plant.
A. armenum 'Warley Ruber' (E)
This is a much darker form which came from the same source otherwise similar in all respects and suitable for the rock or small garden.
A. coridifolium (E). (Syns. *Iberis jucunda; A. jucundum*)
A fine plant rarely above 10 cm. high and with a spread of 20 cm. Stems in branches from a woody many stemmed base. Leaves crowded linear, blue-grey. Flowers in large rounded congested racemes, bright pink. May–June.
A. creticum, see *A. saxatile*
A. grandiflorum (E)
The flowers of this species, a native of Persia, are the largest of the genus making it an attractive plant up to 30 cm. high and 23 cm. across. It forms a loose bush of undivided stems from a woody base, clothed with long narrow ovate-oblong glaucous leaves obtuse at apex. Flowers large, in loose terminal racemes of brilliant pale rose. July. Unfortunately plants often supplied by nurserymen are only hybrids

between this plant and *A. coridifolium* but the true plant can be distinguished by its fruits being almost round, while those of *coridifolium* are boat shaped.

A. iberideum (E)
A native of the Levant, this is a dwarf shrublet about 15 cm. high and with a spread of 30 cm. Stems branching, erect from a woody base, leaves wide ovate, tapered to stem, acute to apex, blue-grey. Flowers in terminal racemes, white. May.

A. jucundum, see *A. coridifolium*

A. kotschyi (E)
An outstanding dwarf species from Asia Minor forming a dense compact mound of small congested branches about 10 cm. high and 15 cm. across. Leaves arranged in whorls around stems, thick long, narrow linear tapered to point at apex. Flowers in terminal racemes, pink. June.

Aethionema pulchellum

A. pulchellum (E)
This plant, a native of Asia Minor, is sometimes confused with both *A. coridifolium* and *A. grandiflorum* but if it is remembered that in *coridifolium* the fruits are boat shaped, *grandiflorum*, nearly round and in *pulchellum* heart shaped no difficulty in differentiation should arise. It makes a

45

dwarf bush only 15 cm. high by 23 cm. wide of branching stems from a woody rootstock. Leaves crowded, linear, grey-green. Flowers in large rounded congested racemes, bright pink. June.

A. saxatile (E). (Syn. *A. creticum*)
Another plant which requires a warm spot to give of its best being a native of Crete and Anatolia. Only about 10 cm. high and wide with small erect stems from a woody base, rarely branches. Leaves vary from ovate-spatulate to oblong-elliptic, obtuse, bluey-grey. Flowers small in elongated racemes, bright rose. June.

ALYSSUM (Cruciferae)

The Madworts have provided the gardener with a number of worthwhile easy species and cultivars which in common with the indomitable *Arabis* and *Aubrieta* forms are the attraction of countless rock and small gardens in early spring.

Cultivation. All do well in a light open well-drained soil in full sun, the *A. saxatile* forms make good plants but these must be cut hard back after flowering to allow them to retain not only a compact habit but also to keep them from occupying too much valuable space. All benefit from a topdressing in early spring with a light sandy compost.

Propagation. The species can be increased by seed sown when ripe or in the following March. Cuttings can also be used, these being taken with a heel of the old wood in August or green in late June.

A. alpestre (E)
A native of many European Alps, this is a prostrate creeping sub-shrub, less than 8 cm. high and a spread of 23 cm. with grey, oblong leaves covered with stellate hairs. Flowers in unbranched racemes the petals orbicular, pale yellow. May.

A. gemonense, see *A. petraeum*

A. montanum (E)
A small tufted shrublet about 8 cm. high with prostrate grey-green branches, spreading to 30 cm. Leaves crowded, small, obovate to oblong, hairy, silver-grey. Flowers in a loose raceme, fragrant golden-yellow. May. A native of Europe.

A. petraeum (E). (Syn. *A. gemonense*)
A native of Austria, this is a more compact plant than *A. saxatile,* which it resembles. It makes a shrubby, semi-ascending plant up to 15 cm. high and 23 cm. wide with soft silvery grey lanceolate leaves. Flowers large in a crowded corymb, golden-yellow, petals almost cut to base. May–June.

A. pyrenaicum, see *Ptilotrichum pyrenaicum*

A. saxatile (E)
This species has given pleasure to countless gardeners all over the country and with its named forms must be considered one of the backbone plants of the rock or small garden. It has one failing, if it can be called a failing, and that is that it is one of the easiest and strongest growing of all dwarf shrubs. It makes a sub-shrub of up to 23 cm. high with a spread of over 60 cm. if allowed, of ascending tortuous stems with many laterals. Leaves entire, crowded, oblanceolate to ovate-lanceolate, covered with hoary hairs, the whole a bright silver-grey. Flowers in a close crowded corymb, golden-yellow. April–May. A native of E. Europe. There are several named cultivars and the following are representative:

'Citrinum'. Lemon-yellow.
'Compactum'. More compact, bright yellow.
'Dudley Nevill'. Wiry, yellow coloured flowers.
'Plenum'. A double form of bright yellow.
'Tom Thumb'. A smaller form in all its parts, only 8 cm. high, bright yellow.
'Variegatum'. This has leaves of yellow and grey-green.
A. serpyllifolium (E)
A native of S.W. Europe, this makes a delightful plant and, although not difficult, for some unknown reason it is not often seen these days. It forms a prostrate, rarely above 5 cm. mat of congested branchlets with a spread of 20 cm. densely covered with narrow obtuse grey foliage. Each lateral bears terminal racemes of bright golden-yellow flowers in June.
A. spinosum, see *Ptilotrichum spinosum*
A. spinosum 'Roseum', see *Ptilotrichum spinosum* 'Roseum'
A. tortuosum (E)
This makes a small shrublet only 15 cm. high of tortuous stems densely clothed with the linear-lanceolate hoary, grey-green foliage, the bushlet having a spread of 25 cm. Flowers in a loose flat terminal raceme, bright yellow. May. A native of Hungary.
A. wulfenianum (E)
A native of Asia Minor this is a small soft sub-shrub up to 8 cm. high with prostrate lax grey-green branches spreading to 45 cm. across, covered with stellate grey hairs. Leaves in small whorls, oval to ovate, fleshy dull green patterned on both sides with silvery stellate hairs. Flowers in large corymbs bright yellow, usual crucifer shape with notched petals. June to September.

ANAPHALIS (Compositae)

A small genus of semi-shrubby plants of which there is one species that is suitable for the small garden.
Cultivation. A warm dry spot in full sun is ideal for this plant.
Propagation. This is by seed sown in March.
A. cuneifolia (E)
A small sub-shrub up to 20 cm. high and a spread of 38 cm. with ascending grey woolly stems. Leaves linear to lanceolate, ribbed on upper surface, silvery grey due to intense covering of white wool. Flowers in terminal clusters on 20 cm. leafy scapes, many petalled silvery white. May–June. A native of Kashmir.

ANDROMEDA (Ericaceae)

There have been at different times a good number of plants classified under this generic name but there is only one true *Andromeda, A. polifolia,* with pale pink flowers and having a wide distribution in the Arctic and temperate regions of the Northern hemisphere including N. Britain and Scotland. A number of forms have been described at different times but only three are likely to be found in cultivation today. The true *A. polifolia* var. *compacta* is a native of N.E. Asia and N. America and bears white flowers, but is extremely rare and seldom seen in cultivation. It is well illustrated in Homer D. House's *Wild Flowers,* an outstanding monograph of American plants in natural colour. However a form with pink flowers and labelled *compacta* has been introduced into this country from Japan and most plants under this name have originated from that country. Recently a white form named *A. polifolia alba* was given an Award of Merit by the Royal Horticultural Society, whether this is the true Asian form or a white variant of the Japanese is hard to say.

Cultivation. This is definitely a plant for a cool spot in the peat garden, amongst other ericaceous plants. It requires some shade in southern counties but will endure more sun in the cooler, moister atmosphere of the north. Should not be allowed to suffer from drought and a lime free soil is a necessity. Topdress in early spring with peat or leafmould, working this well down amongst the branches.

Propagation. By green cuttings taken in July.

A. caerulea, see *Phyllodoce caerulea*

A. nana, see *Arcterica nana*

A. polifolia (E)

This makes a low straggling plant rarely above 15 cm. high and 30 cm. wide, with linear to narrow oblong entire leaves, tapered to base and apex, dark green above with reticulate veinings, strongly recurved margins, white below. Flowers in small terminal umbels, pendant, urn shaped, pink. May.

Andromeda polifolia compacta

A. polifolia var. *compacta* (E)
A native of Japan, forming an attractive shrublet up to 23 cm. high and 30 cm. wide, leaves leathery, long narrow almost linear, tapered to base and apex, margins strongly recurved, upper surface grey-green, silvery grey beneath. Bears terminal umbels of light pink urn shaped flowers in May. There is a much dwarfer form of this plant about 10 cm. high and wide which is being distributed in the trade and is an exact replica in miniature.

A. polifolia var. *minima* (E)
Another Japanese plant, much smaller than *compacta* rarely exceeding 5 cm. in height with a spread of 23 cm. and very scarce in cultivation. Branches prostrate smooth, new growth almost white, adult light brown. Leaves alternate, thick, long narrow, tapered towards base and apex, deeply recurved margins, heavily reticulated veinings, midrib sunken; deep shiny green above, silver grey beneath with pronounced midrib; petiole short, almost appressed. Flowers in terminal clusters, large pendant, urn shaped, deep rose-pink. May.

ANTHYLLIS (Leguminosae)
The Kidney Vetches are a small race of plants containing both shrubs and herbs, natives of central and southern Europe providing the rock or small garden with a number which are both charming and delightful.
Cultivation. All like a position in a warm sunny dry spot and the soil should be both light and open for stagnant moisture is fatal. It should be remembered that like most members of the pea family these plants resent disturbance once they are established.
Propagation. This is best by cuttings taken with a heel in August, or if seed is set, sow it in March.
A. erinacea, see *Erinacea anthyllis*
A. hermanniae (D)
This is a compact much branched shrublet up to 30 cm. high and across, with spine tufted, congested branches covered with a fine grey down. Leaves sessile, simple or tri-foliate, oblong, wedge shaped, grey due to covering of fine down. Flowers few in terminal clusters, small, pea shaped, golden-yellow. July–August. A native of Corsica, it is surprising how hardy this is provided it gets all available sun and perfect drainage.
A. montana (D)
A native of south and south-east Europe it forms a much branched prostrate sub-shrub up to 10 cm. high and a spread of 23 cm. Leaves pinnate, consisting of eight to twelve leaflets, leaflets sessile, narrow, long linear-oblong, acute, the upper surface covered with whitish hairs. Flowers on 10 cm. hairy stems in globular heads tightly packed, small typical pea shaped, rose-pink with a central dark stain. May. A white form *A. montana* 'Alba' is also known.
A. montana 'Rubra' (D)
This is from south and south-east Europe and is similar to the species but with deep rich rose flowers. May. There are also two other colour forms which have been named, these being 'Atropurpurea', rose-purple and 'Carminea', bright ruby-pink.

ARCTERICA (Ericaceae)
This is a monotypic genus native of Japan, Kamchatka and the Bering

Islands, closely related to *Pieris* and has been included in that genus at different times.

Cultivation. It is a plant that requires a cool root run in half shade, such as is afforded by a peat garden; drought in any form is fatal and the soil must be lime free. Requires topdressing in early spring with equal parts of leaf-mould and sharp sand which should be worked down amongst the prostrate stems.

Propagation. This is best carried out by cuttings of half-ripened wood in late June. If seed is obtainable sow in late February.

Arcterica nana

A. nana (E). (Syn. *Andromeda nana*)
This is a dwarf, prostrate shrublet only 2 cm. or so high and 24 cm. wide forming a mat of tight congested branchlets, which are wiry, brownish and thinly covered with a white down when young. Leaves alternate, crowded, small, thick, oval to oblong, leathery, pointed with a minute tooth, tapered towards base, margins slightly recurved and sparsely ciliate, deep glossy green. Flowers fragrant, white up to four in terminal clusters, pendant, urn shaped; calyx lobes pink or green, ovate, acute, margins ciliate. April.

50

ARCTOSTAPHYLOS (Ericaceae)

A genus composed generally of large shrubs or small trees, but there are a number of the smaller species which are suitable for the rock or small garden. The genus is confined to America and Mexico with the exception of two species, these being native of arctic or alpine regions of the northern hemisphere.

Cultivation. All species require a moist cool root run in half-shade in a lime free soil which has been enriched with leaf-mould. They make good subjects for the peat garden and require plenty of water during the growing season. A topdressing of equal parts loam, leaf-mould and sand, well worked down amongst the prostrate branches is beneficial in early spring.

Propagation. This is best by green cuttings struck in bottom heat. July. Or if available seed in February.

A. alpina (D). (Syn. *Arctous alpina*)

This plant has a wide distribution over the northern hemisphere including Scotland where I found it while taking a party up Ben Ledi during an Alpine Garden Society's tour. It forms a dwarf prostrate plant less than 5 cm. high, spreading slowly into a tufted wiry mat about 30 cm. across. Leaves small, obovate to oblanceolate, tapered to base, apex obtuse, margins ciliate and serrate, bright green. Flowers terminal in clusters up to four oval urn shaped, white flushed pink, sometimes white with a greenish tinge; anthers chocolate brown. April–May. These are followed by black-purple fruits, $1\frac{1}{2}$ cm. across. The autumn coloration is outstanding.

A. alpina var. *ruber* (D). (Syn. *Arctous a.* var. *ruber*)

This is near to the type in form and habit but the leaves are lighter green and obovate, the flowers narrower and longer. The fruits are bright red. April–May. A native of north America and west China.

A. nummularia (E). (Syn. *A. myrtifolia*)

A rare and far from easy plant to keep in good health, it seems to miss the wide open, damp peaty moors and drought or cold drying winds in any form are fatal in cultivation. It makes a plant up to 23 cm. high with slender slightly contorted, brown hairy branches. Leaves alternate, leathery, crowded, generally entire, sometimes with few minute irregular serrations, obovate, rounded at base, apex acute, bright glossy green, margins ciliate. Flowers in small pendant terminal racemes urn shaped, white, calyes deep rose. May. Fruit oblong dark brown. A native of California.

A. myrtifolia does not seem to have any botanical standing and has been made synonymous with *A. nummularia* but I have grown a plant under that name, which although similar in all other respects to the species differs in that the flowers are pink followed by red drupes. A native of California.

A. uva-ursi (E)

A good ground cover for small fastigiate rhododendrons where it will quickly spread forming a mat up to 15 cm. high and 60 cm across. The prostrate shoots root where they come in contact with the ground and then produce ascending puberulent laterals. Leaves obovate or oval, apex sub-scute or retuse, tapered to base, leathery, margins ciliate, glossy deep green. Flowers in small terminal racemes, pendant, urn shaped, pinkish or white flushed pink. April–May. Fruit globose, bright glossy red. Widely distributed over the northern hemisphere.

ARCTOUS, see *Arctostaphylos alpina*

BERBERIS (Berberidaceae)

The Barberries are a large and widely distributed genus found in most countries of the world but absent from Australia and Dr L. W. A. Ahrendt in his recent taxonomic revision of Berberis and Mahonia, Journal of The Linnean Society of London, vol. 57 (No. 369), May 1961, lists 497 species. Unfortunately with but a few exceptions they are too large for the small garden, although those listed here can be relied upon for inclusion in the small garden.

Cultivation. A warm spot in a well-drained loamy soil suits them, and it should be remembered that once established these plants resent root disturbance.

Propagation. This is carried out by taking cuttings of the current year's growth with a heel attached in July and rooting them in a propagating frame.

B. buxifolia var. *nana* (E)

This is a native of Chile and the type plant will reach 2 m. but the dwarf form rarely exceeds 30 cm. in cultivation, and about 60 cm. across when mature. It makes an erect shrub of brown hairy, spine clad branches. Leaves crowded, entire, cuneate elliptic-obovate, deep yellow. May. Berries globose, blue, pruinose.

B. darwinii 'Nana' (E)

A seedling from *B.* x *stenophylla* that outstanding hybrid between *B. darwinii* and *B. empetrifolia,* its form is near to the female parent *B. darwinii* while it has inherited its dwarf stature from the male. A garden hybrid, it rarely exceeds 30 cm. in height and up to 60 cm. across, with erect twiggy brown hairy shoots armed with short sharp spines. Leaves small, oblong, bright glossy green with three marginal teeth on each side. Flowers clustered on large racemes, pendant, petals entire, elliptic-obovate, rounded orange-yellow. May. Berries dark purple, pruinose.

B. empetrifolia (E)

A native of Chile it makes a sub-prostrate shrub under 30 cm. high and 45 cm. across, with rounded puberulous juvenile stems, which become glabrous deep red when mature. Leaves entire, revolute, spine tipped, shiny deep green, grey below, covered with a waxy powder. Flowers solitary, petals oblong-obovate, golden-yellow. May. Berries globose deep purple, pruinose.

B. osmastonii (E)

A fairly recent introduction from Garhwal, this is a dwarf species close to *B. candidula* only 15 cm. high and 30 cm. across with glabrous semi-rounded stems, puberulous in juvenile state, bright yellow, glabrous when mature, spines soft. Leaves crowded linear-oblong, revolute entire, deep green above, pruinose, white below. Flowers solitary on the smallest of pedicels, petals narrow obovate, entire, deep yellow. May. Berries ovoid deep red.

B. repens, see *Mahonia repens*

B. x *stenophylla* (E). (*B. darwinii* x *B. empetrifolia*)

This hybrid has produced a number of dwarf forms of which three are eminently suitable for cultivating in the rock or small garden. These are all close to their parents and give a brilliant floral display in May and June.

B. x *stenophylla* 'Coccinea' (E)
A good dwarf form about 23 cm. high and 30 cm. across, with crimson buds opening to coral flowers. Berries purple.
B. x *stenophylla* 'Corallina Compacta' (E)
Rarely above 15 cm. high and 23 cm. across this has the typical foliage of its female parent, buds coral, flowers yellow, fruits purple-white, pruinose.
B. x *stenophylla* 'Gracilis Nana' (E)
This is a dwarf shrub about 15 cm. high and 23 cm. across with holly shaped, spiny mid-green yellow flecked leaves. The young foliage is a brilliant orange-red. Flowers deep orange-yellow, berries purple.

CALLUNA (Ericaceae)
A genus containing but one species, the Common Ling or Scottish Heather, depending on whether you come from this side or the other side of the Border, must with its wide geographical habitat have produced more cultivars than any other monotypic genus. This plant is widely distributed over the northern hemisphere from Europe to Siberia and into Lapland, so one can realise how difficult it is to specify the typical plant, each country having great variations within the species. They differ from *Erica* in that the coloured calyx is longer than the corolla.
Cultivation and Propagation. The same as for *Erica.*
C. vulgaris (E)
This is a shrublet ranging from 5 cm. to 60 cm. in height with linear-oblong, sub-acute or obtuse semi-erect, congested, sessile foliage, more or less ciliate. Flowers in terminal racemes from 8 to 15 cm. long with purplish pink calyx and corolla. August to September.
C. vulgaris 'Alba' (E)
The white form, which in its wild state, is much sort after as a bringer of good luck is a more or less shrublet up to 30 cm. high with pale green to yellowish foliage. Flowers in long terminal racemes are pure white. August to September.
C. vulgaris 'Alba Aurea' (E)
Is similar to the type about 15 cm. high with bright green, yellow tipped leaves and pure white flowers. September to October.
C. vulgaris 'Alba Carlton' (e)
Raised by Mrs Ward of Malton, this is an improvement on the type with its freely produced racemes of white flowers from both terminal and lateral branches. August to September.
C. vulgaris 'Alba Elegans' (E)
This is a form which often produces double flowers of a pure white on compact bushes. August to September.
C. vulgaris 'Alba Minor' (E)
This bushlet is only 15 cm. high with bright green foliage and ample sprays of white flowers. July to August.
C. vulgaris 'Alba Plena' (E)
Reputed to be a sport of *c.v.* 'Alba Elegans' which originated in Germany this is an outstanding double flowered form. It makes an upright bush about 38 cm. high with 24 cm. spikes of purest white, double flowers. September to October.
C. vulgaris 'Alba Pumila' (E)
A really outstanding dwarf, suitable for the smallest garden, where it

will not exceed 8 cm. in height and produces dainty spikes of white flowers. August to September.

C. vulgaris 'Argentea' (E)
A plant which makes a more or less erect bush up to 30 cm. high with outstanding new foliage of silver-grey in spring followed by flowers of a light mauve. August to September.

C. vulgaris 'Aurea' (E)
A charming foliage plant with rambling habit often only reaching 23 cm. high. It forms outstanding light golden leaves during the growing season, maturing to a deeper bronze-gold, tipped red in winter. Flowers in sprays are purple. September.

C. vulgaris 'Ben Rhadda' (E)
This form originated in Scotland and is up to 30 cm. high of semi-erect branches. Its beauty lies in that it bears both white and pink flowers, mixed on the same spire. August to September.

C. vulgaris 'Blazeaway' (E)
A plant of recent introduction about 30 cm. high, grown more for its outstanding foliage effect, with leaves that are of bronze, orange and red mostly during the dull months when colour is at a premium. Flowers in spires, light mauve. August to September.

C. vulgaris 'Californian Midge' (E)
An introduction from America this form is suitable for the smallest gardens or troughs being only 2 cm. or so high. Leaves minute, mid-green. Flowers small rose-purple. August to September.

C. vulgaris 'Camla' (E)
This originated from an introduction by the well-known firm of nurserymen, Ingwersen, making a rambling semi-erect plant up to 23 cm. high of mid grey-green foliage. Flowers pink, fully double on erect spikes in great profusion. August to September.

C. vulgaris 'Coccinea' (E)
Flowers in spikes, deep crimson-red. August to September. A fine form making a rambling bushlet of grey hairy foliage about 25 cm. high.

C. vulgaris 'Cupraea' (E)
A good form, making a compact bush about 30 cm. high with copper coloured foliage, turning through rich red to deep red-brown during the winter. Flowers in spikes are purple. August to September.

C. vulgaris 'Darkness' (E)
A recent introduction making a compact bushlet about 20 cm. high and 40 cm. wide with bright green foliage and large spikes of deep red flowers. August to September.

C. vulgaris 'David Eason' (E)
A more or less spreading bushlet up to 30 cm. high with light green foliage. Flowers in spikes are deep red, tinged purple fading to a much deeper colour. September to November.

C. vulgaris 'Gnome' (E)
A good form for the small garden with its erect growth, making a bushlet about 15 cm. high. Foliage is light green, which is enhanced when the new foliage appears in spring being of an even paler green. Flowers sparingly, white. September to October.

C. vulgaris 'Hibernica' (E)
A small form of prostrate growth from Ireland rarely up to 15 cm. high and mid-green foliage. Flowers in profusion are of a really bright pink. October to November.

C. vulgaris 'Hirsuta Compacta' (E). (Syn. *C.v.* 'Sister Anne')
This variety was found by a Miss Anne Moseley in the Lizard district of Cornwall and is an outstanding plant. Never more than 20 cm. or so high especially if planted in the scree, which is the best home for it, it will make a really fine cushion plant of grey-green, due to the intense covering of fine hairs, turning to a reddish bronze in winter. Flowers are of a bright pink. August to September.
C. vulgaris 'Humilis Compacta', see *C. vulgaris* 'Mrs Ronald Gray'
C. vulgaris 'Joan Sparkes' (E)
Another fine variety only up to 23 cm. high with deep green foliage. Flowers in must branched spires, are of a pleasing double mauve. August to September.
C. vulgaris 'Kynance' (E)
A form which makes a bushlet up to 30 cm. high with dark dull green foliage. Flowers in elongated feathery spikes, bright pink. August to September.
C. vulgaris 'Minima' (E)
A real dwarf, making close mats of deep green foliage only 2 cm. or so high. Flowers are purple. August to September.
C. vulgaris 'Mrs Pat' (E)
A small Ling rarely above 15 cm. high with bright green foliage. The attraction of this plant is that the new growth is of a pleasing shade of light pink. Flowers light purple. August to September.
C. vulgaris 'Mrs Ronald Gray' (E). (Syn. *C. vulgaris* 'Humilis Compacta')
Another very dwarf, hugging Ling only 6 cm. or so high with much branched laterals and green foliage. Flowers are reddish purple. August to September.
C. vulgaris 'Multicolor' (E)
An outstanding form from America, this is a good foliage plant rarely above 10 cm. high with semi-prostrate branches. Leaves are of different hues of orange, yellow and reddish brown giving the plant an overall look of many colours. Flowers are purple. August to September.
C. vulgaris 'Nana Compacta' (E)
A small prostrate mat of intertwining branches and laterals only about 8 cm. high with bright green foliage. Flowers small, are borne in great profusion, often turning the mat into a complete mass of deep pink. August to September.
C. vulgaris 'Penhale' (E)
A close semi-erect plant up to 30 cm. high with deep green foliage, this turning to a fine shade of reddish brown in winter. Flowers in feathered spikes are reddish purple. August to September.
C. vulgaris 'Ruth Sparkes' (E)
A small compact plant up to 23 cm. high with outstanding foliage of golden-yellow. Flowers are large, double white. August to September.
C. vulgaris 'Sister Anne', see *C. vulgaris* 'Hirsuta Compacta'
C. vulgaris 'Tenuis' (E)
An early flowering form, this is a prostrate shrublet of loose habit rarely above 15 cm. high with mid-green foliage. Flowers in narrow spires are of a deep red-purple. June to September.
C. vulgaris 'Tom Thumb' (E)
An outstanding dwarf form up to 15 cm. high of erect branches giving it the appearance of a dwarf conifer out of flower. Foliage congested, is of

a light yellow-green. Flowers are but sparsely borne and these are pink. August to September.

C. vulgaris 'White Mite' (E)

A small early flowering bushlet about 23 cm. high with outstanding light green foliage. Flowers in profusion are of a good clear white. July to August.

CARMICHAELIA (*Leguminosae*)

A small genus of shrubs which are with one exception endemic to New Zealand, but there are only two suitable for our purpose as the majority range from 1–3 m. in height.

Cultivation. A dryish spot in a light poor soil over faultless drainage in the rock or small garden. Resents disturbance once established.

Propagation. This is by seed sown in February, or cuttings with a heel in July.

C. enysii (E)

This is a small dense shrub rarely above 8 cm. high and a spread of 20 cm. from a stout taproot, quite leafless when adult; branches erect glabrous, flattened, finely striate, light green. Leaves on juvenile wood minute, sub-orbicular, emarginate. Flowers are the usual leguminose, either solitary or up to four in racemes on short peduncles, standards purple with darker veins, keel green flushed purple, fragrant. June. A native of New Zealand and quite hardy in this country.

C. monroi (E)

A charming congested dwarf shrub up to 15 cm. high and a spread of 30 cm. across, from a central stout rootstock with erect rigid grooved flattened branches, obtuse to sub-acute at apex, leaves non existent. Flowers pea shaped, solitary, rarely in pairs, in a two to five flowered slender raceme on short hairy peduncles; standards white, veined purple, suffused purple at base, whitish with basal greenish blotch; pedicels small hairy. June. A native of New Zealand.

CASSANDRA (*Ericaceae*)

This is a monotypic genus being near to *Leucothoe* and *Lyonia,* and the one species and variety are ideal plants for a semi-shady lime free soil.

Cultivation. A good well drained moist soil enriched with leaf-mould and a site in half shade is suitable.

Propagation. By seed in March; green cuttings in June or layering.

C. calyculata (E). (Syn. *Chamaedaphne calyculata*)

This is a small erect shrub about 36 cm. high and a similar width with spreading branches. Leaves alternate, leathery, thinnish, acute, oblanceolate to oblong, margins obscurely dentate, petiole small, covered with round scurfy scales, bright green ageing to bronze. Flowers solitary in the upper axils of small bract like leaves, forming a one sided raceme, cylindrical narrowed at throat, fragrant. Five recurved teeth, white. April to June. A native of the northern hemisphere.

C. calyculata 'Nana' (E)

A smaller more compact shrub with all its parts, including leaves and flowers, smaller than the type. April to June.

CASSIOPE (*Ericaceae*)

A race of dwarf, often prostrate acid loving shrubs characterised by the appressed foliage which is present, giving the branches the appearance

56

of whipcord. As a genus with an alpine arctic distribution in the northern hemisphere, climbing high in the Himalayas and down to the sea shores in Alaska, they are rather difficult to please, especially in the hot dry atmosphere of the south. Many of them do well in the cooler conditions and greater atmospheric moisture which prevails in the north of England and Scotland, where they will tolerate more sun than in the south.

Cultivation. These are all definitely plants for the peat garden in a well enriched humus laden, lime-free soil and they need half shade, more so in the southern half of the country. They appreciate a topdressing of equal parts of sand and flaked leaf-mould, carefully worked in amongst their branches in early March.

Propagation. This is by green cuttings, taken in August and rooted in a propagating frame; detached prostrate branches which root where they touch the soil from the procumbent species, treating these as cuttings until re-established. Seed is also a means of increase, this should be sown in February.

C. 'Edinburgh' (*C. fastigiata* x *C. tetragona*) (E)
This outstanding hybrid which appeared in the Royal Botanic Gardens at Edinburgh is a decided improvement on either of its parents. It makes a close compact bushlet less than 30 cm. high and a spread of 38 cm., only slightly branched, these being small. Leaves dense, bright green, closely imbricated, lanceolate, slightly keeled, margined with white bristles. Flowers in terminal or axillary racemes, crowded large pendant, campanulate, slightly puckered at mouth, lobes recurved, white. Borne on light green, thin hairy pedicels, calyces greenish brown with red margins. April.

C. fastigiata (E)
A native of the Himalayas, less than 30 cm. high with a spread of 30 cm. across, and erect four sided branches in appearance, due to the four parallel vertical lines of imbricated foliage. Leaves small lanceolate, sessile, grooved on reverse, margined with a white membrane and silky hairs. Flowers from the leaf axils, solitary, pendant on slender downy green or pinkish red pedicels, campanulate with reflexed small lobes; calyx lobes narrow-lanceolate, green or red. April.

C. fastigiata x *lycopodioides* (E)
A charming hybrid between the two species with the upright growth of the former and the red pedicels and pinkish green calyx lobes of the latter. April.

C. lycopodioides (E)
Possibly the easiest of the difficult genus; here in west Kent I have a mat of this species, over 1 m. across, rooting as it spreads and providing a delightful sight in early spring when in flower. It is growing in a peat garden amongst other choice ericaceous and kindred plants under semi-woodland conditions in half shade and certainly looks as if it is here to stay, after a period of fifteen years. It makes a completely prostrate shrublet only 2 cm. or so high of smooth interwoven branches and branchlets. Leaves ovate or ovate-lanceolate, entire, keeled glaucous deep glossy green in four vertical, parallel rows, tightly appressed to the branch, concave on inner surface, paler and glaucous margins membranaceous. Flowers solitary on glabrous threadlike red pedicels from the leaf axils, white, pendant, oval bell shaped with five reflexed lobes; calyx pinkish green. April. A native of Japan.

Cassiope lycopodioides

C. mertensiana (E)

An erect species making a slender bushlet up to 23 cm. high and across of roundish wiry branches. Leaves glabrous, dark green, entire, oblong, sub-acute convex sometimes keeled on back, concave inside, lighter, in four vertical rows, less imbricated than in *C. fastigiata*. Flowers solitary pendant, round bell shaped, white, from the leaf axils with recurved lobes, calyx reddish. A native of N. America. April.

C. 'Muirhead' (*C. wardii* x *C. lycopodioides*) (E)

A charming hybrid raised by that noted grower of dwarf *Ericaceae* the late Mr R. B. Cooke, V.M.H. of Northumberland. It is intermediate between the two species, the rounded light brown rigid, erect branches and branchlets are thicker than in *C. lycopodioides* but much less than *C. wardii* these are spotted deeper brown with small bristly hairs, the whole is about 15 cm. high and 23 cm. across. Leaves narrow ovate to ovate-lanceolate, appressed to the branches in four vertical parallel rows, deeply grooved on two thirds of reverse, pale dull green with sparse hairs, margins membranaceous and sparsely ciliate, tapered to apex, tipped with a long bristly hair. Flowers solitary on pinkish thread like hairy pedicels both terminal and axillary, white roundish campanulate, lobes reflexed, calyx coral. April. There is also a prostrate form which instead of having erect branches, these are more procum-

58

bent like *C. lycopodioides* only 5 cm. high, otherwise similar to the hybrid.

C. species aff. *selaginoides* L.S. 13284 (E)

This is an introduction by Ludlow and Sherriff and is proving a good useful and extremely floriferous plant. It is up to 15 cm. high with erect branches and laterals. Leaves bright green, lanceolate with bristly margins, edged with white membrane deeply keeled on back, here it differs from the species, closely appressed to branches in vertical rows of four. Flowers large, solitary from almost the whole length of the branches from the leaf axils on long thickish hairy pedicels, pendant, large globular with deeper cut reflexed lobes, creamy white, May.

C. tetragona (E)

An erect or semi-erect dwarf shrublet up to 23 cm. high, and as much across. Leaves deep green, ovate lanceolate, grooved closely imbricated in four vertical rows on the branches, margins slightly ciliate. Flowers on downy pedicels, white tinged pink, large, solitary, pendant, rounded bell shaped, lobes recurved, calyx pale green, tipped red. This plant has a tendency to go brown at the base of the stems with age. A native of the Arctic region. May.

Cassiope tetragona

CEANOTHUS (Rhamnaceae)

A genus which is much favoured for its large plants and wall climbers with blue flowers, an uncommon colour in shrubs. There are two species which can be tried in the small garden that will grow much wider than high but are easy to keep in check by pruning.

Cultivation. A warm sheltered spot in full sun is required and a not too lean medium to grow in. They are quite hardy once established and a little protection the first winter is advisable in cold bleak gardens.

Propagation. This is by green cuttings taken with a heel and rooted in the propagating frame in August.

C. divergens (E)

A native of California this is a slow-growing dwarf shrub more prostrate than erect although it will reach a metre after many years but can be kept dwarf with careful pruning. Branches lax, leaves opposite, obovate margined with spiny teeth, bright green. Flowers on a short scape in corymbs greyish blue. June.

C. thyrsiflorus prostratus (E)

A native of California, it is only a few cm. high but with a spread of 45 cm. across, making a mat of tangled downy branches. Leaves holly shaped, dense, small, opposite, thick, oval, sharply serrate, margins revolute, deep green. Flowers bright blue borne in terminal clusters up to twenty on the end of short leafy twigs. June.

CHAMAECYTISUS (Leguminosae)

These were until recently grouped together under the generic heading of *Cytisus* but the botanists have now decided to place them in a genus of their own.

Cultivation. They require a light open well-drained soil in full sun. It must be remembered that when planting the position should be chosen with care for they have the family dislike of root disturbance and transplanting.

Propagation. Seed sown when ripe, but where a number of species are grown in close proximity, vegetative increase is probably safer, due to the tendency with which they will cross with each other. Cuttings of firm wood should be placed in the propagating frame in early August and allowed to remain until rooted the following spring.

C. albus (D). (Syn. *Cytisus leucanthus* var. *albus*)

This species makes a low hummock of trailing rounded hairy branches about 15 cm. high and 30 cm. across. Leaves trifoliate on short stems, leaflets oval to elliptic, glabrous, mid-green, hairy below, margins ciliate. Flowers in terminal clusters up to eight pea shaped, light cream. June. A native of S.E. Europe.

C. hirsutus (D). (Syn. *Cytisus hirsutus*)

A very variable shrub in its native habitat with a wide geographical distribution Central S.E. Europe from Germany to the Caucasus and the Maritime Alps. The plant ranges from 30 cm. to over 60 cm. in height and a spread of 45 cm., but in its dwarfer forms it makes ideal small garden plants. The branches are slender erect or semi-erect, hairy. Leaves trifoliate, leaflets oval, obovate or obovate-oblong, with few hairs on upper surface, dense rough below. Flowers from the leaf axils up to four generally in pairs, large pea-shaped, yellow flushed brown, calyx tubular hairy. May to June.

C. purpureus (D)

The 'Purple Broom' is a small shrub up to 30 cm. high and as much wide, from C and S.E. Europe with flexible nearly smooth branches. Leaves tri-foliate, leaflets obovate, generally ciliate, light green. Flowers large in up to three axillary clusters, light purple. May.

C. pygmaeus (D)

This is a small shrub from 5 to 10 cm. high of more or less prostrate branches clad with appressed soft silky grey hairs. Leaves trifoliate, elliptical to linear, margins and midrib hairy. Flowers large usual pea-shaped bright yellow. June. A native of Turkey.

CHAMAEDAPHNE, see *CASSANDRA*

CHAMAESPARTIUM (Leguminosae)

The two species mentioned here have recently been transferred from *Genista* by botanists, the main difference is that the stems are winged and the leaves simple or absent.

Cultivation. They require a hot dry sunny position in a well-drained medium, the warmer the site the greater the floral display. This must be chosen with care, for once planted they resent root disturbance.

Chameaspartium delphinensis

Propagation. By green cuttings in June, hard-wood cuttings with a heel in late July or early August, or seed sown in March.

C. delphinensis (D). (Syn. *Genista delphinensis*)
At one time considered only a dwarf variety of *C. sagittale*, it has now been given specific status. It is a very prostrate shrublet only 2 cm. or so high and about 30 cm. across with zig-zagged winged branches. Leaves grey-green, appressed to the stems. Flowers up to three in erect, terminal clusters of a light golden-yellow. June. A native of the Pyrenees.

C. sagittale (D). (Syn. *Genista sagittalis*)
A small shrub, the 'Arrow Broom' is about 23 cm. high and a spread of 45 cm. with yellow glabrous corolla, calyx hairy. June. A native of S.E. Europe and France.

CISTUS (Cistaceae)

This is a small genus of shrubs containing about twenty species mostly from the Mediterranean region and all are avid sun-lovers. Many are only half hardy but the plants listed here can be expected to survive all but the hardest of winters. The species will root easily from cuttings so that a stock of young plants can be kept going to replace casualties.

Cultivation. A good open light loam in a sunny sheltered spot is suitable, dryness holds no terrors for these plants when established but any stagnant moisture is fatal. All are also suitable for the small garden or sunny ledges in the rock garden where the roots finding their way under the rocks are protected during extreme cold spells. The Rock Roses are lime-lovers but will do well in neutral soil.

Propagation. This is by green cuttings taken in late June and rooted in the propagating frame.

C. crispus (E)
A small compact densely branched shrub rarely up to 60 cm. high and a similar spread, new growth covered with long white hairs. Leaves opposite, crowded at the apex of the shoots, almost in whorls, ovate to oblong, obtuse, rarely acute, tapered to base which is appressed to the branchlets; thick heavily veined, margins undulate, light bright green, covered with glistening down. Underneath three-nerved at base, nerves pronounced. Flowers in terminal clusters opening in rapid succession on short hairy pedicels, five rounded overlapping petals, bright red. June to July. A native of S.W. Europe.

C. palhinhae (E)
This is a tidy much branched smooth woody shrub up to 45 cm. high and a spread of 60 cm. Leaves opposite crowded, thick, obovate, obtuse, tapered to an almost non-existing petiole, veining pronounced, deep green above, white below due to an intense covering of white down. Flowers white, produced singly from the apex of the shoots, petals five, ovate. June. A native of Portugal.

C. parviflorus (E)
A small crowded roundish shrub up to 30 cm. high and a spread of 60 cm. with densely hairy juvenile growth. Leaves opposite, thickish, ovate to ovate-cordate, petiolate covered with appressed downy hairs. Flowers large in terminal clusters up to five fleeting, five petalled, light rose. May to June. A native of Sicily and E. Mediterranean.

C. parviflorus 'Albiflorus' (E)
This form differs only from the type in having white flowers. May to June.

Cistus 'Silver Pink'

C. 'Silver Pink' (E)
A garden hybrid between *C. laurifolius* and *C. incanus* (Syn. *C. villosus*) which originated in the nursery of Messrs Hillier and Sons, Winchester. It forms a compact shrub up to 60 cm. high and as much across with downy laterals. Leaves opposite, thick, crowded, lanceolate, tapered to base, margins undulate, deep green above, greyish green below, midrib prominent with two paralleled nerves. Flowers in terminal clusters on short hairy pedicels, five rounded petals, of a bright shiny pink. June.

CONVOLVULUS (Convolvulaceae)
A genus of plants which contains amongst its members some of the most persistent weeds that the gardener has to contend with in this country, especially on light sandy loams. Of these the 'Lesser Bindweed', *C. arvenis* is almost impossible to eradicate once it has gained a foothold and I would say that this is the one plant which will cause more heartbreak in the garden than any other. It is a large genus with a wide geographical distribution over both temperate and subtropical zones but the centre is around the Mediterranean region. There is only one suitable for the rock or small garden.

Cultivation. It requires a light well-drained soil in full sun, in fact too much sun cannot be given.

Propagation. By seed if obtainable in March; green cuttings in July, rooting these with bottom heat or layering non-flowering shoots in early June.

C. cneorum (E)

A charming dwarf sub-shrub rarely attaining 60 cm. in height and having a similar spread, but this can be kept to a reasonable size by pruning or it will often be cut back to the base during cold winters. Branches slender semi-prostrate, branching greyish green, covered with appressed hairs. Leaves large, congested almost in whorls, lanceolate tapered to base, pale grey-green, silvered with a dense covering of flat silky hairs. Flowers in umbels, terminal individually fleeting, lasting only a few hours but produced in quantity over a period; open funnel shaped, hairy without, white striped pink on reverse of the petals and the whole having a delightful silvery sheen. June–July. A native of Spain.

CORIS (*Coridaceae*)

A genus of two sub-shrubs from the Mediterranean region and both are suitable for a hot dry spot in the rock garden.

Cultivation. A well-drained sandy loam in full sun and shelter in the open bleak gardens, otherwise quite easy.

Propagation. This is by seed sown in March.

C. hispanica (E)

A native of S. Spain, this is a more or less erect plant up to 10 cm. high and 20 cm. across with branching stems. Leaves grey, aromatic, thick linear, glabrous, reflexed at apex. Flowers in a long elongated raceme, two pink lobes, backed by spiny calyx lobes, marked with black dots. June.

C. monspeliensis (E)

A native of the Mediterranean region, this is a sub-shrub with slender semi-erect branches up to 15 cm. high and 23 cm. across. Leaves grey, aromatic, thick, linear, glabrous, reflexed at apex. Flowers in congested racemes, two lobed, deep rose, calyx having larger spines than lobes. June.

CORONILLA (*Leguminosae*)

A race of plants inhabiting warm spots in central and southern Europe, the Orient and N. Africa, there are two which are quite hardy in the garden here and are attractive when in flower.

Cultivation. A warm spot in full sun is essential and the soil should be light and well drained. A sheltered spot is required in bleak, exposed gardens.

Propagation. This is by half-ripened cuttings taken in July or layering of the plants in May.

C. cappadocica (E)

A native of Asia Minor, this is a dwarf plant only 15 cm. high and a spread of 30 cm. across with prostrate stems. Leaves up to eleven, leaflets grey-green, obcordate, ciliate, stipules roundish toothed. Flowers in a congested umbel up to eight large, pea-shaped, yellow. July.

C. minima (E)
This is a native of S.W. Europe and is a small dwarf sub-shrub with prostrate stems about 10 cm. high and a spread of 23 cm. across. Leaflets from seven to thirteen grey-green, roundish-ovate, obtuse with small two stipules. Flowers up to eight in a close umbel, fragrant, yellow. June–July. Needs a sheltered, hot dry spot to give of its best.

COTONEASTER (Rosaceae)
A large genus of shrubs indigenous to many parts of Europe, N. Asia and N. Africa with the hub in west, central China and the Himalayas. For the most part they are too large for the small or rock garden but there are a number which can be used. Their great attraction is that they provide colour in the garden at a time when it is most needed, during late summer and autumn, for these plants bear fruit prolifically and the colour of the berries gives them the appearance of molten fire.
Cultivation. A good open loam or poor stony medium is suitable; they seem to flower and fruit better in a poor medium and they like nothing better than a rock to clamber over. They can be kept in check by drastic pruning of the leading shoots once they have filled their allotted space.
Propagation. This is by cuttings of half-ripened wood in the propagating frame in July. Seed is not recommended, for they will cross with most other species and the resultant plants are likely to bear poor coloured fruits, or to be large growing forms.
C. adpressus (D)
This is a small congested shrub which follows and adheres to the contours of a large rock, if provided for it to clamber over, about 30 cm. high, spreading to 1 metre. Branches rigid, leaves alternate, entire, ovate to obovate small, dull green. Flowers solitary, small five petal-sepals white margined rose, followed by bright red globose berries. May–June. A native of N. China.
C. congestus (E). (Syns. *C. microphyllus glacialis; C. pyrenaicus*)
A dwarf evergreen shrub up to 30 cm. in height and about 1 m. across of congested much branched erect habit. Leaves alternate entire, oval to obovate, dull green, glabrous, white beneath. Flowers white tinged pink followed by bright red rounded fruits. June. A native of the Himalayas.
C. microphyllus var. *cochleatus* (E)
This species, although a low-growing plant, is much too large in its spread for inclusion in the normal small or rock garden, whereas this variety is less invasive. Only about 6 cm. high it will drape rocks, following their contours with slender woolly shoots. Leaves small ovate, glossy green, grey with woolly hairs below. Flowers small white in June followed by globose red berries. A native of the Himalayas.
C. microphyllus glacialis, see *C. congestus*
C. pyrenaicus, see *C. congestus*
C. thymifolius (E)
A tight congested shrub with numerous stiff branchlets up to 38 cm. high and a spread of 60 cm. Leaves alternate, narrow obovate, bright green, margins incurved, white below. Flowers solitary, rarely in pairs, white flushed pink, followed by brilliant globose red fruit. May–June. A native of the Himalayas, this is close to *C. microphyllus* and sometimes classed as a variety of that species.

65

Cyathodes colensoi

CYATHODES (*Epacridaceae*)

This is a genus of extremely decorative Australasian shrubs, unfortunately there are only two hardy in this country and these are all endemic to New Zealand.

Cultivation. An open soil well drained, but containing a good deal of peat or leaf-mould. A west-facing position is best and all require protection from cold searing winds in bleak gardens.

Propagation. By green cuttings taken with a heel in mid July.

C. colensoi (E)

This is a decumbent neat shrub with ascending branchlets up to 30 cm.

high and as much across. Leaves opposite arranged in whorls along the whole of the steam, sessile, narrow oblong concave-convex, apex obtuse apiculate, margins thick recurved ciliolate, bluish silver-grey above, white beneath with three to five parallel blue-grey lines. Growth buds pinkish. Flowers in short terminal racemes, pitcher shaped, cream in colour densely hairy on upper surface fragrant; calyx lobes elliptic-oblong, obtuse, ciliolate, June. In late summer this bears deep pink or white berry like globose drupes. A native of New Zealand.

C. fraseri (E) (Syn. *Leucopogon fraseri*)
This forms a dense close mat only a few centimetres high but with a spread of 30 cm. branches wiry, semi-erect clothed with very fine hairs. Leaves crowded alternate, sessile, obovate, thick, abruptly tapered to pungent tip, margins cartilaginous ciliolate brownish green above paler below. Flowers solitary from leaf axils, sessile, rounded, tubular, five short acute lobes, densely hairy on upper surface white flushed pink, fragrant, calyx lobes acute. May. Fruit edible, broad-oblong, deep reddish yellow.

CYTISUS (Leguminosae)
A genus of sun-loving plants which are extremely floriferous and useful for providing colour in early summer, it is a genus for which I have had more than a sneaking regard. I always remember in the late forties when I showed a 30 cm. pan of *C. procumbens* that was given the Royal Horticultural Society's Award of Merit, so covered with flowers that it was impossible to see any foliage. They are with few exceptions natives of Europe especially the southern half but there are several in N. Africa, the majority of these being taller and less hardy. Botanically the genus is near to *Genista,* the difference between the two being that in *Cytisus* the seed has a small wart like growth near its base, this is absent in *Genista.*

Cultivation. This presents no difficulty in a light open well-drained soil in full sun. They also do quite well if planted at the rear of a rock where their trailing shoots can grow over this. A point to remember is that when planting, the position should be chosen with care for they have the family dislike of transplanting: all are intolerant of root distur-bance.

Propagation. Seed germinates freely and should be sown soon as ripe but where there are a number of species growing in close proximity, vegetative means of increase is possibly safer, due to the readiness with which the species will cross with each other. Cuttings of firm wood should be inserted in the propagating frame in early August and allowed to remain until rooted the following spring.

C. ardoinii (D)
This is a native of the Maritime Alps, making a dwarf prostrate mat forming shrublet rarely above 10 cm. high and a spread of 20 cm. with octagonal grooved hairy branches. Leaves narrow oblong in threes on short pedicels, hairy on both sides and bright green. Flowers solitary or up to three on a short hairy stalk from the joint of the previous year's growth, pea-shaped, golden-yellow. May.

C. x 'Beanii' (D). *(C. ardoinii* x *C. purgans)*
Where space is available this is a first rate plant for the small garden: named after the late W. J. Bean of Kew, where it originated in 1900. It is a semi-procumbent shrub up to 38 cm. high and a spread of 45 cm.

Cytisus ardoinii

with interwoven branches and branchlets. Leaves small, simple, linear-lanceolate, hirsute. Flowers in axillary clusters up to three sometimes solitary, pea-shaped, deep bright yellow. May. Can be cut back after flowering but only the new wood, as it will rarely break from the old.

C. decumbens (D). (Syn. *Genista prostrata*)
A prostrate species hugging the ground rarely above a few cm. high but up to 30 cm. across with wiry five angled hairy shoots. Leaves simple, oblong, pointed at apex, tapered to base, grey-green and hairy on both sides, margins ciliate. Flowers in pairs from the leaf axils of the previous year's growth, bright rich yellow, pea-shaped. May. A native of S. Europe.

C. hirustus, see *Chamaecytisus hirsutus*
C. leucanthus var. *albus,* see *Chamaecytisus albus*
C. procumbens (D). (Syn. *Genista procumbens*)
A charming species with interwoven slender long branching stems covered with appressed hairs about 23 cm. high and a spread of 45 cm. Leaves simple, oblong-obovate on short petioles, apex obtuse, grey-green, hairy below. Flowers in pairs from the leaf axils, brilliant yellow. May. A native of S.E. Europe including Hungary.

Cytisus procumbens

DABOECIA (*Ericaceae*)

A small genus of heath-like shrubs with two species and a number of varieties which are ideal plants for inclusion in the heather garden where they make individual specimens. *D. cantabrica* has produced a number of different forms which with their variety of colours increase the value of these dwarf shrubs.

Cultivation. They can be grown as specimens in a lime-free medium, well enriched with peat or leaf-mould, or planted amongst dwarf heathers in a heather garden. All benefit from an annual topdressing of leaf-mould or peat in late spring.

Propagation. The species by seed or cuttings, and the varieties from cuttings. Seed should be sown in March, and cuttings of the side shoots taken in June and kept in a closed frame until rooted.

D. azorica (E)

A native of the Azores, making a dwarf shrub up to 23 cm. high and a spread of 30 cm. with very slender glandular, hairy stems. Leaves oblong, narrow tipped incurved, dark green, white woolly below. Flowers pendant, egg-shaped with four reflexed lobes, up to ten in erect racemes, ruby-crimson on red stems. June.

D. cantabrica (E). (Syn. *D. polifolia*)
This is an erect bushlet which will eventually reach 45 cm. high and having a similar spread with glandular slender stems. Leaves alternate, oval to oblong-lanceolate, sub-acute, callus tipped, only slightly recurved, deep green and bristly white tomentose below. Flowers pendant in loose terminal racemes egg-shaped with restricted mouth and four reflexed lobes, reddish purple. June–November. A native of S.W. Europe and W. Ireland.
D. cantabrica 'Alba' (E)
From Connemara, W. Ireland, is similar to the type but with large glistening white flowers.
D. cantabrica 'Alba Globosa' (E)
Also from Connemara, it is a dwarf form up to 23 cm. high with larger more rounded pure white flowers.
D. cantabrica 'Atropurpurea' (E)
This is similar to the type plant but has rich wine coloured flowers.
D. cantabrica 'Bicolor' (E)
A remarkable form with variously marked flowers of white and purple, all on the same plant.
D. cantabrica 'Nana' (E)
This is a very dwarf form not more than 15 cm. high with the usual bright purple flowers.
D. cantabrica 'Praegerae' (E)
An outstanding plant of recent introduction from W. Ireland about 30 cm. high similar to the type but with clear deep rose bells. July.
D. polifolia, see *D. cantabrica*

DAPHNE (Thymelaeaceae)
A large and interesting genus containing a good number of dwarf shrubs suitable for the small garden. Evergreen and deciduous species are included in the family and with one exception, all are intensely fragrant and when suited provide an interesting display over a period in late spring. The genus as a whole has over a number of years built up a reputation for being difficult in cultivation but with reasonable and intelligent care they can be grown successfully. There is no doubt that once a daphne starts to die back there is as far as I know no cure and these plants can beat most other plants at the rate at which they will fade away.
Cultivation. The plants like a fairly retentive lime-free soil with plenty of humus in the form of leaf-mould and with few exceptions prefer full sun. A number are natural makers of long straggling stems and these should not be exposed to too much sun. Where they need special cultural hints these will be given when describing the plants. One thing all daphnes have in common is their intense dislike of root disturbance and any moving of established plants is likely to result in failure.
Propagation. Most of the species will strike from cuttings of the previous year's wood taken in late July or early August and placed in the propagating frame until rooted. *D. arbuscula* and *D. cneorum* can be increased by layering and *D. alpina* from seed if sown as soon as ripe.
D. alpina (D)
A small shrublet up to 30 cm. high in nature but rarely above 15 cm. high in cultivation with a spread of 20 cm. with short erect tangled hairy branches. Leaves long, crowded towards apex, lanceolate,

ABIES
balsamea var. *hudsonii*

AETHIONEMA
aureum 'Warley Rose'

ACER
palmatum 'Dissectum Aureum'

AETHIONEMA
grandiflorum

BERBERIS
x *stenophylla 'coccinea'*

CALLUNA
'Mrs. Ronald Gray'

CALLUNA
'Darkness'

PENSTEMON
rupicola

CHAMAECYPARIS
obtusa 'Caespitosa'

CHAMAECYPARIS
pisifera 'Plumosa Rogersii'

CHAMAECYTISUS purpureus
purpureus

CISTUS
'Silver Pink'

CRYPTOMERIA
japonica 'Knaptonensis'

CHAMAECYTISUS
hirsutus

DAPHNE
cneorum 'Exima'

DRYAS
drummondii

EURYOPS
acraeus

GAULTHERIA
miqueliana (fruit)

GAULTHERIA
procumbens (fruit)

GENISTA
lydia

HEBE
ochracea

HEBE
(in small garden)

HELIANTHEMUM
'Cupreum'

HELIANTHEMUMS
(in small bed)

HELIANTHEMUM
'Wisley Primrose'

HELICHRYSUM
sibthorpii (virgineum)

HYPERICUM
empetrifolium 'Prostratum'

JUNIPERUS
communis 'Compressa'

JUNIPERUS
chinensis 'Echinformis'

KALMIA
angustifolia 'Pumila'

LINUM
arboreum

LITHODORA
oleifolia

MINIATURE ROSES

PENTSTEMON
newberryi

PERNETTYA
mucronata 'Nana'

PICEA
abies 'Gregoryana'

POTENTILLA
fruticosa var. *beesii*

RHODODENDRON
'Carmen'

RHODODENDRON
charitopes

RHODODENDRON
'Chikor'

RHODODENDRON
obtusum (forms)

RHODODENDRON
radicans

SALIX
sepyllifolia

THUJA
orientalis 'Minima Glauca'

THYMUS
caespititius

VERBASCUM
'Letitia'

HYDRANGEA
'Pia'

VINCA MINOR
var. *'Bowles'*

obtuse, grey-green, downy on both sides. Flowers in terminal clusters, large tubular, lanceolate lobes, white, fragrant. May. Fruits ovoid red, a native of many European Alps.

D. arbuscula (E)

This is a low-growing shrublet about 15 cm. high and 30 cm. across with radiating branches from a central rootstock, semi-erect and reddish in the juvenile state. Leaves long, crowded towards apex, wide-linear, obtuse, mid-green, downy beneath. Flowers in terminal clusters of four ovate-oblong lobes over a short tube, lilac-pink, fragrant. May. A native of Hungary.

D. buxifolia, see *D. oleoides*.

D. cneorum (E)

The Garland Flower is the well-known species much in demand before the last war and imported from Holland in large quantities by florists and nurserymen. Most of these plants were raised in almost pure peat, the whole a congested mass and it was invariably impossible to induce rooting in a normal compost, consequently they languished for a period then died, this gave the species an undeserved bad name. Under normal conditions it makes a trailing shrub rarely above 15 cm. high and a spread of 30 cm. with hairy flexible branches. Leaves not crowded but spaced along the branches, narrow oblong to oblanceolate, obtuse, tapered to base, recurved, deep green, glaucous grey below. Flowers in crowded terminal clusters with small downy tube, four ovate lobes, rich deep pink, fragrant. May. A little protection from midday sun is advisable and all trailing shoots should be covered with pieces of rock to help retain this plant in good health. A native of central and southern Europe.

D. cneorum 'Alba' (E)

A white form of the species, slightly smaller in all its parts and far from vigorous. Like so many albinos it has a weak constitution and is difficult in cultivation but worth all the trouble spent when it produces its fragrant glistening white flowers. May. A native of the Jura Mountains.

D. cneorum 'Eximia' (E)

A larger plant than the species up to 23 cm. high, very robust, flowers larger and a deeper red-rose. May.

D. collina, see *D, sericea* var. collina

D. fioniana, see *D.* x *neapolitana*

D. laureola var *philippi* (E). (Syn. *D. philippi*)

The Spurge Laurel is much too big for the small garden but there is a good dwarf variant from the Pyrenees in var. *philippi* which is ideal for our purpose. It forms a procumbent plant rarely above 20 cm. high and a spread of 30 cm. with smooth branches. Leaves small obovate, acute, tapered to base, deep glossy green above, lighter below. Flowers in small racemes on a short peduncle, tubular four lobed, yellow-green, marked violet on exterior, very fragrant. May.

D. x *neapolitana* (E). (Syn. *D. fioniana*)

This is near to *D. oleoides* but is given by some authorities as only a natural hybrid between *D. oleoides* and *D. cneorum* for it occurs where these two species meet in nature. It makes a good robust shrub reaching 60 cm. after many years and it is about 38 cm. across with erect hairy branches. Leaves not congested, oblanceolate sub-acute, dark glossy green above, lighter and hairy below on short petioles. Flowers in terminal clusters tubular with spreading lobes, downy on outside, red-purple, paling with age, sweetly scented. March to May. This is one of the easiest of a temperamental genus.

D. oleoides (E). (Syn. *D. buxifolia*)
A fine dwarf shrub, tree-like in habit with an erect stoutish short trunk up to 38 cm. high and as much across, much branched firm twigs, silky grey in juvenile state. Leaves lanceolate or oblanceolate tapered to base, apex mucronulate, glabrous, mid-green, covered with silky hairs below, petiole minute. The flowers in terminal clusters, tubular with four ovate or lanceolate pointed lobes, covered with fine hairs on the exterior. The normal colour is white or pale cream although all colours to rose have been recorded. A plant in my possession has flowers of a dirty off-white, these are cleistogemous, flowers which never open but are self-fertilised, but it always sets a 100% crop of globose fruits which are extremely attractive, the colour being a rich orange-red. May–June. A native of S. Europe, N. Africa and Asia Minor.

D. petraea (E). (Syn. *D. rupestris*)
The gem of the race as far as alpine shrubs go, this species rewards all the care and attention needed to bring it to perfection. All that a choice alpine should be, dwarf in habit, extremely floriferous with large flowers covering the whole plant and with a delightful fragrance. A native of the southern Tyrol inhabiting crevices in high perpendicular

Daphne petraea 'Grandiflora'

cliffs in full sun, it requires the same conditions in cultivation and should be wedged between rocks in a light well-drained soil in which there is a fair amount of humus. It makes a spreading prostrate shrub only 10 cm. high and about 20 cm. across with slightly downy, stiff woody shoots. Leaves thick, crowded towards apex, sessile, oblong or narrow spatulate, obtuse or sub-acute, tapered to base, dark glossy green. Flowers in terminal clusters up to six with small tube having longitudinal markings and four spreading oval, obtuse lobes; the whole covered with a white down on the exterior, deep rose. May–June.

D. petraea 'Grandiflora' (E)
This form is generally the one met with in cultivation under *D. petraea*, it is similar to the species but is more robust and with larger brilliant flowers of a deep rose. May–June.

D. philippi, see *D. laureola* var *philippi*

D. retusa (E)
An Asiatic species which requires at least half shade in the gardens of the southern half of the country, to grow successfully. Although reputed to grow to 1 m. I cannot bear this out for a specimen which I obtained in 1946, kept in a pan for nine years then planted out is today, in semi-woodland still only 50 cm. high, and wide. Many complaints that this plant soon outgrows its station in the garden makes me believe

Daphne retusa

that *D. tangutica* is doing service for *D. retusa*. This is a much stronger growing species up to 2 m. high closely allied to *D. retusa* with only minor botanical differences. In *D. tangutica* the leaves are longer and more tapered towards apex and unlike *D. retusa* the stigma is not downy.

It makes a much branched shrublet with stout erect branches, young wood downy. Leaves crowded towards apex of shoots, oblong-obovate to elliptic-oblong, thick, leathery, notched at apex, dark glossy green, paler below, margins slightly recurved, midrib depressed. Flowers in terminal clusters, tube small, four spreading thick ovate lobes, deep purple on reverse, inside brilliant white sometimes tinged pink, intensely fragrant. May. Fruits large oval, orange-red. A native of W. China.

D. rupestris, see *D. petraea*

D. sericea (E)

A native of Crete and Asia Minor, this rare species needs protection from cold winds in bleak gardens. It makes a small bushlet up to 30 cm. high and about 23 cm. across with smooth slender branches. Leaves lanceolate or spatulate- lanceolate, tapered to apex, mid-green, glabrous above, paler and downy below. Flowers in terminal clusters

Daphne sericea var. collina

74

up to eight with small tube and four spreading oval blunt lobes, rose-pink, fragrant. May.

D. sericea var. *collina* (E) (Syn. *D. collina*)

This is a native of the Mediterranean area and requires a position that is sheltered from cold winds in the garden. It is up to 60 cm. high when mature and about 30 cm. across with erect much branched downy wood especially when young. Leaves oblong-lanceolate to oblanceolate, obtuse, dark glossy green above, paler beneath, covered with fine heairs, corolla lobes ovate, blunt open notched silky hairy outside, lilac-pink, fragrant. May.

D. striata (E)

A rare plant less than 15 cm. high and a spread of 20 cm. with a loose straggling habit, branches smooth. Leaves sessile, linear-lanceolate, pointed and sharply tipped, tapered to base, glossy green. Flowers in largish terminal clusters, narrow tubular, tube striped pink and four ovate-lanceolate lobes deep pink, heavily perfumed. May. This is a difficult plant to grow successfully in cultivation and rarely becomes established for long. A native of the European Alps.

D. striata 'Alba' (E)

Similar to the species, just as temperamental, rare in gardens, but with glistening white flowers. May.

Dryas octopetala

DRYAS (*Rosaceae*)
A small genus of plants containing three species natives of high ground in the northern hemisphere of which two are ideal subjects for the small garden.
Cultivation. All are easy in an open medium in the garden in full sun with some humus in the form of leaf-mould in the soil. They benefit from topdressing in early spring with equal parts of leaf-mould, loam and coarse sand.
Propagation. By seed sown when ripe, or green cuttings in June.
D. drummondii (D)
A native of nothern regions of N. America, this is a prostrate trailing plant, forming a mat only a few centimetres high with a spread of 45 cm. across. Leaves elliptic-oblong, margins crenate-dentate, recurved wedge like at base with a long petiole, deep green above turning purple-bronze in winter, white below with covering of hairs. Flowers on 8 cm. scapes, semi-pendant open bell shaped, creamy white with central boss of golden stamens. May–June.
D. octopetala (D)
The Mountain Aven is a native of N. Europe, America and Britain including Scotland, in fact it is the emblem of the Scottish Rock Garden Club. This is a prostrate trailing plant forming a mat about 10 cm. high and a spread of 25 cm. Leaves elliptic-oblong, obtuse, deep glossy green, margins deeply crenate, recurved, white below with a dense covering of white wool. Flowers solitary on 8 cm. hairy scapes, open saucer shaped, white with large central boss of golden stamens, followed by dainty fluffy silvery seed heads in a conical spiral. May–July.
D. octopetala var. *integrifolia* (D). (Syn. *D. tenella*)
This is a smaller plant only 2 cm. or so high with a spread of 30 cm. Leaves entire or only minutely crenate, margins revolute, flowers similar but smaller. May–July.
D. octopetala 'Lanata' (D)
Another smaller edition with all its parts covered with a fine silvery grey down. May–July.
D. octopetala 'Minor' (D)
A much smaller plant suitable for the sunny raised scree, being only 2 cm. high and about 15 cm. across, otherwise similar to the type, white. May–July.
D. tenella, see *D. octopetala integrifolia*

ECHINOSPARTUM (*Leguminosae*)
Another small genus of plants which have now been removed from *Genista* into a genus of their own with opposite spiny branches. Of the three European species one is suitable for the small garden.
Cultivation. A hot dry well-drained light soil with full sun is ideal. The planting should be permanent as it resents root disturbance.
Propagation. By green cuttings in June, or seed sown in March.
E. horridum (D). (Syn. *Genista horrida*)
This is a native of S.W. Europe including the mountains of central Spain, requires all the sun it can obtain here to get it to flower at all well. A small shrublet less than 30 cm. high and a similar spread and interlaced stems of grey-green terminating in a sharp spine. Leaves trifoliate, opposite, segments linear-lanceolate, grey-green covered with

silky hairs. Flowers in small terminal clusters, bright yellow; standard glabrous, keel downy. June.

EPIGAEA (Ericaceae)

There are three species, one colour variant and a single hybrid between them in this genus; these are desirable plants but not easy of culture in the drier parts of the country where shade is essential.

Cultivation. A cool spot in shade, in a lime-free medium with plenty of humus in the soil. They are ideal plants for the peat garden where they must never suffer from drought at any period.

Propagation. This is by seed sown in March, rooted layers or careful division in early September, the pieces treated as cuttings until re-established.

E. asiatica (E)

This is a dwarf growing, creeping shrublet making a prostrate mat about 8 cm. high and a spread of 50 cm. of rough bristle-haired branches. Leaves coriaceous, ovate tapering to apex, cordate at base, veining reticulated, petiole long pinkish red, margins ciliate, dull deep green, lighter below with pronounced reddish midrib, sparsely clothed with bristly hairs. Flowers fragrant up to ten in congested racemes on a

Epigaea asiatica

short hairy scape, globose five lobed, white flushed pink, reddish in bud, calyx lobes deep rose-pink, broadly lanceolate, acute. March–April. A native of Japan.

E. 'Aurora', see *E.* 'Intertexta'

E. 'Intertexta' (E). (Syn. *E.* 'Aurora')
A hybrid between *E. asiatica* and *E. repens* but not so difficult to cultivate with smaller foliage but large delightful open five lobed flowers almost rose-red at tip lobes. April.

E. gaultherioides (E). (Syn. *Orphanidesia gaultherioides*)
A native of the Lazic Pontus in the Black Sea region, where in woodland glades it forms a semi-procumbent dwarf shrub rarely above 30 cm. high and as much across with reddish brown stems covered with brownish hairs. Leaves alternate, large, up to 8 cm., ovate to oblong, pointed with a short spine, heavily reticulate veining, covered with rough bristles, margins ciliate, dull mid-green. Flowers from the terminal leaf axils, generally in pairs, calyx five pointed lobes, green flushed crimson, corolla large, entire, open funnel shape, with undulating margins, rose-pink, April.

E. repens (E)
This is the Mayflower, making a prostrate creeping rooting shrublet with bristly branches about 8 cm. high and 45 cm. across. Leaves ovate or sub-orbicular tapered to apex, cordate at base, rugose, heavily veined, dull deep green, lighter below, margins ciliate and undulate. Flowers in crowded terminal racemes up to six globose five lobed fragrant, white flushed green at base, pink in bud; calyx lobes ovate, pink. April. A native of N.E. America.

E. repens 'Rosea' (E)
This is the extremely rare rose coloured form in all other respects similar to the type. April.

ERICA *(Ericaceae)*
The heaths, which is the common name for the species and forms of *Erica* as opposed to heathers, which are the forms and varieties of *Calluna vulgaris,* are a must for small gardens irrespective of size or shape. The smallest of gardens, this includes troughs and sinks, should have their quota as there are many dwarf forms that will not look out of place amongst their more aristocratic brethren. Not by any means are they less attractive with their diversity of colour forms, often enhanced by attractive protruding anthers, but they also offer a great variety of beautifully coloured foliage which gives them added charm. Even during the dull days of winter the *herbacea (carnea)* types will enhance the small garden, flowering in all weathers with the exception of in the snow when they are hidden, for neither wind, rain, nor frost can harm the hardy species and forms.

There is no doubt that they look better when massed and interplanted with some of the *Calluna* varieties, so as to have twelve months floral display; the dead flower heads can also be retained until the following spring, as these in themselves are attractive. In chapter 1 I discussed the making of a heath and heather garden as an adjunct to the rock garden proper but *Ericas* can also be planted as specimens, there being few dwarf shrubs to equal them.

Cultivation. First it must be remembered that with the exception of the *herbacea (carnea)* varieties most heaths are intolerant of lime. Naturally if planted in the garden as specimens, beds can be dug and the soil replaced with a lime-free compost which if made above the level of the surrounding soil, it should be possible to grow them successfully. There is on the market today, a compound based on the Geigy iron chelate, Sequestrene, with magnesium and manganese added, this corrects iron deficiency in limy soils. It must be used according to the maker's instructions, which state that two applications should be given in the first season, during March or April for the first and September for the second, dissolving the dosage in water and watering each plant individually. After the first season one annual application should be sufficient, this is given in early spring. If the normal soil is alkaline and it is desired to create a heath and heather garden it is essential to apply Sequestrene annually in order to grow a representative collection of plants but the annual cost of applying this iron chelate substance is far from cheap at present.

All heaths prefer an open sunny spot away from the drips of evergreens and the falling foliage of deciduous trees. If only a shady spot is available one must be prepared not only to lose a percentage of flowers but also the colour of the foliage is much less pronounced under these conditions. A light sandy soil well mixed with plenty of humus in the form of rotted leaf-mould or peat is the best medium. The first year after planting they must not suffer from drought and mulching in late May is beneficial. This annual mulch should be given until the plants have covered all available open space when no further mulching should be necessary. They are their own weed suppressors and once the plants have knitted together they only require an annual clipping over to remove the dead flower heads. Naturally the summer and autumn flowering varieties need not be cut over until the following spring as the dead flower heads add colour and background to the winter flowering varieties.

Propagation. This is by green cuttings taken in June and if placed in a very light sandy medium under a bell glass or in the propagating frame will soon root.

E. carnea, see *E. herbacea*

E. ciliaris (E). (The Dorset Heath)

The Dorset Heath has not such a widespread distribution as *E. herbacea (carnea)* being found in Cornwall and parts of western France, Spain and Portugal. It prefers a moister spot than *herbacea (carnea)* but even then the soil must be well drained. Does not object to half shade. It forms a somewhat lax trailing shrub up to 30 cm. high, but slightly less under sunny poor conditions. The foliage is in whorls of three, slightly sticky, hirsute, narrow oval, glaucous green. Flowers in spikes, large, urn shaped, beaked at mouth, bright reddish purple. July to August.

E. ciliaris Forms: (E).

'Alba'.

This is similar to the type with a sprawling trailing habit. Flowers not quite so large but of a good white. July to October.

'Aurea'

A good form with attractive deep yellow leaves, less than 30 cm. high. Flowers similar to the type, unfortunately not freely borne but this failing is offset by the fine foliage coloration. Flowers mid-pink. July to October.

'Maweana'

A natural form from Portugal found by the late Mr George Maw many years ago, it is about 45 cm. high depending on situation and it prefers a dry spot. If forms an upright shrublet with whorls of deep green, narrow oval leaves. Flowers in long racemes, large, rich crimson. July to September.

'Mrs C. H. Gill'
A small shrublet about 30 cm. high of crowded deep grey-green leaves. Flowers in congested terminal racemes, deep rose-red. June to September.

'Stapehill'
A good form rarely up to 30 cm. high with glaucous green foliage. Flowers in long terminal racemes of creamy white, and pale purple flushings deepening to purple at mouth. August to September.

'Stoborough'
The best white in the *ciliaris* clan up to 45 cm. in height with glaucous green glandular foliage in whorls. Flowers in long terminal racemes, round, pale cream in bud opening to pure white. July to September.

E. cinerea (E) (Bell Heather, Scotch Heather)
This is of course the best known of our native heathers and can be seen staining the moorlands especially in thge northern counties and Scotland with a sheet of purple in summer and autumn. It is very variable and it is difficult to point out the typical plant, for the variation is to a large extent geographical and a number of forms have been found and propagated for the benefit of gardeners. The plant is from 15 to 30 cm. high of erect twiggy branches with linear, fine, crowded foliage in whorls of four often with clusters of smaller leaves in the leaf axils, ranging through mid to deep green. Flowers in small upright racemes are oval, deep purple in colour. July to September. This species does well in full sun which it requires to form flowering shoots. Needs topdressing with peat before the weather gets really warm in the south, for it must not suffer from drought. The following forms are representative of the species:

'Alba'
A more erect form about 23 cm. high with foliage that can be from apple to dark green, in the latter the contrast between this and the flowers is remarkable. Flowers on long terminal spikes egg shaped, pure white. June to August.

'Alba Minor'
An ideal plant for the small garden as it rarely reaches 15 cm. high and is quite compact. Foliage is congested, mid-green. Flowers profusely, these are large, rounded, pure white and produced over a long period. June to October.

'Atrorubens'
Another vigorous grower up to 30 cm. high but more spreading. Foliage mid to dark green. Flowers large, borne on terminal spikes in profusion are of a striking ruby-red, which are outstanding. July to September.

'Atrosanguinea Reuthe's'
A smaller plant, rarely above 15cm. high with close compact habit. Foliage crowded, mid-green. Flowers bright carmine-red with a tinge of purple. July to August.

'Atrosanguinea Smith's'
A more recent form of close crowded branches about 15 cm. high.

Foliage deep green. Flowers in long terminal sprays of a glorious bright scarlet. July to September.

'Carnea'
This is a more open bushlet up to 30 cm. high with mid-green foliage. Flowers in terminal spires, light silver-pink. July to September.

'C. D. Eason'
An outstanding form up to 23 cm. high of erect sturdy growth. Foliage bright dark green, flowers of good substance, light pinkish red. June to August.

'Coccinea'
A dwarf spreading shrublet rarely up to 10 cm. high with close compact laterals. Foliage mid-green, crowded. Flowers good of a deep carmine-red. This is another form which is very suitable for the rock garden. July to September.

'Domino'
An outstanding white form which originated as a sport on a shoot of an ordinary *E. cinerea*. It is a close compact shrublet rarely up to 23 cm. high with crowded deep green foliage. The flowers are a distinct break in having black stems and sepals and a pure white corolla. July to September.

'Eden Valley'
A form which originated in Eden Valley in Cornwall and must be considered as one of the best. It is a more spreading than erect shrublet rarely up to 15 cm. high with light green foliage. Flowers in elongated terminal sprays are bi-coloured, the base of the corolla being white, turning to a deepish pink at the mouth. July to September.

'G. Osmond'
A good shrub of erect bushy habit about 30 cm. high with deepish green foliage. Flowers in terminal spires are pale mauve on almost black stems and sepals, both contrasting well. June to September.

'Janet'
A charming form of recent introduction, making a low spreading mat up to 15 cm. high. Foliage is pale green and flowers an attractive shade of pearl white. July to August.

'Mrs Dill'
A small procumbent shrublet very compact less than 10 cm. high with erect branches. Foliage mid-green, crowded, flowers in terminal sprays of a glowing pink and profusely borne. June to August.

'Pentreath'
This form, a small compact bush rarely up to 23 cm. high with crowded deep green foliage. Flowers, which are borne freely, are bright purple. July to September.

'P. S. Patrick'
A fine robust form growing up to 30 cm. high and quite erect. Foliage deep green and long sprays of deep rich purple flowers. July to September.

'Pygmaea'
One of the old reliable forms with a close compact habit rarely 15 cm. high with deep green foliage. Flowers of a good substance, bright rich pink. June to August.

'Rosea'
A fine plant which has stood the test of time making a robust shrublet up to 30 cm. high with crowded deep green foliage. Flowers in terminal

clusters a good shade of rich pink. June to July.
'Ruby'
A free flowering form rarely above 15 cm. high of a compact bushy habit and crowded deep green foliage. Flowers in terminal 15 cm. sprays of a deep glowing ruby. July to August.
'Schizopetala'
A distinct break forming a bushlet about 30 cm. high with green flecked bronze leaves. Flowers pale purple are curious in having the petals split to the base.
'Startler'
A fine dwarf form up to 15 cm. high with crowded bright green foliage. Flowers of good substance, rich pink. June to July.
'Victoria'
An upright form of sturdy growth and deep green foliage, about 30 cm. high. Flowers in long spikes are of a deep rich purple. June to July.
E. herbacea (E) (The Alpine Forest Heath) (Syn. *E. carnea*)
The type plant of the Alpine Forest Heath is found in many parts of Europe, on the high open woodlands in France, Switzerland, Austria and Italy; the further south one travels the better the colour, which reaches its peak in Italy. It is a low-growing shrub in exposed positions, rarely above 15 cm. high with both prostrate and ascending laterals densely clothed with narrow, linear, pointed stiff leaves arranged in whorls of three sometimes four around the stems. The foliage ranges in colour from dark to light green. The flowers are borne at the apex of the shoots in congested clusters pointing downwards, bell shaped, pale green in the bud state, changing to pale carmine with protruding anthers. December to April.
E. herbacea Forms: (E)
'Alba'
A garden form 15 cm. high which is near to white but still has a slight greenish tinge with dark brown protruding anthers. December to April. This has now been superseded by better white forms but it is still a charming, easy, good tempered plant.
'Ann Sparkes'
A new form said to be a sport from E. 'Vivellii' which is a compact bushlet only 15 cm. high and yellow-bronze with reddish tipped foliage and clusters of deep carmine-red flowers in late March and April.
'Atrorubra'
An old and well-tried favourite still to be desired with its deep glaucous green foliage and dark rich carmine flowers in late March and April. The height varies from 15 to 23 cm. according to position.
'Aurea'
A fairly new form up to 15 cm. high with bright golden-yellow foliage in spring becoming flecked with rust during the winter months. Flowers in tight clusters, pale rose. February to March. A good foil if grown among the other *herbacea (carnea)* types, but it is just as outstanding on its own.
'Cecilia M. Beale'
One of the good whites making an upright compact bushlet about 15 cm. high with freely produced very prominent flower spikes, the individual flowers are large for the size of plant. January to March.
'Furzey'
A prostrate rambling sub-shrub up to 15 cm. high with crowded deep

green foliage. Flowers in clusters, large rose-pink. November to April.
'James Backhouse'
Another of the outstanding Backhouse clan, up to 20 cm. high with the largest flowers of the many forms. Foliage crowded, mid-green. Flowers greenish in the bud stage opening to a very pale pink. March to April.
'King George'
A fine form this of tight congested branches densely packed with deep green foliage about 15 cm. high. Flowers crowded, light green buds turning to deep rich crimson. December to February.
'Loughrigg'
A fairly new form up to 23 cm. high with glaucous light green foliage, tipped reddish brown. Flowers pale purple. February to March.
'Praecox Rubra'
An old favourite, this is a mat-forming form rarely above 15 cm. high with dark green foliage. Flowers of good substance, deep rich red. December to March.
'Prince of Wales'
One of the last of the *herbacea (carnea)* types to flower, it is a dwarf plant about 15 cm. high with crowded mid-green foliage. Flowers congested light greenish pink in bud, opening to pale pink, late March to April.
'Queen Mary'
A charming dwarf shrublet rarely above 15 cm. high with congested dark glaucous green foliage. Flowers a fine shade of rich pink. November to January.
'Rosy Gem'
A fine form about 15 cm. high of close compact habit and crowded minute rich green foliage. Flowers good of a rich pink. March to April.
'Rubra'
An outstanding dwarf shrublet rarely 15 cm. high of crowded laterals and deep green foliage. Flowers in abundance of a really deep red. December to January.
'Springwood Pink'
This first originated as a sport from 'Springwood' but there are a number of different colour forms of this now, ranging from a large clear pink to a dark pink. Foliage of glaucous green of an open trailing habit. January to March.
'Springwood White'
A form discovered on Monte Corregio Italy of a low spreading habit and glaucous green foliage. Flowers in long spikes of a good substance and a really fine white. January to March.
'Startler'
A fairly new form about 15 cm. high of compact bushy habit. Leaves dull green, flowers light coral-pink. February to March.
'Vivellii'
This form originally came from Italy and makes a close compact bush up to 15 cm. high. Foliage is bright deep bronzy green to deep green in summer. Flowers pink in bud stage, changing to deep carmine-red. February to March.
'White Glow'
A charming form of upstanding branchlets about 23 cm. high with young foliage deep yellowish green turning to deep green, flowers large, pure white. February to April.

Erica carnea 'Springwood'

E. tetralix (E)
This is the Crossed-leaved Heath, a native of marshy spots on moorlands and is found all over England, but more especially in the western counties and Ireland. In gardens it does as well as other species and forms and provided there is a sufficiency of humus or peat in the soil it does not require a damp place. The first year after planting care must be taken that the plants do not suffer from drought. The species is a variable plant ranging according to geographical location from 15 cm. to 45 cm. high of both open and close compact bushes, the whole covered with a fine down. Foliage is in whorls of fours, grey-green, smallish linear with obtuse apex, margins covered with wiry erect hairs. Flowers in terminal umbels ranging from light to bright pink. June to October.

E. tetralix Forms (E)
'Alba'
This is the albino which is sometimes found wild amongst the species, up to 23 cm. high of much branched bushlets, foliage grey-green and drooping, terminal clusters of glistening white bells. June to August.
'Darleyensis'
A less compact form, more spreading than upright about 15 cm. high

and much branched. Leaves grey-green. Flowers in semi-pendant clusters, salmon-pink. July to August.

'Mary Grace'
This is a curious form but quite attractive with the calyx split into distinct segments. It is rarely above 10 cm. high with more spreading than upright branches, densely clothed with the linear whorled foliage of silver-grey and the quaint, bright pink flowers. June to October.

'Pink Star'
A plant of recent introduction, of an open loose habit, rarely up to 23 cm. high with soft, woolly, grey linear foliage. Flowers in erect loose terminal clusters, large glowing pink. June to September.

'Praecox Alba'
Another loose-growing form about 23 cm. high with many lax branches. Foliage wide, linear in whorls of four, grey-green. Flowers in loose terminal clusters, white. July–August.

'Praegeri'
A form from Ireland of close compact habit up to 15 cm. high with dense congested branches. Foliage wide linear, soft, downy, grey-green. Flowers in profusion, borne in terminal clusters, large, bright pink. July to October.

'Rubra'
Another fine form with close compact branches rarely up to 15 cm. high. Leaves attractive, linear in whorls of four, covered with a soft down, grey. Flowers in large terminal clusters of a fine deep rich red. July to October.

'Ruby's Variety'
This is a good form and unusual in that when in flower there is a combination of different colours. It forms a low growing shrublet rarely up to 15 cm. high with many lax stems. Foliage is the typical *tetralix* type of soft downy grey-green. Flowers in umbels, white at first, changing to rose when mature with deep purple mouth, so that each umbel will bear different coloured bells at the same time. July to October.

E. vagans (E)
The Cornish Heath, a British native, has a tendency to become large and often straggly but the many forms from this species are both dwarf and suitable for the rock or small heather garden. The type plant is a much branched, glabrous shrublet running up to 60 cm. in rich soil but only 30 cm. in a poor medium. Leaves glossy green, linear in whorls of four to five, apex obtuse, margins recurved. Flowers in erect terminal roundish racemes, globular, urn shaped. Pale lilac with deep exserted anthers. August to October. The following forms are representative:

'Alba'
This is similar to the type with a tendency to sprawl, but it should be grown for its free flowering habit of terminal racemes of white flowers enhanced by the deep exserted anther. August to September.

'Carnea'
A more compact form rarely above 30 cm. high with typical foliage and close terminal racemes of small flesh pink flowers. August to September.

'Cream'
A more open shrublet with semi-erect branches up to 45 cm. high. Flowers borne in profusion are creamy white on very long racemes. One of the advantages of this form is that it has a late flowering period.

August to November.
'Kevernensis' (Syn. 'St Keverne')
One of the old timers but still one of the best provided it is obtained true as it has a habit of reverting to type. It makes a close compact plant up to 30 cm. high and whorls of deep green leaves. Flowers in racemes of up to 30 cm. long, deep rose-pink. August to October.
'Kevernensis Alba' (Syn. 'St Keverne Alba')
Similar in its close compact habit to 'Kevernensis' but with shorter terminal racemes of smaller flowers of a good clear white. August to September.
'Mrs Donaldson'
Another form with a close compact habit rarely above 30 cm. high with crowded branches and deep green leaves in whorls. Flowers on terminal racemes of a creamy salmon-pink. August to September.
'Mrs D. F. Maxwell'
Another old favourite making a compact dwarf shrublet up to 30 cm. high and with deep green leaves. Flowers in long terminal racemes, these can be up to 30 cm. long under ideal conditions, large globular, deep cerise-rose. August to October.
'Nana'
A dwarf sport, the smallest of the cultivars reaching 15 cm. when mature, of a close compact habit and mid-green leaves. Flowers in small terminal racemes globular urn shaped, creamy white with exserted chocolate anthers. August to October.
'St Keverne', see 'Kevernensis'
'St Keverne Alba', see 'Kevernensis Alba'

E. × *watsonii.* (E). *(E. ciliaris* × *E. tetralix)*
A natural hybrid discovered by Mr H. C. Watson near Truro in Cornwall. It stands halfway between the species making a more or less erect bush up to 23 cm. high with many branches. Leaves arranged in whorls of four round the stems, linear, glaucous green. Flowers in terminal rounded heads, globular urn shaped, slightly beaked at mouth. July to September.
E. × *williamsii* (E). *(E. vagans* × *tetralix)*
Another natural hybrid discovered near the Lizard by Mr P. D. Williams, making a shrub up to 30 cm. high with whorls of bright green linear, obtuse foliage, new laterals yellow-green. Flowers terminal from the current year's growth globular, reddish pink. August to September.

ERINACEA (Leguminosae)

A monotypic genus with a natural distribution in France, Spain and Algeria, this is an ideal plant for the rock or small garden.
Cultivation. A hot dry spot is best but the plant must be placed so that its roots are protected from the sun in its first few years of life and although it comes from hot dry sites it should not be allowed to suffer from drought until established. It should be borne in mind that this plant is intolerant of root disturbance and the spot chosen should be the permanent one.
Propagation. By seed in March, the ensuing seedlings should be pricked out with care for any injury to the roots is invariably fatal.

Erinacea anthyllis

E. anthyllis (E). (Syn. *E. pungens; Anthyllis erinacea*)
In its native habitat the Hedgehog Broom makes hard spiny hummocks
up to 1 m. across and as much high, but in cultivation a gardener who
has a specimen 23 cm. high and 30 cm. across has indeed a fine
specimen, for it is extremely slow growing. It forms an upright hard
wooded shrub up to 30 cm. high of erect much branched, rigid, spine
tipped, grey-green smooth branches. Leaves few, simple, small, linear-
lanceolate, petiolate, silver-grey due to intense covering of silky hairs.
Flowers carried just below the needle sharp apex of branches, up to
four large, leguminose, violet-blue with a red tinge. May.
E. pungens, see *E. anthyllis*.

ERIOGONUM (*Polygonaceae*)

A large genus of plants from the New World of which there are a
number that can be used in the small garden.
Cultivation. A sunny well-drained spot is required for these plants and
care is needed in damp gardens for the woolly species.
Propagation. By seed when ripe or green cuttings taken with a heel in
July.

87

E. arborescens (E)

A dwarf shrub reputed to be 1 m. in its native habitat but in cultivation rarely grows above 30 cm. high and 38 cm. wide, tree-like with spreading almost contorted branches, reddish brown, striated grey. Leaves arranged in whorls at apex of stems, linear to oblong, mid-green, smooth above, white below due to intense covering of white hairs, margins recurved. Flowers clustered in terminal cymes, bright rose in bud, opening to white with green median line and pink stamens. July. A native of California. Not an exceptionally hardy plant and requires protection in all except warm gardens.

E. microthecum (E)

A dwarf much branched shrublet about 15 cm. high and the same across. Leaves alternate, linear to oblong, grey-green covered with white hairs. Flowers on much forked peduncles, citron-yellow. July. A native of California.

E. ovalifolium (E)

A small congested plant of short white hairy stems about 15 cm. high and 30 cm. across. Leaves elliptic to orbicular, tapered to base, silver-grey due to intense covering of hairs. Flowers on 10 cm. scapes in close umbels, white turning to pink with age, backed with bell shaped involucres. June. A native of N. America.

E. racemosum (E)

A native of W. America, this is a small few branched sub-shrub about 12 cm. high and 23 cm. across. Leaves crowded, oval to orbicular, light green, pale beneath with covering of white hairs. Flowers on small branched spikes, pink. July.

EURYOPS (Compositae)

A race of shrubs confined to Africa, not hardy except in a cool greenhouse, yet there is one which will survive an average English winter outside provided it is sheltered from cold searing winds.

Cultivation. A warm dry spot in a well-drained soil is ideal and it should be planted in a position where it is protected from cold winds.

Propagation. By green cuttings taken in July and rooted in the propagating frame.

E. acraeus (E). (Syn. *E. evansii*)

This is a native of the Drakensberg Mountains, S. Africa, where it makes a dwarf but erect much branched shrublet rarely above 23 cm. high and as much across. Leaves crowded, especially towards apex of twigs, long narrow, grooved, recurved, top third dentate, silver-grey. Flowers solitary on short terminal scapes, bright golden-yellow daisies. May to June.

E. evansii, see *E. acraeus*

FORSYTHIA (Oleaceae)

A small genus of flowering shrubs which are grown extensively for their early spring beauty but are much too large for the small garden, with the exception of one variety of *F. viridissima* that is small enough for inclusion.

Cultivation. Any well-drained loam will suit this plant and a site in full sun is best.

Propagation. By green cuttings in late June.

F. viridissima 'Bronxensis' (D)
This form originated in America and makes an erect much branched shrublet of glabrous stems about 20 cm. high and 23 cm. across. Leaves after flowers are lanceolate, entire, acute, pale green. Flowers up to three from lateral buds, four lobed, petals revolute, primrose-yellow. April.

FUCHSIA (*Onagraceae*)

A genus of shrubs and small trees, natives of Central and South America and New Zealand. There is no doubt that with their long flowering season, right until the frost cuts them off, they have an added attraction all of their own, in their delightful flowers.

The species, *F. procumbens* mentioned here is not reliably hardy except in the most favoured of gardens, but it can be kept going by rooted cuttings, over-wintered in the frame and is included because of its extraordinary flowers and fruits.
Cultivation. A sheltered position in a light loam to which has been added leaf-mould, in full sun is ideal. They need protection from cold winds.
Propagation. By cuttings taken at any time from June onwards and they root in a matter of a few weeks.
F. magellanica (D)
The species from Magellan, S. America, is too large but has provided us with two suitable forms for the small garden.
F. magellanica 'Prunella' (D)
Another delightful dwarf fuchsia less than 30 cm. high and 38 cm. across with charming hanging flowers of scarlet sepals and purple petals. June to September. Garden origin.
F. magellanica 'Pumila' (D)
A small compact shrublet about 15 cm. high and as much across with red stained branches. Leaves lanceolate-ovate, deep green, veined red. Flowers on slender scapes, red sepals and purple petals. June to September. Garden origin.
F. procumbens (D)
A native of New Zealand, making a dwarf prostrate shrub about 15 cm. high and 30 cm. across with slender stems. Leaves alternate, almost circular, cordate at base, margins slightly dentate, deep green. Flowers solitary, erect on small peduncles, calyx tube yellow with green base, sepals recurved, tinged purple at apex, petals absent. July to September. Bears in late September large ovoid-oblong red berries ageing to purple.

GAULTHERIA (*Ericaceae*)

This is an extremely interesting as well as being a very decorative genus of evergreen woodland plants having an extensive global distribution with the exception of Europe. There are representatives in Australia, New Zealand, the Himalayas, China and America. All are floriferous and the flowers are generally succeeded by extremely decorative fruits making the genus a very useful addition to a collection of dwarf shrubs, providing one attends to their few simple needs. The fruits are formed by the seed being enclosed by the enlarged and succulent calyx.
Cultivation. These plants have one thing in common, the need of an open, lime free medium well enriched with leaf-mould and in the south

at any rate, protection from the early morning sun. They are ideal for planting among dwarf rhododendrons with which they associate well. All require an annual topdressing of equal parts of loam, leaf-mould and coarse sand in early spring. *Gaultherias* are impatient of root disturbance and should be planted in their permanent position when small.

Propagation. Detach small shoots of the current year's growth in August and root in the propagating frame. Seed is another method of increase and it should be sown in March.

G. *adenothrix* (E)

A dwarf shrub up to 30 cm. on height and about 45 cm. across with much branched almost contorted slender stems. Leaves alternate, thick leathery, ovate, glossy green, margins ciliate, reddish brown, hairy below. Flowers solitary on reddish brown pedicels, pendant urn shaped, white flushed pink. June. Berries large, deep red. A native of Japan.

G. *antipoda* var. *depressa*, see G. *depressa*

G. *cuneata* (E). (Syn. G. *pyroloides* var. *cuneata*)

A low compact shrublet rarely above 30 cm. high but with a spread of over 60 cm. in time, with slender semi-procumbent stems, hairy when young. Leaves narrow, ovate, leathery, dark green above, paler below, margins serrate. Flowers in terminal racemes, pendant urn shaped, white, similar to sprays of lily of the valley. June. Fruits globular in clusters, white. A native of China.

G. *depressa* (E). (Syn. G. *antipoda* var. *depressa*)

A small species botanically near to G. *antipoda* and was at one time considered only a dwarf variety. It is smaller in all its parts, rarely up to 15 cm. high and a spread of 45 cm. making a mat, this forming a mass of interlacing rooting, bristly branchlets. Leaves alternate, coriaceous, elliptic to elliptic-oblong to sub-orbicular, all on the same plant, deep green, shortly petiolate, margins crenulate and bristly hairy. Flowers sub-sessile, solitary from the upper leaf axils; corolla five small obtuse lobes, recurved, pendant, white. June. Fruits large globose, pale pink. A native of New Zealand.

G. *humifusa* (E). (Syn. G. *myrsinites*)

This species is botanically near to G. *ovatifolia* but is smaller in all its parts. It forms a dwarf shrublet of tufted habit with erect branches up to 10 cm. high and about 30 cm. across, sparsely clothed with long hairs. Leaves oval, cordate at base, coriaceous, margins serrate, dark green, slightly hairy. Flowers solitary on short pedicels, urn shaped, white flushed pink. June. Fruits globular, scarlet. A native of British Columbia.

G. *miqueliana* (E)

A native of Japan, this is a dwarf shrublet rarely above 20 cm. high, but more likely to be less than 10 cm. and about 30 cm. across. This is much branched with semi-prostrate wiry stems. Leaves oval to ovate, coriaceous, margins serrate, deeply veined, glossy deep green above, paler beneath. Flowers in terminal racemes up to six white, green based or red flushed, urn shaped, June. Fruits rounded, white, well marked with depressions.

G. *myrsinites*, see G. *humifusa*

G. *ovatifolia* (E)

An outstanding dwarf trailing shrublet rarely above 10 cm. high and 30 cm. across with semi-erect branchlets. Leaves oval, rounded at base, very coriaceous, bright dark green, heavily marked, margins serrate. Flowers solitary from the leaf axils, urn shaped with five rounded lobes, pink. June. Fruit flattish, scarlet. A native of N.W. America.

G. procumbens (E)

A native of N. America, this is a prostrate plant of tufted habit, up to 10 cm. high and 60 cm. across with slender, reddish, hairy stems. Leaves borne at the apex of the branches, oval, minutely serrate, leathery, dark glossy green above, paler beneath, margins bristly turning to shade of bronze and red in autumn. Flowers pendulous urn shaped, both axillary and terminal, corolla lobes broad-ovate, pinkish white. June. Fruits globular, scarlet.

G. pyrolifolia (E). (Syn. *G. pyroloides*)

A dwarf creeping plant of tufted habit, a native of the Himalayas, where it makes dense mats of slender stems, rarely up to 10 cm. high and 45 cm. across. Leaves at apex of shoots, oval, thick dark glossy green above, hairy beneath, margins serrate. Flowers up to six in terminal or axillary racemes, corolla oval, urn shaped, white, flushed pink. May. Fruits globular, black.

G. pyroloides, see *G. pyrolifolia*

G. pyroloides var. *cuneata*, see *G. cuneata*

G. rupestris (E)

A more or less erect shrub up to 30 cm. high and as much across with scattered bristly hairs. Leaves on stout petioles, coriaceous, dull green above, paler below, elliptic to elliptic-oblong, apiculate, margins serrate. Flowers on pendant, hairy, reddish pedicels in terminal racemes, corolla urceolate, lobes broad-ovate, recurved, white, tinged pink. June. Globular, bright red. A native of New Zealand, needs shelter from cold winds.

G. sinensis (E)

A Chinese species, up to 30 cm. high and 45 cm. across with congested slender stems covered with appressed reddish hairs. Leaves oblong to ovate, dark glossy green, margins bristly, serrate. Flowers solitary from the leaf axils on short pedicels, white with recurved petal lobes. May. Fruit globular, bright blue.

G. thymifolia (E)

This is an outstanding dwarf shrublet from N. China rarely above 15 cm. high and having a spread of 45 cm. with prostrate reddish stems, sparsely clothed with long hairs. Leaves small, long narrow oblanceolate, recurved towards apex, tapered at both ends, margins serrate, glossy green above turning reddish in the adult stage, paler below. Flowers solitary from terminal axils, white urn shaped. June. Fruits large roundish, lilac-blue with persistent five lobed, fleshy deep violet calyx, an attractive combination.

G. trichophylla (E)

A good, dwarf, compact shrublet with lax stems up to 8 cm. high and 30 cm. across. Leaves sessile, oblong to oval, deep bright green above, paler beneath, margins ciliate and slightly serrulate. Flowers solitary from the leaf axils, bell shaped, pinkish white. June. Fruit globular, lapis-lazuli blue. A native of W. China.

X *GAULTHETTYA* (*Ericaceae*)

This is a bigeneric hybrid between *Gaultheria* and *Pernettya* and the one

plant mentioned here originated in the R.H.S. Gardens at Wisley.
Cultivation and propagation. Same cultural needs as for *Gaultheria*.
X *G.* 'Wisleyensis' (E)
A hybrid between *Gaultheria shallon* and *Pernettya mucronata*, it is a dwarf
shrub up to 45 cm. high and as much across. Leaves elliptic-oblong to
oblong-ovate, broad, cuneate at base, margins dentate. Flowers in
small racemes, up to fifteen, urn shaped, covered with a glandular
down, pearly white. May to June. Followed by rounded maroon fruits.

GAYLUSSACIA *(Ericaceae)*

A genus of plants confined to America, the Huckleberry has a close
affinity to *Vaccinium* producing two species suitable for the small
garden.
Cultivation. These require a cool position in a lime-free soil, some shade
in hot dry gardens, and are ideal for the peat garden. They must not be
allowed to suffer from drought.
Propagation. By green cuttings in June, rooting these in the propagating
frame, or seed when ripe.
G. brachycera (E). (Syn. *Vaccinium brachycerum*)
A close compact shrub up to 30 cm. high and as much across with
erect, wiry, triangular downy stems. Leaves small, crowded, oval to
ovate, leathery, bright glossy green, lightly dentate, margins revolute,
turning a brilliant red in autumn. Flowers erect in small dense clusters
on top third of laterals, from the leaf axils, urn shaped, white flushed
pink. April–May. Fruits bluish, pear shaped. A native of E. America.
G. dumosa (D). (Syn. *Vaccinium hirtellum*)
The dwarf Huckleberry is a small much branched shrub rarely 30 cm.
high and 45 cm. across, young wood glandular, hairy. Leaves entire,
obovate, pointed at apex, green covered with glandular down. Flowers
pendant, campanulate, in small axillary racemes, white, flushed pink.
May–June. Fruit globose, black. A native of N.E. America.

GENISTA *(Leguminosae)*

The Brooms have a wide distribution although almost exclusively
European, but there are one or two outlying species in Asia and N.
Africa. It is a large genus of flowering shrubs; the wild species are
generally some hue of yellow, ranging from pale to golden. *Genista* is
closely allied to *Cytisus* (p. 67) there being only a slight botanical
difference between the two genera.
Cultivation. All do well in hot dry sunny spots, they cannot have too
much sun in this country and the warmer the position the greater the
floral display. The species are best planted as young specimens. The
chosen site should be the permanent one as they dislike any root disturbance.
Propagation. By green cuttings in June, rooting these in the propagating
frame; hard-wood cuttings with a heel in late July or early August, or
seed sown in March.
G. aspalathoides (D)
A tiny prostrate shrublet rarely above 8 cm. high and about 30 cm.
across with grooved branches, hairy when young, smooth and spiny
tipped when mature. Leaves minute, linear-lanceolate, grey-green with
appressed hairs. Flowers from the leaf axils, in small clusters up to four

Genista hispanica

pea-shaped, light yellow. June. A native of S.W. Europe and N. Africa.
G. delphinensis, see *Chamaespartium delphinensis*
G. hispanica (D)
Where room can be found for this species the Spanish Gorse is one of
the finest of all shrubs but needs siting away from cold searing winds in
bleak gardens. It makes a plant from 30 to 60 cm. high and as much
across with semi-erect branches. The much branched laterals are
densely covered with long white hairs. Leaves simple, basal, oblong-
lanceolate, obtuse, upper linear-lanceolate, acute, grey-green, hairy.

Flowers in terminal clusters from erect leafy laterals bright golden-yellow with glabrous standard and downy keel. June to July. A native of S.W. Europe.

G. horrida, see *Echinospartum horridum*

G. januensis (D). (Syn. *G. triangularis*)
A species with a fairly wide distribution in Central and S.E. Europe which has given rise to the many synonyms under which it is known. The Genoa Broom makes a small prostrate shrub only 8 cm. high and about 38 cm. wide, with glabrous, three angled stems. Leaves short, narrow-ovate, dark green, smooth, sub-acute. Flowers solitary from the terminal leaf axils on 5 cm. pedicels in a small raceme, smooth, bright yellow. June.

G. lydia (D)
A semi-procumbent plant up to 30 cm. high and a spread of 45 cm. with first ascending then arching slender branches. Leaves simple, linear-elliptic or linear-obovate, acute, glabrous. Flowers in sub-terminal racemes on topmost branchlets which terminate in a spine, bright yellow, glabrous. May. A native of E., S.E. Europe and Syria. This makes a good wall plant.

G. pilosa (D)
A fine dwarf shrub rarely above 15 cm. high and a spread of 30 cm. in cultivation, although it is much taller in its native habitat. Stems slender, prostrate when young, more erect when mature. Leaves simple, small, elliptic-oblong or obovate, obtuse, sometimes pointed, bright green above, lighter beneath due to the covering of greyish white hairs. Flowers solitary from the leaf axils on small pedicels, clear yellow. June. A native of S.E. Europe including S. England.

G. pilosa 'Procumbens' (D)
A much smaller form only a few centimetres high but spreading into a wide mat of woody stems, covered in due season with the clear yellow flowers. June.

G. procumbens, see *Cytisus procumbens*

G. prostrata, see *Cytisus decumbens*

G. pulchella (D). (Syn. *G. villarsii*)
From Dalmatia and S.E. France, this species is a charming plant only 2 cm. or so high forming a mat about 23 cm. across of interlaced grooved hairy twigs. Leaves thin, minute, linear, hairy on both sides, grey. Flowers solitary from the leaf axils at the apex of the laterals, deep golden-yellow, corolla silky hairy. June.

G. sagittalis, see Chamaespartium sagittale

G. sericea (D)
A dwarf shrublet about 23 cm. high and 30 cm. across with erect, twiggy hairy growth. Leaves simple, small, narrow oblong to elliptic, bright green, glabrous above, hairy beneath, margins ciliate. Flowers in terminal racemes clustered together, golden-yellow, standard and keel hairy. June. A native of Tyrol and Dalmatia.

G. sylvestris 'Procumbens' (D)
A dwarf rock-loving form of the species up to 8 cm. high and 23 cm. across with angular twiggy stems. Leaves simple, minute, linear, crowded, deep green. Flowers in terminal racemes, golden-yellow. June.

G. tinctoria (D)
This species is too large for the small garden but it has produced two dwarf varieties which are suitable.

G. tinctoria var. *anxantica* (D)
A native of Italy, it forms a mass of grooved, twiggy stems only 8 cm. high and 23 cm. across. Leaves narrow, linear, pointed, deep green. Flowers in erect, terminal racemes, clear yellow. June.
G. tinctoria var. *hungarica* (D)
This is a prostrate shrublet up to 8 cm. high and 23 cm. across with closely congested twiggy branches. Leaves minute, ovate, pointed, bright green. Flowers in terminal clusters, bright yellow. June. A native of S.E. Europe.
G. triangularis, see *G. januensis*
G. villarsii, see *G. pulchella*

HALIMIUM (Cistaceae)
A small genus of flowering shrubs of which some members are suitable for culture in the small garden. They have a close affinity to *Helianthemum* and the majority will be found under this name in the catalogues. There are only slight botanical differences between the genera. In *Halimium* the style is short and straight and there are three or five sepals, in *Helianthemum* the style is long, curved and there are five sepals. Natives of the Mediterranean regions and W. Asia.
Cultivation. All members of this family require an open light soil in full sun and they do well against a sunny bank facing south where the wood can be well ripened, a safeguard against our changeable winter climate. They will tolerate a large amount of lime in the soil and although the presence of this is not essential it does enhance the foliage to a much greater degree than when planted in a neutral medium.
Propagation. This is easy by soft cuttings taken in late June, placed in the propagating frame where they will root in a week or so.
H. alyssoides (E)
Makes a dwarf shrub up to 45 cm. high and 60 cm. wide, grey due to the intense covering of woolly down. Leaves oblong to ovate-lanceolate, tapered to apex, sessile covered with a fine down, grey. Flowers terminal and axillary on branched stems, large rounded golden-yellow, unblotched. May. A native of Spain.
H. lasianthum sub-species *formosum* (E)
Makes a dwarf shrub about 45 cm. high and a spread of 60 cm. with erect grey branches and a mixture of small downy and longish hairs. Leaves oblong to obovate, obtuse, silver-grey in colour, three nerved. Flowers are large, golden-yellow with a brownish red blotch near the base of each petal and are borne in clusters on side branches. May. A native of Portugal.
H. lasianthum sub-species *formosum* 'Concolor' (E)
This is similar to the type but the flowers are of a clear yellow without the petal markings. May.
H. ocymoides (E). (Syn. *Helianthemum algarvense*)
Another charming shrublet about 45 cm. high and a spread of 60 cm. with erect grey downy branches. Leaves narrow obovate to oblong, slightly wedge-shaped covered with fine hairs, grey when young, turning green on maturity. Flowers in erect few flowered panicles, golden-yellow with purplish black blotch at base of petals. May. A native of Spain and Portugal.
H. umbellatum (E)
A distinctive dwarf shrub about 30 cm. high and 45 cm. wide of erect

open downy, sticky branches. Leaves sessile, linear, deep green above, white below. Flowers clustered in ascending umbels arranged on a 10 cm. scape, white with a yellow blotch at base of petals. May. A native of the Mediterranean region.

HAPLOPAPPUS (Compositae)

A large genus of plants containing over a hundred species, natives of N. and S. America of which there are two species hardy enough for the small garden.
Cultivation. Is best in a poorish well-drained soil in full sun.
Propagation. By division in March or green cuttings in June.
H. coronopifolius (E)
This is a native of the Andes, with prostrate woody stems forming a mat only 2 cm. or so high and about 20 cm. across. Leaves crowded, deep green, oblanceolate, acute, dentate on upper third. Flowers solitary on slender 15 cm. penduncles, golden-yellow, many-rayed daisy shaped. June to August.
H. spinulosus (E)
An erect sub-shrub about 30 cm. high and as much across with grey woolly stems. Leaves pinnate, lobes linear, acute. Flowers on leafy scapes in a corymbose panicle, daisy like with crowded overlapping ray florets, golden-yellow. August. N.W. and Central United States.

HEBE (Scrophulariaceae)

I have been interested in this complex genus over a good number of years and have grown all the species and varieties noted here in my garden in west Kent. This is not a warm area by any standard, often suffering from late spring frosts but to date not one has failed through cold winters or frost. Even the notorious winter of 1962–3 did nothing more than cut back a number of growths and these soon regenerated themselves when spring arrived.

They are useful in the small or rock garden not only for their floral effect but also with their diverse shapes and forms, one can state without exaggeration both are interesting and satisfying. They can hold their own against such plants as dwarf conifers to give grace and form in the garden, to say nothing of the many shapes and sizes of their foliage. These are then in due season enhanced with flowers of both grace and elegance.

The genus was at one time included in *Veronica* and even today are found under this generic name not only in nurserymen's catalogues but in text books. But whereas *Veronica* is distributed over a wide area of the globe *Hebe* is confined to the southern hemisphere and of the approximate hundred species known the large majority are endemic to New Zealand. Of the others, two are found in S. America, one in the Falkland Islands and a few in East Australia and New Guinea.

In this work the plants are listed under their correct genera *Hebe*, and *Parahebe*.
Cultivation. It provides no difficulty as all are easy in a well-drained medium such as one would find in a normal garden. A little shade is desirable in hot sunny gardens but this should only be needed when the sun is at its zenith. Gold bleak gardens present a problem for although hardy a number of the species resent cold drying winds which have a

Hebe armstrongii

tendency to defoliate the plants if exposed over a long period.

Propagation. By green cuttings taken in late July and early August which quickly root if kept close in the propagating frame, or seed of the species in March. All species can be cut back to retain a close compact habit if necessary which is characteristic of a number of these plants. It will be found that they readily break from either a bud on the old wood or from the base of the plant.

H. allanii (E)

A charming small spreading shrub up to 24 cm. high 45 cm. across, branches thick, covered with long hairs. Basal stem leaves stout, oblong, glaucous; upper broader ovate, sub-cordate at base, apex obtuse, entire, margins reddish, both sides of leaf covered with a dense hairy pubescence. Flowers in a simple lateral dense spike well clear of the foliage on shaggy hairy peduncles, sessile, corolla tube narrow larger than calyx, with four spreading, narrow, white lobes. July to August. New Zealand.

H. armstrongii (E)

An upright much branched shrub about 38 cm. high and a similar spread with thin roundish whipcord golden-yellow stems. Leaves appressed joined to two thirds of length when juvenile, roundish with acute, keeled tip, margins yellow, becoming less appressed when mature and at apex of branches. Flowers in terminal spikes up to six, corolla tube fused into broad obtuse segments, four lobed white. July to August. New Zealand.

H. astonii, see *H. subsimilis* var. *astonii*

H. balfouriana (E)

This plant was raised from seed, source unknown, at Edinburgh Botanic Gardens. Type specimen at Kew from Sir J. D. Hooker's garden 28 June 1894. Specimens sent from Edinburgh by Prof J. B. Balfour to New Zealand were recorded as a hybrid with *H. vernicosa* as one parent and *H. pimeleoides* could be the other.

It makes a compact spreading shrub up to 60 cm. high and as much across of purplish-brown branches and branchlets the under parts which are covered with a fine down. Leaves opposite in alternate lines, entire, thick, narrow oval to ovate, abrupt at base, recurving from a small appressed petiole, apex acute, glabrous, bright green. Flowers opposite in terminal racemes with four acute corolla lobes on short pedicels, purplish blue. June to July.

H. bidwillii, see *Parahebe* x *bidwillii*

H. buchananii (E)

This is a small compact shrublet, much branched up to 20 cm. high and about the same across with thick roundish black stems, branchlets round deep glossy green with a pair of well marked pubescent stripes. Leaves spreading broadly ovate, thick, glaucous, concave, sub-acute, dull green, margins thick, purple in juvenile state, midrib prominent, keeled towards apex. Flowers in up to four spikes from laterals, crowded, sessile; corolla tube small, four lobes narrow, white. June to July. New Zealand.

H. buchananii var. *exigua* (E)

This is a much smaller variety found on the Hooker Glacier, New Zealand, at 1,500 m. and differs in that the foliage is smaller, in fact the whole plant rarely grows up to 15 cm. high, otherwise it is similar to the type.

H. buchananii 'Nana' (E). (Hort.)

One of the mysteries of this complex genus, quite distinct, it is probably only a microform which has been perpetuated by vegetative means, as I have never seen this in flower. Here it makes a minute 'bun' in the raised scree, and is only 8 cm. across by 4 cm. high after four years, no doubt in a richer medium it would be larger. It differs from the species in that the foliage is narrow-oval with sub-acute base, dull green, midrib not pronounced.

H. canterburiensis (E). (Syn. *Hebe vernicosa* var. *canterburiensis*)

This is a small prostrate shrublet rarely above 30 cm. high and the same across with semi-erect branches covered with fine down. Leaves entire, semi-imbricated, arranged in two rows, thickish obovate, sub-acute, apex obtuse, glossy green above, duller below, petiole and leaf margins covered with a very fine down. Flowers lateral congested in small racemes, peduncle minute, pedicels small; corolla lobes spreading smaller than tube, white. June to July. A native of New Zealand.

H. 'Carl Teschner' (E)

A garden hybrid reputed to be between *H. elliptica* and *H. pimeleoides* from the garden of Mr James Speden, New Zealand. This makes a much branched compact shrub with semi-procumbent deep purple stems up to 15 cm. high and a spread of 45 cm. Leaves narrow oval, sub-acute, glossy green. Flowers in axillary and terminal racemes are violet; lobes wide ovate, pointed, with a white throat. June.

H. carnosula (E)

A small compact dwarf shrub rarely up to 30 cm. high and as much across of firm woody thickish branches having a distinct pubescence towards apex. Leaves entire, wide obovate, thick more or less concave, reflexed at apex, glaucous green, petiole broad, midrib obscure. Flowers crowded in laterals forming a terminal spire, pedicels downy. Corolla has long spreading lobes, white. New Zealand. July–August. Not a distinct species and as noted by Cockayne and Allan is best regarded as a hybrid.

H. catarractae, see *Parahebe catarractae*

H. catarractae var. *diffusa*, see *Parahebe catarractae* var. *diffusa*

H. ciliolata (E). (Syn. *Veronica gilliesiana*)

A shrub up to 30 cm. high and 38 cm. across of much branched semi-procumbent habit; branchlets deeply grooved. Foliage arranged closely in vertical rows of four round the stems, narrow-oblong, concave, base broad, apex thick, squarish, appressed, dull green; margins have short wiry hairs. Flowers lateral in one to three pairs, sessile with rounded corolla lobes, tube smaller than calyx, white. June. A native of New Zealand.

H. colensoi (E)

A small growing compact shrublet rarely up to 45 cm. high and 30 cm. across with stout glaucous smooth branchlets. Leaves crowded, obovate to elliptic-oblong, thick, recurved at apex, glaucous green both sides, sub-acute, margins sometimes toothed, slightly revolute. Flowers lateral or terminal, lower racemes often tripartite, sessile. Corolla tube same size as calyx, lobes longer, narrow sub-acute, white. July to August. A native of the North Island, New Zealand.

H. colensoi var. *hillii* (E)

This variety is a small edition, only about 23 to 30 cm. high and 23 cm. across with elliptic leaves, three to ten pairs of marginal teeth otherwise similar to the type. A native of the Kaweka Range, North Island, New Zealand.

A small shrub with decumbent branches about 30 cm. high and a spread of 38 cm. branchlets slender usually erect, dark glossy purple-black with two rows of pubescence. Leaves spreading, entire, elliptic to broad-elliptic, slightly concave, margins red, tapered to base, glabrous, midrib obscure. Flowers lateral in congested racemes on pubescent peduncles; bracts and pedicels short, corolla tube narrow, lobes rounded, spreading, white. July to August. A native of the South Island, New Zealand.

H. 'Edinensis' (E)

This hybrid is a cross between *H. hectori* and *H. pimeleoides* but seems to be nearer to *pimeleoides*. It forms a roundish bushlet about 23 cm. high with a 30 cm. spread, much branched from the base with regular roundish branchlets, bright green and glabrous. Leaves in opposite alternate pairs, entire, erecto-patent, thick, wide lanceolate, sub-acute, narrowing leaf base, clasping, concave slightly keeled, glabrous bright shiny green above paler below. Flowers on axillary laterals almost sessile with keeled ovate thickish bracts. Corolla lobes spreading with smallish tube bright blue. June to July.

H. epacridea (E)
A prostrate creeping shrublet with woody stems only a few centimetres high and a spread of 20 cm. Leaves crowded entire sub-acute, recurved, keeled, broad ovate, glabrous dull green, margins thick reddish covered with short hairs on lower third. Flowers in compact spikes from the leaf axils, end of shoots almost terminal; bracts elliptic, keeled with long hairs. Corolla tube narrow, lobes short, white. July. A native of South Island, New Zealand.

H. 'Fairfieldii' (E)
This is a garden hybrid that was accorded specific rank by Hook, f. in *Botanical Mag.*, 49, 1893 t. 7323, basing description on a plant sent to Dr Balfour from a Mr Martin of the Fairfield Nursery, New Zealand, to date it has never been found in the wild. Is reputed to be a hybrid between *H. hulkeana* × *H. lavaudiana* and certainly shows characteristics of both species. It forms a small erect slender branched shrublet up to 30 cm. high and as much across. Leaves grey-green, sparse, fleshy ovate to sub-orbicular, margins pubescent, crenate dentate, reddish; slight pubescence on lamina, and midrib, petioles long, channelled; this foliage is similar to *lavaudiana*. The flowers are a replica of *huikeana* just as decorative, of a bright lavender; bracts and calyx lobes covered with pubescence and the calyx has a fifth lobe smaller than the rest. July.

H. haastii (E)
A dwarf prostrate shrub with many procumbent or ascending branches and laterals up to 24 cm. or so high and about 30 cm. across. Branches glabrous or slightly hairy below leaf nodes. Leaves thickish and fleshy, closely imbricated, broad ovate to ovate-spatulate, concave, united at base, hairy margins, ridged, generally entire sometimes with a few notches on upper third, dull green. Flowers in spikes from axils of upper leaves, also terminal making a compact ovoid cluster. Bracts lanceolate to linear, obtuse, hairy on lower third, calyx lobes longer but similar. Corolla tube long narrow with small lobes, white. July to August. A native of South Island, New Zealand.

H. hectori (E)
Another whipcord species with erect stiff roundish glossy stems about 45 cm. high and a 23 cm. spread, only occasionally branched which become erect. Leaves glossy green densely imbricated, joined up to two thirds; wide ovate-deltoid, fleshy, rounded on back, convexly incurved, apex obtuse to sub-acute sometimes with small obtuse mid-rib, margins ciliate when young. Flowers in terminal spikes, bracts broadly ovate, mucronate, faintly ribbed. Calyx lobes ovate-oblong, sub-acute, faintly ribbed lower third joined. Corolla tube similar to calyx, lobes spreading, white, sometimes tinged pink. July. A very variable species with a number of forms that have yet to find a permanent home. A native of New Zealand in the South Island.

H. hookeriana, see *Parahebe hookeriana*

H. hulkeana (E)
One of the best of all the many *Hebe* species making a grand decorative plant for the small garden, needing only shelter from the cold biting east winds in exposed positions. It forms a soft-wooded slender shrublet up to a maximum of 60 cm. high and a spread of 45 cm., much branched, branchlets lax, rugose, reddish brown, glabrous. Leaves spreading sub-orbicular, sub-acute, margins widely bi-serrate, deep

glossy green above paler below, upper surface shows veining, midrib sunken with a light brownish pubescence, petiole long, channelled. Flowers in a broad terminal panicle up to 45 cm. long, branched towards base with slender spikes, sessile. Corolla lobes ovate, lavender with extended style, stigma lobed. May to June. A native of South Island, New Zealand.

H. lavaudiana (E)

A smallish soft wooded shrub up to 30 cm. high and the same across with lax semi-procumbent branches which later become erect, covered with soft glandular pubescence. Leaves fleshy, grey-green, spreading, obovate to sub-orbicular, obtuse to sub-acute, margins crenate-dentate, reddish with soft sparse pubescence; midrib and on young leaves, lamina pubescent. Petiole short, stout, pubescent, channelled. Flowers in terminal corymbose slender stalked panicles, sessile, peduncle leaves generally alternate, densely pubescent. Calyx lobes acute, ciliate, front pair fused, often small fifth one present. Corolla tube equal to calyx, lobes obtuse pinkish lilac, style glabrous, stigma lobes. May. A native of South Island, New Zealand.

H. lyallii, see *Parahebe lyallii*

H. lycopodioides (E)

An erect stiff shrub ranging from 30 to 60 cm. in height and a spread of 38 cm. but there are a number of smaller forms, with four-angled many

Hebe macrantha

101

branchlets; bright yellow-green. Leaves thick, appressed, joined in pairs to one third of their length, wide deltoid to semi-circular, strongly convex and rounded; apex obtuse or sub-acute, green ribbed yellow; margins sinewy yellow, narrowed into a wide blunt yellow spine. Flowers in lateral spikes up to twelve with spreading corolla, lobes white, anthers blue. June. A native of South Island, New Zealand. This species shows great variation and is very complex, sometimes bears foliage which is not appressed and is much narrower that the type.

H. macrantha (E)
A rather untidy rambling shrub up to 45 cm. high and as much across with few erect branches and branchlets, these being glabrous except near the apex which has a small pubescence. Leaves spreading, elliptic to sub-orbicular, leathery, narrowing wedge shaped to petiole, apex obtuse to sub-acute, margins cartilaginous with obtuse teeth, glabrous bright green. Flowers on small pedicels, lateral in axillary racemes, peduncle leaf pubsecent. Corolla tube shorter than calyx, lobes rounded and spreading, white. June to July. A native of South Island, New Zealand.

H. ochracea (E)
An upright, rigid flat topped or roundish shrub about 20 cm. high and 40 cm. wide with stout stems and arching branches, ochre coloured at tip. Leaves joined together for about one third of length broadly triangular, ochre-yellow when young. Flowers in a ten flowered spike, white. June. A native of New Zealand.

H. olsenii, see *Parahebe hookeriana* var. *olsenii*

H. parviflora (E)
This is a shrubby much branched shrublet up to 60 cm. high and 45 cm. across with roundish glabrous branches. Leaves close, entire, linear-lanceolate, stiff smooth glabrous, acute, dull green. Flowers from the upper axils in racemes on a stout rounded peduncle. Corolla lobes obtuse, white flushed lilac. July–August. A native of South Island, New Zealand.

H. pimeleoides (E)
A dwarf shrub rarely up to 30 cm. high, often only 15 cm. and a spread of 23 cm. with decumbent or semi-erect branches, these being dark bronzy green. Leaves entire, glabrous, fleshy, semi-erect, decurved, narrow lanceolate to broad-obovate, sub-acute, margins reddish, leaf base slightly concave, midrib shows below. Leaves generally of one type on individual plants. Flowers lateral on a slender hairy pubescent peduncle in pairs almost sessile or on very short pedicels. Corolla tube small, lobes outstanding, purplish. June to August. A native of South Island, New Zealand.

H. pimeleoides var. *minor* (E)
This is a dwarf form only a few centimetres high and about 15 cm. across with hairy pubescent branchlets; leaves smaller, lanceolate, acute otherwise similar to the type. First discovered in the shingle beds near Lake Heron, Middle Island, New Zealand.

H. pinguifolia (E)
A variable shrub which can be either erect or prostrate from 15 to 60 cm. high and a spread of 30 cm. with stout branchlets covered with a fine pubescence. Leaves thick and glaucous, entire, either imbricated or open, wide ovate, concave, obtuse glabrous, tapered to base, midrib indefined. Flowers lateral, simple, crowded, sessile. Corolla tube small,

Hebe pimeleoides

lobes long and narrow, white with blue anthers. June to August. Native of South Island, New Zealand.

H. pinguifolia 'Pagei' (E)
A plant which has had a varied career there being great uncertainty as to its place of origin for many years. It has now been decided that it came to Kew from the Dunedin Botanic Garden 1925. Whatever its origin it is a first-class plant and well worthy of the Award of Merit it received at Chelsea 1958. It makes a compact shrub up to 30 cm. high and about 24 cm. across with ascending purplish glaucous, glabrous branchlets with bi-farious pubescence, these ageing to green but colour persisting at nodes. Leaves sessile, entire, spreading, reflexed elliptic-obovate, obtuse, concave, glaucous, margins purplish, cuneate; midrib not prominent. Flowers lateral in spike almost sessile with small corolla tube, lobes spreading, basal elliptic others ovate, white, anthers purple. June

H. propinqua (E)
A small dwarf plant up to 30 cm. high and a spread of 45 cm. forming a close bush of congested roundish branches. Leaves thick entire, joined up to half their length, broad ovate, obtuse, rounded on back, top half standing away sharply from branchlet, green. Flowers in terminal spikes up to eight. Corolla lobes narrow ovate-oblong, obtuse, joined

103

one third of their length, spreading, white. July–August. A native of the South Island, New Zealand.

H. salicornioides (E)
An erect shrub up to 60 cm. in height and as much across, but rarely reaching this stature in cultivation, of pliable rounded dull branches and branchlets. Leaves green, entire, fleshy, joined to half their length in pairs, appressed, obtuse, slightly convex and incurved, light green marginal rim. Flowers in terminal spikes up to twelve; corolla lobes spreading, white. July to August. A native of South Island, New Zealand.

H. subsimilis var. *astonii* (E). (Syn. *H. astonii*)
This forms a dwarf lax tuft of slender stems much branched near apex and slightly four-angled, about 15 cm. high and 23 cm. across. Leaves deltoid-oblong, obtuse, appressed at base but apex standing clear in juvenile state; more imbricated when mature, concave, thick leathery but not keeled, rich golden-yellow. Flowers in small axillary clusters near the apex of the stems; corolla lobes spreading, tube small, white. July. A native of the North Island, New Zealand.

H. tetragona (E)
A fine upright shrublet about 30 cm. high and as much across with yellow-green, four-angled branches. Leaves crowded, simple, deltoid to subulate, joined at base, thick concave, keeled, pointed apex, flat inside apex, yellow-green. Flowers in terminal spikes up to twelve; corolla tube small, lobes spreading, white. July. A native of North Island, New Zealand.

H. tetrasticha (E)
A small slender erect shrublet up to 15 cm. high and 23 cm. across with four-angled grooved branches, these being much sub-divided into slender laterals. Leaves dull very congested, appressed to stem, imbricated in four vertical lines, deltoid above wide base, concave, apex obtuse, not acute, margins minute ciliate, stiff, dull dark green. Flowers on small spikes from terminal leaf axils on one to three pairs sessile; corolla tube flat, lobes rounded, white. May to June. A native of South Island, New Zealand.

H. vernicosa var. *canterburiensis*, see *H. canterburiensis*

HEDERA (*Araliaceae*)
The common ivy is so well known that it needs no description here for it abounds everywhere in the British Isles, giving colour during the winter months, even though it be of a somewhat sombre mantle of deep green, and also hiding what would often be a hideous piece of architecture with its close-fitting robe of foliage. It has sported a number of forms, of which three are suitable for the rock or small garden, retaining their compact dwarf habit over a number of years, also looking well when placed against a buff of rock in a shady spot where little else will grow.
Cultivation. This is easy in any type of soil either in sun or shade where the plants will soon adapt themselves to such conditions. Naturally they make better specimens in a more generous medium.
Propagation. This is by cuttings taken with a heel and rooted in the propagating frame in August.

H. helix 'Conglomerata' (e)
A very dwarf slow-growing form usually not more than 30 cm. high and

a spread of 38 cm. but taking a number of years before this stature is reached. Leaves crowded, alternate, thick, typical ivy shape, dark glossy green.

H. helix 'Maple Leaf' (E)
This I do not know, but have been informed that it is an even smaller leaf form than *H. helix* 'Minima' with foliage similar in shape to the foliage of the maples. Is in cultivation.

H. helix 'Minima' (E)
One of the smallest of the forms, making a small congested ivy only a few centimetres high and a spread of 23 cm. with crowded, little greyish green tri-lobed, triangular leaves.

HELIANTHEMUM *(Cistaceae)*

The sun Roses are delightful plants for the small or rock garden, providing a fine display of colour when the early flush of spring flowers is over. Although the individual flowers are fleeting, lasting but a few hours or so, they are produced so prodigiously that for weeks on end there is a continuous display. They are closely allied to *Halimium,* with only slight botanical differences. (See *Halimium* p. 95). The genus is a large one containing over a hundred species of evergreen shrubs or sub-shrubs also herbaceous perennials distributed over Europe, N. Africa, W. Asia and N. America.

Cultivation. All these plants require sunshine; too much cannot be given in this country and a bank facing full south is essential for them to give of their best. Any good well-drained sandy loam is best and they are admirably suited to furnishing dry walls. After flowering the shoots can be reduced to two thirds of their length; this treatment will keep the plants compact and tidy.

Propagation. Is by green cuttings in June, placed in the propagating frame where they will root in a matter of weeks or so.

H. algarvense, see *Halimium ocymoides*

H. alpestre, see *H. oelandicum* sub-species *alpestre*

H. apenninum (E). (Syn. *H. polifolium*)
A semi-prostrate shrub up to 45 cm. in height and a spread of 60 cm., much branched, the branches covered with a fine white down. Leaves linear to linear-oblong, margins recurved, grey-green. Flowers in terminal racemes borne in succession over a long period, these are a clear white. June. A native of Europe, Asia Minor and Britain.

H. apenninum var. *rhodanthum,* see *H. apenninum* var *roseum*

H. apenninum var. *roseum* (E). (Syn. *H.a.* var. *rhodanthum*)
A similar plant to the type with flatter foliage and bright deep rose-pink flowers in June. A native of the Rhodope Mountains.

H. apenninum 'Versicolor' (E)
A variety with smaller lanceolate grey-green leaves and reddish flowers in June.

H. canum (E). (Syn. *H. vineale*)
A dense congested shrub only a few centimetres high, the slightly spreading branchlets covered with fine hairs, with a 30 cm. spread. Leaves ovate-oblong to lanceolate, mid-green, hairy above, light grey beneath due to the intense covering of down. Flowers in small terminal racemes, pedicels hairy, golden-yellow, unblotched. June. A native of Europe, Britain and Ireland.

H. chamaecistus, see *H. nummularium*

H. croceum (E)

This is a dwarf species about 5 cm. high and a spread of 45 cm. with silvery white, linear-lanceolate foliage and brilliant deep yellow flowers in June and July. A native of S.W. Europe.

H. lunulatum (E)

A compact hummock of congested downy shoots less than 15 cm. high and 20 cm. across. Leaves oval-oblong to obovate, drab green, smooth above, hairy below and on margins. Flowers terminal, solitary on hairy pedicels rounded, brilliant yellow with a crescent shaped blotch at base. June to July. A native of Italy.

H. nummularium (E). (Syns. *H. chamaecistus*; *H. vulgare*)

This is the *H. vulgare* of catalogues and there are many delightful colour forms. These are an asset to the small garden, at the front of borders or raised scree beds, and appended is a list from which a selection can be made to suit one's taste.

The type plant is a native of Europe and the British Isles and it makes a dwarf spreading mound rarely above 15 cm. high but up to 60 cm. across of much branched hairy laterals. Leaves oblong green above, hairy, silvery grey below. Flowers clear yellow borne in terminal racemes over a long period. June to July. Varieties of *H. nummularium* (All evergreen). June to July.

'Amy Baring'. A good dwarf form with large bright orange flowers.

'Apricot'. Fine apricot flowers with a deeper eye.

'Ben Heckla'. A good flowering plant with bright red brick flowers.

'Ben Dearing'. Rich crimson flowers.

'Ben Hope'. A good bright carmine.

'Ben Lawers'. A deep crimson form.

'Bronze Jubilee'. A double flowered form of brownish yellow.

'Coccineum'. A double brilliant deep red.

'Cupreum'. A single with deep bronze flowers.

'Firedragon'. Makes a sheet of deep crimson.

'Golden Queen'. A good clear golden-yellow.

'Jock Scott'. Has flowers of a light rose.

'Miss Mould'. Fringed blooms of a good salmon-pink.

'Mrs Earle'. A good double red with a spot of yellow at the base of petals.

'Rose of Leeswood'. A fine double light pink.

'The Bride'. Striking grey foliage and single white flowers.

'Venustum'. A bright deep red.

'Wisley Primrose'. Grey-green foliage and bright yellow flowers.

This list could be lengthened almost indefinitely, all to good purpose, or personal choice, but any good nurseryman's catalogue will furnish particulars of many forms not mentioned here.

H. oelandicum sub-species *alpestre* (E). (Syn. *H. alpestre*)

A congested dwarf shrub less than 15 cm. high and 30 cm. across with running branches densely clothed with very small greyish hairs. Leaves oval-lanceolate, wedge shaped, wide, green, hairy on both sides. Terminal racemes of clear yellow flowers on slender hairy pedicels. June. A native of Central Europe.

H. polifolium, see *H. apenninum*

H. tuberaria, see *Tuberaria lignosa*

H. vineale, see *H. canum*

H. vulgare, see *H. nummularium*

HELICHRYSUM (*Compositae*)

A race of plants of mostly white foliage due to covering of downy felt-like wool. Some are only sub-shrubs with thick persistent woody stems, while others are either herbaceous perennials or shrubs. It is a large genus containing over 300 species distributed over both warm and temperate regions of the Old World with the main groups being in S. Africa and Australasia. Their foliage is very decorative and the everlasting flowers are far from insignificant.

Cultivation. In the garden an open but sheltered spot in full sun is necessary for their well being, especially in the bleaker districts of the British Isles. Good drainage coupled with an adequate amount of water is essential during late spring and early summer. Some of the plants mentioned here are best in the raised scree bed and when grown under these conditions half shade is a necessity.

Propagation. The Whipcord species can be increased by cuttings pulled from the plant, not cut, and rooted in the propagating frame in May. All others can be increased by detaching rosettes which will quickly root in the cutting frame. June to August.

H. bellidioides (E)
This is a native of New Zealand and is quite an easy and delightful plant for the small garden. It forms a prostrate congested hummock of slender branches covered with a loose tomentum about 15 cm. high and a spread of 30 cm. Leaves crowded, broadly rounded, abrupt, mucronate at apex, base cuneate, petiole flat, glabrous, mid-green above, white below due to interlaced covering of tomentum. Flowers on short slender woolly scapes, with numerous narrow-oblanceolate, white bracts, terminal, small white florets. June to July.

H. bellidiodes var. *prostratum* (E)
This is a more compact dwarf form only a few centimetres high and 15 cm. across. Similar to the type but with sessile clusters of white florets at the tips of the branches. June. A native of Campbell Island, New Zealand.

H. confertum (E)
A small dwarf sub-shrub rarely above 15 cm. high and a spread of 23 cm. with erect stiff woolly branches. Leaves in whorls, oblong to spatulate, thick felted, white petiolate, veined on reverse. Flowers sessile in a small corymb white with a delightful golden centre. June. A native of S. Africa. Only hardy in very sheltered gardens.

H. coralloides (E)
A native of New Zealand where it inhabits high cliff faces in the mountains. It forms an erect stout main stem and thick tomentose branches with persistent leaves up to 24 cm. high and 15 cm. across. Leaves closely imbricate, oblong, obtuse, symmetrical, appressed, coriaceous on upper half, glabrous dark green; underneath concave densely clad in long tangled white hairs; margins revolute, apex hooded. The arrangement of the leaves is such that the appearance of the plant is similar to that of coral stems. Flowers solitary terminal, cream, florets numerous, 'everlasting' June. Peaty raised scree.

H. orientale (E)
This species is about 23 cm. high and 15 cm. across, very woody at the

107

base and producing loose rosettes of long obovate, extremely woolly greyish white leaves, pointed at apex. The flowers are borne on slender, felted 15 cm. scapes in tight terminal clusters, buds a fine satiny light yellow, opening to white. June. A native of Crete.

H. plicatum (E)
This is a sub-shrub with a woody base up to 30 cm. high and a spread of 23 cm. Leaves narrow spatulate to linear in tufts covered with a downy felt, grey. Flowers on a slender erect grooved downy scape in a terminal corymb, golden-yellow. June. A native of S.E. Europe.

H. selago (E)
This is a much branched shrublet resembling a whipcord *Hebe* up to 20 cm. high and about 23 cm. across with stiff erect branches and crowded branchlets. Leaves appressed ovate-triangular, sub-acute, coriaceous in upper half, apex hooded, glabrous on back, deep green, other side has dense coat of felted white hairs. Flowers solitary, sessile, terminal, creamy white. July. Best in a peaty raised scree. A native of New Zealand.

H. sibthorpii (E). (Syn. *H. virgineum*)
A fine rock garden plant from high cliffs on Mount Olympus in Greece. It forms a hard woody central base and stems up to 23 cm. high and wide. Leaves in elongated rosettes, thick fleshy, intense silver-grey, long obovate, tapering to a blunt point. Flowers in terminal clusters up to twelve on 23 cm. woolly scapes, glistening orange-pink in bud, opening to everlasting creamy white flowers. May.

H. virgineum see *H. sibthorpii*

HYDRANGEA (*Hydrangeaceae*)

A genus of shrubs native of N. and S. America and Asia which have provided a number of good plants for the garden. Unfortunately only one small branch-sport from the 'Hortensia' group of *H. macrophylla* is suitable for the small garden.

Cultivation. Needs a well drained soil enriched with plenty of humus in full sun. Top dress in late spring with a mulch of leaf-mould or peat to protect the surface roots.

Propagation. Is by green cuttings taken in late June.

H. 'Pia' (D)
It forms a close compact bushy shrub 12 to 18 cm. high and a spread of 40 cm. with erect slender branches. Leaves bright green, ovate, texture thick, margins serrate. Flowers white in a compact flat topped rounded cluster of deep rich pink bracts, fading to brick red. July to September. Garden origin.

HYPERICUM (*Guttiferae*)

A large genus of plants, the St John's Worts contain a number of species which are suitable for the small garden. They are for the most part easy, but one or two will test the skill of the grower to make them happy and contented in cultivation. There is a wide diversity in the size of the flowers but all are similar in shape and colour; generally five petalled, golden-yellow with a central boss of long thin deep golden-yellow stamens.

Cultivation. All the *Hypericums* are easy to grow requiring a light open soil in a sunny position. The dwarf prostrate species should be accommodated in a sunny raised scree while the more bushy shrubs are useful as a background for some of the delicate alpines. A word of warning is necessary here, the Rose of Sharon, *H. calycinum,* is sometimes offered in nurserymen's lists of rock plants but it should not be planted in a small garden or near choice plants, for it will soon spread over a wide area by underground runners.

Propagation. Plants can be increased easily by seed, division in many cases, or by green cuttings taken in July.

H. aegypticum (E)

A small erect shrublet about 15 cm. high and as much wide with many branched stems, densely covered with small oval to ovate, pointed, grey-green leaves. Flowers solitary on short pedicels, pale golden-yellow. August. A native of S. Europe. It is only really suited to a warm sheltered spot and is definitely not a plant for cold bleak gardens.

H. balearicum (E)

A more or less erect shrub up to 38 cm. high and a spread of 30 cm. with slightly winged stems. Leaves obovate, rounded at apex, tapered to base, with small protuberances, margins undulate. Flowers solitary from terminal shoots, large, bright yellow. June to September. A native of the Balearic Island, it is a plant that requires a sheltered spot and is unsuited to cold bleak gardens.

H. buckleyi (E)

This makes a dwarf shrub up to 30 cm. high and as much across, with erect much branched four-angled reddish stems. Leaves orbicular, bluish green above, paler below, turning red in autumn. Flowers solitary, rarely in threes, from the apex of the shoots, large typical, golden-yellow. July. A native of America.

H. confertum (E)

A semi-prostrate lax shrublet up to 15 cm. high and about the same across with four-angled stems. Leaves crowded, small lanceolate, obtuse, grey-green, covered with small dots, margins recurved. Flowers from the terminal leaf axils on short pedicels, rich golden-yellow. June. A native of Asia Minor.

H. empetrifolium (E)

The type form makes a dwarf semi-erect shrublet about 30 cm. high and as much across, but there is a much smaller plant only a few centimetres high which is very desirable. Branches slender, much angled. Leaves small, linear in whorls of three, margins recurved, grey-green. Flowers in small tiers, pale yellow. June. A native of Greece. Requires protection from cold winds.

H. hyssopifolium (E)

This is a prostrate shrublet about 15 cm. high and a spread of 30 cm. with lax, congested, red wiry stems. Leaves large linear, grey-green, glaucous below. Flowers in long terminal racemes, deep golden-yellow. June to July. A native of N. Asia.

H. kalmianum (E)

A shrub up to 45 cm. in height and a spread of 38 cm. which is useful in the small garden for it is a late flowering species. It makes a much branched four-angled stemmed plant, clothed with numerous long narrow bright green leaves. Flowers in terminal and axillary cymes, golden-yellow. July. A native of N. America.

H. nummularium (H)

A native of E. France, Italy and Spain, this is a small rambling sub-shrub up to 15 cm. high and 20 cm. across with slender stems, coppery red when young. Leaves orbicular on small petioles, green, glaucous below. Flowers in a small terminal cyme borne in great profusion, golden-yellow. July to August.

H. olympicum (E). (Syn. *H. polyphyllum*)
This makes a small shrub up to 23 cm. high and about the same wide with smooth slender two-edged stems. Leaves long, oblong, pointed at apex, glaucous grey-green with transparent dots. Flowers in small terminal cymes, golden-yellow. A native of S.E. Europe, this species requires protection from cold winds. May to June.

H. olympicum 'Citrinum' (E)
A colour variant, this has even more attractive flowers of a pale lemon-yellow. June.

H. orientale (H)
This is a sub-shrub up to 23 cm. high and as much across with upright flexible slightly crooked stems. Leaves linear-obovate to oblong, obtuse, stem clasping ciliate-glandular. Flowers in small terminal cymes, lemon-yellow. June to August. A native of Asia Minor.

H. polyphyllum, see *H. olympicum*

H. reptans (E)
Possibly the hardiest of the small *hypericums*, it is a native of the Himalayas, making a dwarf creeping sub-shrub only 2 cm. or so high and a spread of 48 cm. with self-rooting, wire like, smooth two edged stems. Leaves congested small, oval, obtuse, mid-green turning red-brown in autumn. Flowers solitary at the end of the shoots, red in bud opening to golden-yellow. July.

IBERIS (*Cruciferae*)

The Candytufts are well-known useful plants for the small and rock garden with their ease of cultivation and display of four-petalled flowers over a long period. They should be reckoned amongst the 'musts' as they only require a little attention. The flowering stems must be reduced by one third after flowering when all can be left alone with the knowledge that the plants will provide a further magnificent display the following spring. It is a comparatively small genus embracing about forty species of mostly sub-shrubs, natives of S. Europe and W. Asia.

Cultivation. Any good light well-drained soil will suit these plants, but the very dwarf saxatile species are best planted in a sunny raised scree bed. A little top-dressing of equal parts of leaf-mould, loam and sand, in early spring is beneficial.

Propagation. This is by seed sown in March, or green cuttings taken in late June.

I. gibraltarica (E)
A much tangled bushlet of branches up to 30 cm. high and as much wide. Leaves crowded, long narrow oval, dentate on upper quarter, apex rounded or obtuse, dark glossy green. Flowers on 10 cm. scapes, often branched, flattish umbels, congested, light lilac-blue. May to June. A native of S. Spain including Gibraltar, this species requires full sun and a position sheltered from cold winds.

I. jordanii, see *I. pruitii*

I. jucunda, see *Aethionema coridifolium*

Iberis pruitii

I. *lagascana* (E)

A dwarf procumbent plant up to 10 cm. high and 20 cm. across with stiff rounded branches. Leaves small, ovate, dentate, deep glossy green. Flowers in crowded terminal umbels, pure white with golden eye. May. S.E. Europe. Now included in *I. pruitii* but is quite distinct.

I. *pruitii* (E). (Syn. *I. jordanii*)

A native of Anatolia, this is a small prostrate sub-shrub less than 8 cm. high and a spread of 20 cm. Leaves alternate, crowded, spatulate, deep green. Flowers in clustered terminal corymbs, large for size of plant, white. May.

I. *saxatilis* (E)

Makes a dwarf prostrate shrub up to 10 cm. high and a spread of 20 cm. Leaves thick, small, crowded, oblong to linear, cylindric, margins ciliate, dull dark green. Flowers on short scapes in small terminal clusters, glistening white. April to May. A native of S. Europe.

I. *sempervirens* 'Little Gem' (E)

The species itself is a prostrate but far too spreading for the small garden. This dwarf form is only a few centimetres high and about 30 cm. across with smooth slender branches. Leaves crowded oblong, apex obtuse, margins ciliate, dull dark green. Flowers on 5 cm. scapes, large in flat terminal racemes, intense white. April. There are a

111

number of garden forms of this species, differing only in the whiteness of the flowers, of which 'Climax' is a good example.

I. simplex (E). (Syn. *I. taurica*)
A charming dwarf compact species with small semi-erect smooth branches only 5 cm. high and 20 cm. across. Leaves crowded, spatulate, apex notched, grey-green, covered with fine hairs. Flowers in a congested small flattish umbel, buds violet-blue, opening to a glistening white. May to June. A native of Asia Minor.

I. taurica, see *I. simplex*

I. tenoreana (E)
This makes a small compact bushlet with erect twisting branches less than 10 cm. high and 20 cm. across. Leaves oblong-linear, thick, rounded at apex, tapered towards base, margins ciliate, green. Flowers in flat terminal clusters, white. April. A native of Spain. Another plant which is now listed in the *I. pruitii* complex.

ILEX (*Aquifoliaceae*)

The Hollies are represented in this country by the many forms and varieties of *I. aquifolium* which in one way or another provide the berried branches for the Yuletide decorations. All are tall and unsuitable for the small garden but a Japanese species, *I. crenata,* has produced several forms which must be considered as some of the slowest growing of all rock or small garden shrubs.

Cultivation. A position midway up in the rock garden, backed by a buff of rock, these plants will help to bring the rock garden into its true perspective. Any well-drained good light soil will suit them, but they need plenty of water during dry spells.

Propagation. Cuttings rooted in the propagating frame July; these are very slow to reach sizeable specimens.

I. crenata 'Bullata' (E)
A dwarf form from Japan, very slow growing, reaching 38 cm. and a similar spread after many years. It makes a rounded stiff congested shrub with small twigs. Leaves crowded, broad, oval, dark glossy green. Flowers inconspicuous, dingy white followed by black fruits on minute pedicels.

I. crenata 'Golden Gem' (E)
This is a new colour form which makes a low rounded shrublet up to 45 cm. high and across. It is similar to 'Bullata' but has small thick leaves that are yellow-green and the coloration is more pronounced during the winter months.

I. crenata 'Mariesii' (E)
This is a very slow-growing form making less than 2 cm. a year to about 23 cm. high and as much wide with short, erect, stiff branches and small twigs. Leaves crowded, broad ovate to orbicular, dark glossy green, marked with two teeth at apex. The fruits are black, rounded on minute pedicels. Japan. This is a very desirable pygmy which will retain its dwarf stature for many years.

JASMINUM (*Oleaceae*)

A large and varied genus of plants mostly climbing or slender branched shrubs, of which only a few that are hardy enough for outdoor culture in this country. There is one small enough for the garden and this is a very desirable plant.

Jasminum parkeri

Cultivation. A light well-drained soil in full sun is suitable. A position flanking a large rock will allow this plant to drape it completely. A little compost of equal parts loam, leaf-mould and sand can with advantage be worked down among the branches in early spring.

Propagation. Is by green cuttings in early spring.

J. parkeri (E)

A low contorted much branched interlaced shrublet only a few centimetres high and spreading slowly to cover 14 cm. with congested smooth grooved stems. Leaves alternate five-foliate mid-green; leaflets oval, pointed at apex, tapered to base. Flowers from apex of the shoots solitary, erect, five lobed, bright yellow with a delightful fragrance. June. These are followed by translucent globular black fruits. A very desirable shrub giving nine months of pleasure with its delightful flowers and its far from inconspicuous fruits. A native of N.W. India.

KALMIA (*Ericaceae*)

A small genus of shrubs from the New World closely allied to *Rhododendron* and containing a few that are suitable for the small or peat garden.

Cultivation. A situation in a moist half shady spot is necessary for this

genus, a well-drained lime-free leafy soil is ideal and all benefit from a biannual top-dressing of peat or leaf-mould in late spring and autumn.
Propagation. By seed, in March, or half ripened cuttings taken with a heel of the old wood in July.

K. angustifolia (E)
This is a very variable shrub ranging from dwarf specimens of 15 cm. to large shrubs of a metre or more. For our purpose it will be necessary to obtain the smaller forms and it is best to get these from a reliable source, where such forms are grown. The type plant is a dwarf tufted shrub of open slender wiry downy stems. Leaves opposite, rarely in threes, oval, tapering to base, smooth, bright green, paler beneath. Flowers in congested clusters on the previous year's growth, open saucer shaped, deep rose-red. June. A native of N. America.

K. angustifolia 'Pumila' (E) (Syn. *K.a.* 'Nan')
A named dwarf form only a few centimetres high with typical foliage and flowers. June.

K. angustifolia 'Rubra' (E)
This is a much deeper coloured variety almost ruby-red and is a fine plant. June.

K. angustifolia 'Nana', see *K.a.* 'Pumila'

K. carolina (E)
A native of S. Carolina, U.S.A. this is similar to *K. angustifolia* but is more erect, up to 30 cm. high and a spread of 45 cm. with upright stiff branches. Leaves opposite or in threes, oval tapered to base, smooth bright green above, grey below due to intense covering of down. Flowers on previous year's growth, terminal clusters of purplish rose, saucer shaped; lobes recurved. June.

K. glauca, see *K. polifolia*

K. glauca var. *microphylla*, see *K. polifolia* var. *microphylla*

K. polifolia (E). (Syn. *K. glauca*)
A small erect shrub rarely above 30 cm. high and with a spread of 38 cm. much branched slender stems and two edged laterals. Leaves opposite rarely in threes, oblong to lanceolate, tapered to base and apex, margins recurved, deep glabrous green, greyish white below. Flowers in terminal umbels, open saucer shaped, rose-lilac. April to May. A native of N. America.

K. polifolia var. *microphylla* (E). (Syn. *K. glauca* var. *microphylla*)
Only 15 cm. high and 23 cm. wide with opposite ovate to oval, deep green leaves, grey below. Flowers in terminal clusters large rosy lilac, saucer shaped. May. A native of America from Yukon to California.

KALMIOPSIS (*Ericaceae*)

A monotypic genus which was discovered by Mrs Leach in the Curry County, Oregon, after whom it has been named. It is rare in its wild state and in cultivation the stock has dwindled with neglect during the war years, although it is becoming a little easier to obtain now. Unfortunately the plant is not easy, but there is hope that a form found in S. Oregon will prove more amenable to cultivation. According to reports this form named var. M Le. Piniec presents no difficulty and flowers profusely, but whether it will be more amenable under cultivation here remains to be seen.
Cultivation. This is best sited in the peat garden with other ericaceous

Lavendula latifolia 'Nana'

plants and the soil must be well enriched with leaf-mould, moist and well drained; half shade is essential.

Propagation. Cuttings taken with a heel in July and rooted in the propagating frame.

K. leachiana (E)

It forms a dwarf erect shrub about 23 cm. high and as much across, the young wood covered with minute hairs. Leaves small oval, leathery, dark glossy green above, spotted with sunken yellow glands below. Flowers in loose terminal clusters on slender hairy stems, saucer shaped, deep rose-pink. April to May.

LAVANDULA (Labiatae)

A genus of intensely aromatic plants, natives of the Mediterranean and sub-tropical regions. The common lavender, *L. latifolia*, has produced two dwarf forms and there is one species which can be considered for the small garden.

Cultivation. A hot dry spot in full sun with perfect drainage is suitable and they need only be clipped slightly back after flowering to enable them to retain a dwarf compact habit.

Propagation. Cuttings should be taken in August and rooted in the propagating frame, or division of the plants in April.

L. latifolia 'Alba' (E)

This is a dwarf shrublet with erect squarish branches about 45 cm. high and 38 cm. wide, grey in colour due to covering of minute hairs. Leaves linear, apex obtuse, margins recurved, greyish green. Flowers in whorls on crowded spikes, each flower having a pair of oval bracts at base, white. July. A native of Mediterranean region.

L. latifolia 'Nana' (E)

A dwarf garden form similar to the type but less than 15 cm. high with square grey downy stems and small linear pale grey downy leaves. Flowers crowded in a spike on a short scape, tubular greyish blue. July.

L. stoechas (E)

A small shrub the 'French Lavender' is generally about 30 cm. high and as much across with grey downy shoots. Leaves sessile, linear, margins recurved greyish green covered with a grey down. Flowers crowded at apex of a slender four angled scape in a spike, tubular deep purple, bracts purple, the whole atopped by a cluster of similar bracts. July. A native of S.W. Europe.

L. stoechas 'Albiflora' (E)

This is a just as beautiful white form similar to the type with both flowers and bracts being white. July.

LEDUM *(Ericaceae)*

A small genus containing a few plants that are suitable for the small garden and although not outstanding where floral display is concerned they are interesting.

Cultivation. Like the majority of ericaceous plants an open lime free medium containing a high percentage of leaf-mould or peat is required in half shade and shelter from drying winds. At no time should the soil be allowed to dry out and the plants should be mulched with half decayed leaves in late spring and again in autumn.

Propagation. This is by green cuttings taken in August and rooted in the propagating frame, or seed in March.

L. buxifolium, see *Leiophyllum buxifolium*

L. groenlandicum (E). (Syn. *L. latifolium*)

An erect shrub up to 60 cm. high and as much across with rust coloured hairy branches. Leaves oblong to narrow oblong, tapering to base, apex obtuse, margins recurved, dull dark green above, rust-red below due to heavy tomentum. Flowers in large terminal clusters, five petalled open, white. May. A native of Greenland and N. America.

L. groenlandicum 'Compactum' (E)

A dwarf compact form rarely 30 cm. high and as much across with typical oval to oblong leaves and stems covered with rust coloured hairs. Flowers smaller, white. May.

L. latifolium, see *L. groenlandicum*

L. minus (e)

A smaller plant near to *L. palustre* from N.E. Asia and differs from the species in being only 30 cm. high with erect branches and linear leaves. White flowers in dense clusters. May.

L. palustre (E)

The Labrador Tea is a small thin erect shrub up to 48 cm. high and

Leiophyllum buxifolium prostratum

wide, stems densely covered with rust coloured down. Leaves small, narrow-oblong, wrinkled, margins recurved, dark dull green above, rust coloured beneath with heavy covering of wool. Flowers in small terminal clusters, white cup shaped, five petalled. May. A native of the Arctic regions, Asia and America.

L. palustre 'Decumbens' (E)
A more prostrate lax form less than 30 cm. high with linear leaves and flowers in much looser terminal heads, white. May.

LEIOPHYLLUM (*Ericaceae*)

This is a monotypic genus related to *Ledum*, from the New World and the one species and two varieties are all suitable for the small garden.
Cultivation. A spot facing west in lime free soil with plenty of humus is ideal and they are good companions for other ericaceous plants. A topdressing of well rotted leaf-mould is beneficial in late spring and again in the autumn.
Propagation. Green cuttings should be taken in July.
L. buxifolium (E). (Syn. *Ledum buxifolium*)
The species is a dwarf shrub rarely above 30 cm. high and 45 cm. across, much branched with reddish young wood. Leaves small,

117

oblong-ovate, obtuse, arranged in whorls of three or four, dark glossy green, lighter beneath. Flowers in congested terminal clusters, buds pink, opening to white; five petalled tinged with pink. May. A native of New Jersey, U.S.A.

L. buxifolium var. *hugeri* (E)
This variety is much dwarfer, rarely above 15 cm. high with alternate long, narrow, deep glossy green leaves and terminal clusters of white flowers. May. A native of E. America.

L. buxifolium var. *prostratum* (E). (Syn. *L. lyonii*)
This form is an even smaller prostrate shrublet less than 15 cm. high and about 23 cm. across, quite compact. Leaves oblong-ovate, opposite, deep glossy green, lighter below. Flowers in small terminal clusters of white flushed pink, five petalled. May. A native of E. America.

L. lyonii, see *L. buxifolium* var. *prostratum*

LEUCANTHEMUM (Compositae)

A small genus containing one species of outstanding beauty of both foliage and flowers.
Cultivation. A well-drained light soil in full sun.
Propagation. This is best by seed sown in March; or green cuttings taken in June.

L. hosmariense (E). (Syn. *Chrysanthemum hosmariense*)
A small woody stemmed, much branched plant about 15 cm. high and a spread of 20 cm. with silver-grey leaves; leaflet trifid. Flowers solitary on a silver 15 cm. scape, large with pure white ray florets, disk yellow shading to green in centre, bracts silvery, margined black. April. A native of Algeria.

LEUCOGENES (Compositae)

This is a small genus containing two species of sub-shrubs endemic to New Zealand, which are a 'must' for any worthwhile collection of small shrubs. *L. grandiceps* is confined to the mountains of the South Island, whereas *L. leontopodium* is native to both North and South Islands and as the specific name of the latter denotes they are the New Zealand counterparts of the European Edelweiss, but even more decorative with their persistent sub-shrubby stems and evergreen glistening silver foliage.
Cultivation. A cool, dryish but not arid spot is needed for these plants and in the south protection from too much direct sunshine is desirable. A position facing west in a well-drained light soil to which a little peat is added will do much to make these aliens feel at home.
Propagation. Green cuttings, taken in June strike easily if rooted in pure sand and kept moist.

L. grandiceps (E)
A soft woody shrublet lax in growth, but not prostrate, up to 10 cm. high and a spread of 15 cm. with stout rounded stems densely clothed with a fine woolly down. Leaves arranged in symmetrical whorls along the whole length of the branches somewhat intricate often apiculate, obovate-cuneate, completely covered with a fine silvery white wool, so that the plant appears to shine. Flowers in a congested terminal

118

cluster, very light yellow, surrounded by a symmetrical collar of woolly, silvery floral bracts. June.

L. leontopodium (E)

A more erect plant than *L. grandiceps* with white woolly rounded stems up to 20 cm. high and a spread of 15 cm. from more or less decumbent branches. Leaves congested in a symmetrical pattern round the stems, sessile, linear to lanceolate-oblong, acute to sub-acute silver-grey in colour due to intense covering of silky shining appressed tomentum. The flowers are produced on short laterals, sparsely clothed with alternate and opposite white woolly leaves, typical composite light yellow, surrounded by radiating silver woolly bracts. June. There is no doubt that both these plants are not easy to keep in good health over long periods in this country, but by taking frequent cuttings and raising new stock it is possible to have fine compact specimens.

LEUCOPOGON fraseri, see *CYATHODES fraseri*

LEUCOTHOË (Ericaceae)

A small genus of hardy shrubs from Japan and N. America but there is only one species which is dwarf enough for the small garden. Although small in stature it has the distinction of having the largest flowers of the genus.

Cultivation. A moist lime-free aspect in part shade although if the humus content is high more sun will be tolerated, giving a fine display of autumnal tints. Topdress twice a year in early spring and late summer with a good mulch of rotted leaves.

Propagation. Is effected by green cuttings taken with a heel of older wood in August and rooted in the propagating frame.

L. keiskei (E)

From a central rootstock radiate the prostrate, zig-zagged smooth shoots, red in juvenile state not more than 15 cm. high but covering an area of 30 to 45 cm. Leaves thick, alternate, large oval to ovate, tapering to a fine point, faintly serrulate, sparsely bristly below, bright shiny red when young turning to deep glossy green when mature. Flowers in small racemes from the terminal of the shoots, pendant, cylindrical, five recurving lobes, white. July. A native of Japan. Colours well in autumn.

LINUM (Linaceae)

A widely distributed genus of plants from the warmer temperate regions containing annuals, perennials and shrubs, a few suitable for the small garden.

Cultivation. A spot in full sun is desirable, for this genus demands sunshine to give of its best. A well-drained medium but not rich, is necessary and an ample supply of water during the growing season.

Propagation. Is easy by green cuttings taken in late June and rooted in the propagating frame. Quick rooting is essential for unless they have become well established before the winter sets in, the rooted cuttings are not easy to bring through this period successfully.

L. arboreum (E)

This is a smooth compact much branched shrub up to 30 cm. high and as much across with glabrous rounded stems. Leaves sessile, spatulate,

119

Linum arboreum

obtuse, recurved, grey-green. Flowers in short stemmed terminal panicles, fleeting, thin textured five petalled, golden-yellow. June to
September. A native of Crete.

L. arboreum 'Gemmells Hybrid' (E)

A fine form only about 23 cm. high and a similar spread with large
clusters of deep rich yellow flowers over a long period. June to
September. A more hardy plant than the species which is often cut
during cold spells in bleak gardens.

L. monogynum (E)

This is a plant up to 30 cm. high and a 23 cm. spread with erect slender
branches from a woody rootstock. Leaves grey, narrow-lanceolate to
linear, acute, sub-glaucous, almost sessile. Flowers in close clusters
from the apex of the branches, numerous, white veined blue. June to
September. A native of New Zealand.

LITHODORA (Syn. *LITHOSPERMUM Boraginaceae*)

This genus contains some of the best of the blue flowered plants rival-
ling the gentians in depth of colour. There are about forty species with
their main hub in the Mediterranean region, but there are also outliers
in other parts of Europe, N. Asia and N. America. Easy to cultivate

120

provided attention is given to their few needs, although *L. diffusa* 'Heavenly Blue' has a bad reputation for suddenly collapsing without warning (who has a specimen of any great age?). There is little on record of its longevity and it is certainly a money spinner for enterprising nurserymen.

Cultivation. All species and varieties with the exception of the lime loving *L. oleifolia* demand a well-drained neutral or slightly acid soil with plenty of humus in the form of rotted leaf-mould or peat. Full sun is often recommended but I have found that a position facing west is more suitable in the south of the country although northern counties and Scottish gardens a bed in full sun may be necessary to ripen the current year's growth. Water is needed in plenty during the growing and flowering periods, for these plants are intolerant of dryness at the roots. Topdress with equal parts of loam, leaf-mould and sand in early spring, working this down amongst the branches in the procumbent species and forms.

Propagation. This is best by seed in March, or green cuttings in June.

L. diffusa (E). (Syn. *L. prostratum*)
The type plant is a native of Spain and has given rise to a number of forms which are noted here. It makes a low spreading soft wooded shrub roughly 15 cm. high and a spread of 45 cm. with long radiating lax branchlets from a central rootstock, often rooting where the shoots are in contact with the ground. Leaves alternate, sessile, arranged round the stems, base appressed, long narrow tapering, rounded at apex, covered with wiry hairs, margins recurved, midrib sunken, prominent below, green. Flowers sessile in small sprays from the leaf axils, short tubular five lobed, gentian-blue. June to September.

L. diffusa 'Album' (E)
This is similar to the type with dainty white flowers, not an improvement but a good foil to the blues of the species and forms. May to July.

L. diffusa 'Erectum' (E)
A similar variety to the type but instead of spreading it is more compact with erect shrubby stems and terminal clusters of gentian-blue flowers. May to June.

L. diffusa 'Grace Ward' (E)
A form with the largest flowers of the types of *L. diffusa*, gentian-blue with a faint tinge of red. Unfortunately 'Heavenly Blue' often has to do duty for it. May to August.

L. diffusa 'Heavenly Blue' (E)
The best known form with gentian-blue flowers enhanced with that indescribable tinge of red. May to August.

L. 'Froebelii', see *Moltkia* 'Froebelii'
L. graminifolium, see *Moltkia suffruticosa*
L. 'Intermedium', see *Moltkia* 'Intermedia'

L. oleifolia (E)
A native of Spain this species is found on limestone formation in nature and is a truly saxatile plant. It is one of the few species which seems to appreciate a little lime rubble mixed with the compost and requires faultless drainage to give of its best. A prostrate or semi-erect shrub rarely 15 cm. high and about 23 cm. across with rounded wiry stems covered with a greenish white wool ageing to brown. Leaves sessile, oval-obovate, tapered to base, arranged alternately round the twigs, forming elongated whorls, grey-green covered with appressed whitish

hairs. Flowers in flattish terminal racemes, five lobed, open funnel shaped, pinkish blue in bud opening to a bright glistening mid-blue. May to June.

L. petraeum, see *Moltkia petraea*

L. prostratum, see *L. diffusa*

L. rosmarinifolia (E)

This is a native of the mountains of central Italy, making a compact bushy shrublet about 30 cm. high and as much across with erect branches. Leaves sessile, alternate, narrow-oblong, obtuse, green. Flowers in small terminal clusters, funnel shaped, five lobed, bright blue, lined white. February. A warm sheltered spot is required for this species.

MAHONIA (*Berberidaceae*)

A genus closely related to *Berberis* and still often quoted under that generic name in catalogues. The main difference between the two genera is that in *Mahonia* the foliage is pinnate, whereas in *Berberis* it is simple. There is only one species and a variety dwarf enough for the small garden at present in cultivation which are described in these notes.

Cultivation. An open well-drained spot in full sun is ideal in a good loam; requires a good supply of water while growing.

Propagation. This is by layering or seed in February.

M. repens (E). (Syn. *Berberis repens*)

A dwarf shrub of erect rigid branches less than 30 cm. high and a spread of 35 cm. Foliage thick pinnate up to nine leaflets, ovate, obtuse ending in a rigid spine, margins edged with long spines, deep bluish green above, grey below. Flowers in erect terminal racemes on short pedicels, golden-yellow. May. Followed by globose berries of deep blue and a similar coloured bloom. A native of Western N. America.

M. repens var. *repens* (E)

This is an even smaller variety with stoloniferous stems only about 15 cm. high and a similar spread with dainty racemes of golden-yellow flowers, followed by blackish berries covered with a blue bloom. May. A native of N.W. America.

MARGYRICARPUS (*Rosaceae*)

A small member of the mighty rose family which will make a decorative if not showy plant in the small garden. Its chief attraction being in the large pearl like berries which the plant bears in profusion in late summer.

Cultivation. A sunny position in well-drained, not too rich soil is ideal.

Propagation. Green cuttings taken in May and rooted in the propagating frame, or seed in February.

M. setosus (E)

It makes a semi-prostrate shrublet up to 15 cm. high and a similar spread, with bright yellow smooth branches. Leaves pinnate, segments awl shaped, reflexed, deep green. Flowers insignificant, produced from the leaf axils, followed by pearl like white globular fruits in late August. A native of Chile.

MENZIESIA (Ericaceae)

A small genus of choice shrubs of American or Japanese origin containing one species and two varieties that are suitable for the small garden or better still in a choice spot in the heather garden; they like cool moist conditions.

Cultivation. A sheltered spot in half shade in bleak gardens is necessary but in a more humid atmosphere they will tolerate a greater amount of sunshine. In the southern parts of the country they do well planted among dwarf *Rhododendrons* and other choice ericaceous plants. On the western seaboard and in Scotland a site facing west should be suitable. Lime free soil is essential for all are lime haters, this coupled with a sufficient supply of water during the growing and flowering season will make these charming plants happy and contented. A light topdressing of equal parts of leaf-mould, loam and sand should be given in both spring and autumn.

Propagation. Take green cuttings in June, or layers in early May.

M. ciliicalyx (D)

A small, slow-growing shrub eventually up to 60 cm. in height and 45 cm. across. Branches spreading, smooth, light brown in the juvenile state, becoming greyish brown, striated white. Leaves alternate near terminals, almost rosettes, oval to obovate, tapered to base, midrib extending past apex, bright light green, paler below; sparsely clothed with bristly hairs especially on the margins, veinings reticulate. Flowers pendant, bell shaped in small umbels from apex of previous year's growth, changing from light green at base to purple at the mouth. May. A native of Japan.

M. ciliicalyx var. *lasiophylla* (D)

This is similar to the type, slow growing, with larger pendant flowers, deeper purple at apex of lobes, shading to yellow-green at base. May. A native of Japan.

M. ciliicalyx var. *multiflora* (D)

This variety differs from the type in having larger flowers, tubular bell shaped, purplish in colour. May.

MOLTKIA (Boraginaceae)

A small genus of plants closely related to *Lithodora* and often found under that generic name in catalogues, there being only small botanical differences between the two genera. They are natives of S. Europe and Asia and include a few that make ideal plants for the small garden.

Cultivation. Their needs are simple; a good light well-drained soil in full sun, the only emphasis is on the drainage which must be perfect, for failure to provide this will mean the almost certain death of plants during a wet winter.

Propagation. By green cuttings in July.

M. caerulea (E)

A native of Asia Minor, this makes an erect shrublet about 23 cm. high and 20 cm. across with hairy branches. Leaves oblong to lanceolate, pointed, grey-green due to covering of silky hairs. Flowers in terminal spikes on 10 cm. scapes, long narrow tubular, five lobed, bluish purple. April.

M. 'Froebelii' (E). (Syn. *Lithospermum* 'Froebelii')
A small much branched, woody sub-shrub stated to be a hybrid
between *M*. *petraea* and *M*. *suffruticosa* about 15 cm. high and 23 cm.
across. Leaves long narrow, lanceolate, covered with long appressed
silky hairs, deep green. Flowers in small branched terminal cymes,
funnel shaped, five lobed, bright blue. May. Garden origin.
M. 'Intermedia' (E). (Syn. *Lithospermum* 'Intermedium')
Another garden hybrid between *M*. *petraea* and *M*. *suffruticosa*, which
forms a dense shrublet of erect grey haired branches up to 38 cm. high
and 30 cm. across. Leaves alternate, long narrow, grey-green due to
covering of appressed silky hairs. Flowers crowded in terminal clusters,
long tubular, five lobed, pinkish blue in bud opening to violet-blue.
June.
M. *petraea* (E). (Syn. *Lithospermum petraeum*)
A native of S. Albania, it is a desirable very floriferous shrublet up to 23
cm. high and about the same across with erect, stiff, rounded branches,
densely clothed with greyish green hairs. Leaves alternate leathery,
long narrow, lanceolate, grey-green covered with smooth grey hairs.
Flowers in congested terminal clusters, opening in succession, narrow
tubular, five lobed with protruding stamens, pinkish blue in bud
opening to a deep blue with a trace of red. June.
M. *suffruticosa* (E). (Syn. *Lithospermum graminifolium*)
A more tufted and less erect shrub, up to 23 cm. high and 30 cm. across
with rounded twiggy stems densely clothed with appressed soft grey
hairs. Leaves alternate, long narrow, linear, pointed at apex, larger
than in *M*. *petraea*, deep green covered with grey hairs on both sides.
Flowers terminal on 10 cm. leafy stems in branched clusters, five lobed,
long narrow, tubular, pendant, pink in bud opening to violet-blue.
Stamens not protruding. June. A native of Italy.

ONONIS (*Leguminosae*)

A genus that contains shrubs, sub-shrubs, annuals and perennials, and
there are a few which can be admitted to the small garden although the
Rest Harrows are not often seen.
Cultivation. All require a hot dry spot in a well-drained poor medium, a
rich compost will certainly shorten the life of these plants; they are intolerant of root disturbance.
Propagation. This is by seed in March, or where available green cuttings
in early June.
O. aragonensis (D)
This is a small shrub up to 45 cm. high and about as much through
with erect, stiff much branched stems, greyish green in colour. The
alternate leaves are tri-foliate, segments oval roundish, unequally
toothed and smooth bright green. Flowers axillary sometimes solitary,
usually more, pea-shaped, yellow, on terminal hairy peduncles. May.
A native of Spain.
O. cenisia, see *O. cristata*
O. cristata (E). (Syn. *O. cenisia*)
A prostrate sub-shrub only 2 cm. or so high but forming a mat of glandular downy stems. Leaves congested, tri-foliate with a small petiole,
segments sessile, serrate on upper third. Flowers solitary from upper
leaf axils on small spreading peduncles, pea-shaped, purplish pink,
124

standards with deep purple veinings. June to August. A native of French Alps, S. Europe and N. Africa.

O. hispanica, see *O. natrix* sub-species *hispanica*

O. natrix (D)

This is a sub-shrub variable in height but in the dwarf forms only about 15 cm. with a spread of 20 cm. and having more or less erect spreading stems. Leaves petiolate, simple at base of stem, tri-foliate on upper part, segments oblong acute, dentate, covered with a fine down. Flowers solitary on more or less leafy sticky peduncles from the leaf axils, pea-shaped, yellow, standard rounded, veined red, emarginate. May to June. A native of S. and central Europe, E. Mediterranean and N.W. Africa.

O. natrix sub-species *hispanica* (E). (Syn. *O. hispanica*)

This is a crowded sub-shrub up to 15 cm. high and about the same across with congested basal tufts. Leaves tri-foliate crowded, segments obovate-cuneate, recurved, sharply serrate. Flowers on long peduncles from the upper leaf axils, smallish, yellow, standards veined rose. June to August. A native of Spain, Sicily, Crete and Asia Minor.

O. rotundifolia (D)

A small sub-shrub up to 30 cm. high and as much across with more or less erect branching glandular hairy stems. Leaves tri-foliate, stalked, segments elliptical to roundish, serrulate; the two outer sessile covered with a glandular down on both sides. Flowers up to three on axillary glandular peduncles, large pea-shaped, rose, standard veined red. June to July. A native of central and S. Europe, and from Spain to Italy.

PARAHEBE (*Scrophulariaceae*)

This is a fairly recent new genus as the species were included with *Hebe* in *Veronica* where Cheeseman 1925 had listed three divisions under *Veronica*; *Hebe*; *Pygmea* and *Euveronica*. These were subsequently returned to genus status *Hebe*, Pennell 1921, *Pygmea*, W. R. B. Oliver 1944 and a new genus for the *Euveronica* division, *Pharahebe*, W. R. B. Oliver 1944.

Cultivation. They are easy in a well-drained medium such as one would find in a normal rock or small garden. A little shade is desirable in hot sunny gardens but this should only be necessary when the sun is high. Cold bleak gardens present a problem for although hardy a number resent cold drying winds which have a tendency to defoliate the plants if exposed to these over a long period.

Propagation. Is by green cuttings in late July and early August which quickly root if kept close. All species can be cut back if required to retain a close compact habit which is characteristic of a number of these plants. It will be found that they readily break from either a growth bud on the old wood or from the base of the plant.

P. × *bidwillii* (E). (Syn. *Hebe bidwillii*)

A natural hybrid between *P. decora* and *P. lyallii*, it is a charming dwarf shrublet up to 15 cm. high and a spread of 30 cm. with glabrous stems, these often having stiff white hairs in the juvenile state and generally rooting where they come in contact with the soil. Leaves small not crowded, bright glossy green. Flowers in axillary, long slender erect racemes on small glandular hairy predicels, corolla tube spreading rounded and unequal, white lined pink. June to July. A native of the South Island, New Zealand.

P. catarractae (E). (Syn. *Hebe catarractae*)
A small semi-erect sub-shrub up to 45 cm. high and as much across
with purplish branches and two rows of pubescence. Leaves distant,
ovate to lanceolate, subsessile, acute, margins coarsely serrate,
glabrous with exception of pubescent midrib, deep glossy green above,
paler, sometimes yellowish below. Flowers in loose terminal racemes
on glabrous peduncles; pedicels clothed with white glandular hairs.
Corolla tube small, four unequal lobes, spreading obtuse, white with a
central zone of crimson. June to July. A native of both North and South
Islands, New Zealand in many stations. A polymorphic species with
many forms that have proved extremely difficult to divide.
P. catarractae var. *diffusa* (E). (Syn. *Hebe catarractae* var. *diffusa*)
This is a more procumbent variety only about 23 cm. high with ovate
leaves and tall glandular racemes of flowers. June to July.
P. hookeriana (E). (Syns. *Hebe hookeriana*; *Veronica nivea*)
A small sub-shrub with stout much branched laterals covered with a
fine pubescence, rarely above 15 cm. high and a spread of 30 cm.
Leaves more or less imbricate erect or recurved on some of the
branches, narrow-ovate to sub-orbicular, thick leathery, coarsely
crenate on short petioles, glandular hairy. Flowers in corymbose
racemes on stout white pubescent peduncles. Corolla tube small, lobes
four unequal, wide ovate oblong, obtuse white streaked pink. June to
July. A native of North Island, New Zealand, Tongariro 1,500 m.
P. hookeriana var. *olsenii* (E). (Syn. *Parahebe olsenii*)
The main difference in this variety is that the leaves are shallowly and
sharply serrate, glabrous and narrowed into flattened petioles. Flowers
only with stiff non glandular pubescence. June to July. A native of
North Island, Ruahine Mountains.
P. lyallii (E). (Syn. *Hebe lyallii*)
Another spreading dwarf shrub with slender prostrate branches
rooting where they come into contact with the soil only a few centimetres high and a spread of 30 cm. covered with crisp white hairs,
sometimes just in two rows. Leaves thick, leathery, glabrous, sub-
orbicular to ovate, apex rounded, base wedge shaped into petiole,
margins deeply crenate, bright green sometimes with a red flush,
midrib slightly pubescent. Flowers in slender racemes, peduncles
generally glabrous, pedicels pubescent. Corolla tube small, lobes four
unequal, spreading rounded, white striped pink, with blue anthers.
July to August. A native of the South Island, Milford Sound.
P. olsenii, see *P. hookeriana* var. *olsenii*

PENSTEMON (*Scrophulariaceae*)

A large genus of plants, the Beard Tongues, are with one exception
wholly American and they make an outstanding contribution to the list
of desirable shrubs for the rock or small garden with an extremely fine
display of floral beauty. They are unfortunately in many instances
short lived and some are of doubtful hardiness, but all are easy to
propagate and there should be no difficulty in keeping a stock going.
Like so many American genera their nomenclature is still very confused, the names used here are as far as possible the accepted ones at
present.
Cultivation. A good loam in a well-drained sunny position will suit these

plants and if possible protection from cold north and east winds by planting on the south or west side of a large rock or shrub. A rich medium is more suitable than a lean stony soil for, given good conditions, these species will make fine, very floriferous specimens. Any attempt to starve them will only weaken their constitution not that their floral display will be impaired but they are likely to suffer from the scourge which often attacks this genus, the dying back of whole branches.

Propagation. This is easy by green cuttings taken in August and rooted in the propagating frame.

P. ambiguus (E)
A neat rounded shrub less than 30 cm. high and about 38 cm. across with congested hairy branches. Leaves thick, narrow, linear to filiform, acute, toothed, mid-green. Flowers in terminal panicles, narrow tubular, lobes five spreading, rose, paler in throat. June to July. A native of W. America.

P. angustifolius (E)
This is a plant up to 23 cm. high and about 30 cm. wide with erect stiff branches. Leaves linear to lanceolate, grey-green. Flowers in an erect panicle, tubular, white in bud, opening pink then turning blue. June to July. A native of W. America.

P. barrettae (E)
From N.W. America, it is an erect shrub up to 30 cm. high and about 23 cm. across. Leaves crowded, oval to oblanceolate, glabrous deep green, margins often coloured red. Flowers in small erect clusters, narrow tubular, bright purple. May.

P. caespitosus (E)
This is a dwarf mat forming plant with trailing procumbent stems only 8 cm. high and about 23 cm. wide. Leaves small lanceolate, grey-green covered with a fine silvery down. Flowers erect on short peduncles, wide tubular, two-lipped, upper bi-lobed, lower three cleft, lilac-purple. June to July. A native of Wyoming. Not an easy species and is best in a leafy raised scree.

P. campanulatus var. *pulchellus* (E). (Syn. *P. pulchellus*)
A dwarf variety of the species it is only a few centimetres high and up to 30 cm. wide, spreading from a branching base. Leaves ovate-lanceolate, toothed, deep green. Flowers tubular, inflated, bright blue. June. A native of Mexico.

P. confertus (E)
A variable species ranging from 10 to 30 cm. high with erect, hairy stems and a spread of 30 cm. Leaves oblong to lanceolate, entire, crowded, glabrous green. Flowers in a narrow spike with long tube, lower lip bearded, creamy yellow. June to July. A native of the Rocky Mountains.

P. corymbosus (d)
This is a much branched erect shrublet up to 30 cm. high and as much across. Leaves opposite, oblong, dentate tapered to base, pointed to apex, deep glossy green. Flowers on hairy scapes in small clusters, two-lipped, tubular bright crimson with a touch of orange. July. A native of California.

P. davidsonii (E)
A small sub-shrub about 8 cm. high and a spread of 30 cm. with creeping running stems and erect branches. Leaves small obovate, acute,

127

entire, smooth glaucous grey. Flowers large on 8 cm. leafy stems, tube inflated, lobes nearly equal, ruby-red. June to July. A native of California.

P. davidsonii 'Alba' (E)
The white form is a much rare plant with pale green oval leaves and flowers of pure ivory white. June to July. A native of California.

P. fruticosus (E)
A very variable shrublet up to 23 cm. high and 30 cm. wide with erect stems. Leaves lanceolate, bright green. Flowers on 23 cm. stems, stem leaves smaller, in short spikes, narrow tubular, purple. July. A native of N.W. America.

P. fruticosus var. *cardwellii* (E)
A small open lax shrub less than 30 cm. high and as much across. Leaves long narrow tapered to apex, and base thick, margins dentate, deep glossy green. Flowers in small terminal clusters tubular, bright blue with a splash of red. July. A native of N. America.

P. hallii (E)
Is a close congested shrublet about 8 cm. high and a spread of 23 cm. with prostrate and ascending stems. Leaves tufted, thick, linear to linear-spatulate, obtuse; stem leaves narrower. Flowers on an erect stiff scape in a short thyrse, wide bell shaped, lilac shot voilet-blue. June to July. A native of Colorado. Best in a leafy well-drained raised scree in full sun.

P. heterophyllus (E)
A semi-dwarf shrub up to 45 cm. high and about 38 cm. wide, lax and wiry in growth. The opposite sessile leaves are oblong, rounded, deep green. Flowers narrow tubular, two-lipped, inflated at mouth, generally solitary on long peduncles, shade of blue through violet to pink. July. A native of California. Not too hardy, stock should be kept going by cuttings.

P. hirsutus (E)
This is a plant up to 38 cm. high and as much through with slender clammy hairy stems. Leaves oblong to linear, deep green, hairy, slightly dentate, upper smaller. Flowers in an open thyrse, semi-pendant, tubular narrow, inflated above, lower lip bearded, lavender ageing to purple. June to July. A native of N. America.

P. hirsutus 'Pygmaeus' (E)
A smaller variety about 23 cm. high and a 38 cm. spread, otherwise similar to the type. June to July.

P. humilis (E)
A small species only about 15 cm. high and 30 cm. across with foliage in congested tufts. Leaves oblong to lanceolate, greyish green; upper smaller, slightly dentate. Flowers in short sprays, narrow tubular, lower lip bearded, bright blue. June to July. A native of the Rocky Mountains.

P. lyallii (E). (Syn. *P. menziesii* var. *lyallii*)
An erect sub-shrub up to 30 cm. high and as much across. Leaves lanceolate, opposite, tapered to apex, dull mid-green. Flowers in terminal clusters, large tubular, purple. May to June. A Native of north America.

P. menziesii (E)
From N.W. America making a small shrublet variable in height but generally less than 23 cm. and a spread of 30 cm. with much branched,

semi-prostrate, slender hairy stems. Leaves thick, opposite, obovate, tapered to base, rounded at apex, dentate, petiole short, bright glossy green. Flowers in a dense raceme up to six from terminal stems, tubular, two-lipped, deep blue with a touch of red. June.

P. menziesii var. *lyallii*, see *P. lyallii*

P. menziesii var. *microphyllus* (E)
This is similar to the type but smaller in all its parts rarely above 8 cm. high, with light purplish flowers, lighter at lip, and makes a good plant for a small garden. June.

P. menziessi var. *scouleri*, see *P. scouleri*

P. newberryi (E)
A native of N.W. America, this is a dwarf sub-shrub with erect slender stems up to 20 cm. high and about the same across. Leaves opposite, orbicular to oval, leathery, dentate, grey-green. Flowers in terminal sprays on short pedicels, two lipped tubular, brilliant red. June.

P. newberryi forma *humilor* (E)
This is a dwarf form only a few cm. high with similar habit and foliage, and flowers of a more intense red. June.

P. pinifolius (E)
A fine dwarf shrublet only 8 cm. high and a spread of 30 cm. with radiating light brown smooth lax branches. Leaves crowded, linear, thick, bright glossy green, arranged in small clusters like pine needles. Flowers on 10 cm. stems sparsely furnished with similar foliage, the upper half bearing up to six long tubular, two-lipped blooms of mandarin red; the basal lip divided into three narrow segments, upper slightly cleft. June. A native of Arizona and New Mexico.

P. pulchellus, see *P. campanulatus* var. *pulchellus*

P. roezlii (E)
A native of California making a small shrublet of slender wiry branches less than 23 cm. high and about 30 cm. wide. Leaves opposite, linear, sessile, rounded at apex, deep green. Flowers in an open panicle, tubular, two-lipped, dark blue with a dash of violet . July.

P. rupicola (E)
A native of W. America, this is one of the best of the genus and is often offered in catalogues as *P. roezlii*. It is a prostrate sub-shrub only a few cm. high and a spread of 30 cm. of crowded, hairy, glandular stems. Leaves alternate, oval to orbicular, basal half dentate, veins hairy, grey-green. Flowers clustered at apex of branches, large, tubular, two-lipped, brilliant crimson. June. When in full flower they will completely obscure the foliage.

P. scouleri (E). (Syn. *P. menziesii* var. *scouleri*)
A small compact shrub up to 30 cm. high and as much across with lax, slender downy stems. Leaves opposite, almost sessile, long narrow lanceolate, acute with small terminal serrations. Flowers in small terminal racemes, two-lipped, tubular, blue shaded red. June. A native of W. America.

P. scouleri 'Albus' (E)
This is a desirable variety similar to the type but with pure white flowers. July.

P, 'Six Hills Hybrid' (e). (*P. davidsonii* × *P. cristatus*)
This is a garden hybrid which originated in the famous Six Hills Nursery and is one of the best dwarf penstemons. Only 15 cm. high and about 30 cm. wide it is a dwarf sub-shrub with slender branches.

Penstemon scouleri 'Albus'

Leaves ovate, opposite, grey-green, margins slightly dentate. Flowers in small terminal racemes, tubular, two-lipped, pale mauve. June.

PERNETTYA (Ericaceae)

This is a genus of mostly dwarf shrubs which contain a number of species and varieties that make delightful subjects for the small garden with their charming flowers followed by outstanding fruits. Botanically it is near to *Gaultheria*, there being only slight differences between the two genera. One is that the fleshy calyx present in *Gaultheria* is much reduced or absent in *Pernettya*.

Cultivation. A lime free, ever moist, but well-drained soil is necessary in half shade, but in the northern counties where the atmosphere is less dry more sun is tolerated. A high content of humus in the form of leaf-mould or peat is essential to their well being and in bleak inland gardens a sheltered spot should be found. Topdress with leaf-mould in early spring.

Propagation. Green cuttings taken in August, rooted in the propagating frame or seed sown in March.

P. empetrifolia, see *P. pumila*

P. leucocarpa (E)

This is a prostrate sub-shrub up to 30 cm. high and 45 cm. across

130

spreading by underground runners; branches congested, wiry, slender. Leaves alternate, oblong on short petioles, margins slightly dentate, deep glossy green, hairy when young. Flowers solitary on short pedicels from the leaf axils, urn-shaped with five spreading lobes, white flushed pink. May. Fruits rounded, white or flushed pink. A native of Chile.

P. leucocarpa var. *linearis* (E)
A smaller variety rarely up to 23 cm. high, branches crowded, leaves dense linear, pointed at apex. Flowers and fruit similar to the species. May. A native of Chile.

P. magellanica, see *P. pumila*

P. mucronata 'Nana' (E)
This is the dwarf form of the well-known species, a plant which rarely exceeds 15 cm. in height and about 30 cm. across, with stiff, wiry, pinkish green stems, sparsely covered with bristly hairs. Leaves alternate, arranged spirally round the stems, long oval, rounded at base, apex terminating in a sharp spine; two to four teeth on each side of leaf, deep glossy green, deep irregular veining, light grey-green below. Flowers produced from the leaf axils, solitary on short pedicels, urn shaped, white flushed pink. May. Fruits globular, reddish blue. Origin unknown, possibly from a dwarf seedling of *P. mucronata*.

P. mucronata var. *rupicola* (E)
A native of Chile, this variety is about 15 cm. high and a spread of 23 cm. with semi-prostrate, lax, wiry stems covered with fine down. Leaves alternate, congested, narrow oval, pointed at apex, toothed towards base, dark glossy green. Flowers solitary from the leaf axils, pendant urn shaped, white, five spreading lobes. Fruit globose, pink to red. May.

P. nana (E)
This is a prostrate shrub about 8 cm. high and a spread of 30 cm. making a close congested mat of creeping rooting branches; branchlets erect slightly hairy. Leaves distant on short petiole, oblong to lanceolate-oblong, thick, acute, margined with two to three pairs of small teeth, hair tipped, glabrous green. Flowers solitary from the upper leaf axils up to five on short pedicels, urceolate with five short lobes, white to pink. May. Fruit rounded depressed, red streaked white with a persisting swollen calyx. A native of the South Island, New Zealand.

P. nigra, see *P. prostrata*

P. prostrata (E). (Syn. *P. nigra*)
From S. America comes this delightful dwarf congested prostrate shrub rarely up to 15 cm. high and a spread of 30 cm. with woolly branches furnished with an occasional stiff hair. Leaves on small petioles, oval, acute, tapered to base, slightly dentate, margins ciliate, deep bright green, paler below. Flowers solitary on short pedicels from the upper leaf axils, semi-pendant, campanulate, five lobed, white. May. Fruit globular, pink to red.

P. prostrata var. *pentlandii* (E).
This is similar to the species but with more erect branches up to 30 cm. high. Flowers from terminal leaf axils solitary, pendant, five ovate lobes, white. June. Fruit globular deep voilet. A native of Chile.

P. pumila (E). (syns. *P. empetrifolia; P. magellanica*)
A native of the Falkland Islands, this increases by underground runners and is rarely above 10 cm. high but with a spread of 45 cm.,

stems stiff, wiry, lightish grey-green in juvenile state, reddish brown when mature. Leaves oval or ovate, deep glossy green. Flowers from upper leaf axils, pendant bell shaped with five oval lobes, white. May. Fruit globular, white or pink.

P. tasmanica (E)

This is a prostrate sub-shrub of crowded, thin wiry lax branches, increasing by underground runners only 5 cm. high and a spread of 30 cm. Leaves alternate, almost in whorls, minute, long narrow oval, tapered to base, apex acute, margins serrulate, glossy green. Flowers solitary on short pedicels from the leaf axils, five lobed, urn shaped, white. May. Fruits borne in abundance, globose, red with a persisting swollen calyx. A native of Tasmania.

PETROPHYTUM (Rosaceae)

A small genus of about four species native of America, closely related to *Spiraea* and they have often been placed in that genus by some authorities. They differ in that the inflorescence of *Spiraea* is generally a panicle or corymb, in *Petrophytum* the flowers are borne in a crowded raceme.

Cultivation. These plants are best suited to an open dry spot in full sun and they will do well in a poor raised scree or planted when young in rock crevices.

Propagation. Green cuttings taken in June and rooted in the propagating frame will soon establish themselves.

P. caespitosum (E). (Syn. *Spiraea caespitosa*)

This is a true alpine shrub and with the possible exception of the rare *Kelseya uniflora*, also of the *Rosaceae* family, must be considered the dwarfest of all shrubs. It makes a tight congested mass of procumbent stiff branches from a central rootstock less than 2 cm. high and about 15 cm. across. Leaves in tight rosettes, spatulate, entire with an acute tip, grey-green in colour due to intense covering of silky hairs. Flowers in dense terminal racemes, very numerous on 5 cm. peduncles, white. July. A native of N. America.

P. hendersonii (E). (Syn. *Spiraea hendersonii*)

A dwarf prostrate shrub endemic to the Olympic Mountains of N. America and near to *P. caespitosum*. It forms a tight congested mat of prostrate branches only 2 cm. high. Leaves dense, alternate, oblanceolate, thick, grey-green. Flowers on 5 cm. peduncles, crowded globular racemes, small fluffy, creamy white. June.

PHYLLODOCE (Ericaceae)

A genus of hardy dwarf shrubs suitable for the small or peat garden amongst choice ericaceous plants. They are confined to the northern hemisphere but are widely distributed over this area, from America through Alaska on to Japan, over North Asia, Iceland, Scotland, Greenland and completing the circle in Northern Canada. Provided their few needs are attended to, no genus with the possible exception of *Rhododendron* is more delightful.

Cultivation. A position among ericaceous shrubs in half shade, a north west or west position is suitable, and protection from early morning sun is necessary. In the south greater shade is required than in the northern counties, where this genus is more tolerant of cultivation, due the higher atmospheric content. A lime-free medium loam, well

Petrophytum hendersonii

enriched with decayed vegetation, either in the form of leaf-mould or peat, with good drainage and in which pieces of sandstone have been buried should be satisfactory for all members of this genus. At all times drought is to be feared, for both dryness in the air or at the roots is fatal, but both can be minimised by spraying in the evenings after hot summer days and providing a good 5 cm. mulch of half rotted leaf-mould in spring before the weather becomes hot.

Propagation. Green cuttings taken in June and rooted in the propagating frame.

P. aleutica. (E) (Syn. *P. pallisiana*).

This is a dwarf semi-procumbent shrublet up to 20 cm. high and as much across, the stems completely clothed with leaves arranged round them. Leaves crowded, small linear, obtuse and minute marginal serrations, recurved, tapered towards base, deep green above, yellowish below with white median line. Flowers in clusters from terminal shoots, each on a short glandular pedicel, pendant, globular, urn shaped, pale yellow. May. A native of Aleutian Islands, Alaska, Japan and Kamchatka.

P. alpina (E)

A native of Japan, this is a semi-prostrate shrub up to 8 cm. high and about 15 cm. across with semi-erect stems. Leaves congested, small linear, minute marginal serrations, obtuse. Flowers in terminal sub-umbellate clusters, globular, urn shaped, reddish blue, May.

P. amabilis, see *P. nipponica* var. *amabilis*.

P. caerulea (E). (syn. *Andromeda caerulea*)

A semi-procumbent much branched shrublet less than 15 cm. high and with a spread of 30 cm. also both erect and horizontal wiry stems. Leaves congested, linear, apex obtuse, minute marginal serrations, dark glossy green. Flowers in terminal clusters up to six pendant, pitcher shaped on short glandular pedicels, light reddish blue. April to May. A native of Europe, Asia, N. America and Ben Lawers, among other Perthshire Hills.

P. empetriformis (E)

One of the finest of the *Phyllodoces* and by far the easiest species of the genus to grow. It makes a low tufted semi-procumbent shrublet rarely above 15 cm. high and 30 cm. across, stems erect in juvenile state. Leaves crowded, small linear, obtuse, tapered to base with minute marginal serrations; recurved, deep glossy green. Flowers in terminal

Phyllodoce caerulea

clusters up to six from the upper leaf axils, each on a small glandular pedicel, urn shaped, pendant, bright red with a touch of blue. April to May. A native of N. America.

P. erecta, see *Phyllothamnus* 'Erectus'

P. glanduliflora (E)

A fine dwarf shrublet up to 15 cm. high and about 23 cm. across of tufted habit with erect branches. Leaves congested, linear, obtuse, tapered to base, deeply recurved margins, slightly dentate, dark green with a median white line beneath. Flowers in terminal, sub-umbellate clusters, each on a slender wiry glandular pedicel, urn shaped pendant, five lobed, yellow with just a trace of green. May. A native of Western N. America and Alaska.

P. nipponica (E)

There is no doubt that this species is the finest of the genus when well grown, as all can testify who saw the magnificent pan of it exhibited by the late Major Walmsley which received a First Class Certificate and the Farrer Memorial Medal for the best plant in the show at a combined Royal Horticultural and Alpine Garden Society's Show in London some years ago. It is a dwarf, compact, erect shrublet rarely above 15 cm. high and 30 cm. across. Leaves crowded, linear, rounded

Phyllodoce empetriformis

at apex, recurved with minute marginal serrations, dark glossy green above, white with an intense covering of down below. Flowers produced from the upper half of the stems in clusters, up to seven from the leaf axils on slender glandular pedicels, bell shaped, glistening white, sepals green. April to May. A native of Japan.

P. nipponica var. *amabilis* (E). (Syn. *P. amabilis*)
Similar to the type with the exception of having red sepals and rose tipped white flowers. April. A native of Japan.

P. tsugifolia (E)
This is a dwarf erect much branched shrub with wiry stems about 30 cm. high and 23 cm. across. Leaves crowded, alternate, linear, tapered to base and apex, margins recurved with minute serrations, deep bright green above, glaucous below. Flowers in stiff terminal sub-umbellate clusters, five part reddish sepals, corolla pitcher shaped, five recurved white lobes, flushed pink, each on a slender reddish erect pedicel. April. A native of Japan.

X PHYLLOTHAMNUS (*Ericaceae*)

Is possibly one of the very few bigeneric hybrids that is grown in the small garden today and is the result of a cross between *Phyllodoce empetriformis* and *Rhodothamnus chamaecistus*, raised over a hundred years ago in the nursery of Messrs Cunningham and Fraser of Edinburgh.
Cultivation. The plant is suited to conditions as advised for *Phyllodoce*, a cool moist but well-drained spot in half shade. A number of authorities recommend more sun for this bigeneric hybrid but here in the south I have found to my cost that sun is undesirable unless accompanied by a moist atmosphere, not an easy combination in many southern counties, topdress with a thick covering of leaf-mould in late spring.
Propagation. By cuttings taken in July and rooted in a shady propagating frame.

x *P.* 'Erectus' (E). (Syn. *Phyllodoce erecta*)
It forms a much branched erect shrub up to 30 cm. high and about as much across. Leaves alternate, crowded, linear, pointed, margins recurved and slightly dentate, dark glossy green. Flowers solitary on slender glandular pedicels at apex of shoots in clusters, from six to ten campanulate, five lobed, rose-pink. May.

PIERIS (*Ericaceae*)

A small genus of highly ornamental shrubs generally too large for the small garden, but there is one variety which is dwarf enough for inclusion.
Cultivation. A position amongst other dwarf ericaceous plants in half shade, sheltered from cold drying winds in a lime free humus, enriched soil. Topdress in early spring with a mulch of leaf-mould or peat.
Propagation. This is by green cuttings in June, these are best rooted with bottom heat if available.

P. japonica 'Variegata' (E)
This is an erect much branched shrub, slow growing, reaching in time 1 m., with glabrous branches and spreading to a similar width. Leaves clustered at apex of laterals, oblanceolate, acute, tapered to both ends, upper half serrulate, smooth, reticulate, yellow-green margined white. Flowers in pendulous panicles, urn shaped, white. April. A native of Japan.

Pieris japonica 'Variegata'

PIMELEA (*Thymelaeaceae*)

A large genus of plants confined to Australasia, there are two that can be used in the small garden and these will endure many degrees of frost without harm. The New Zealand Daphnes are delightful plants with their sweetly scented flowers and glistening white berries.

Cultivation. A warm sunny, but sheltered spot is required in a good light loam to which has been added a fair percentage of peat.

Propagation. Cuttings taken with a heel in July.

P. coarctata, see *P. prostrata* 'Coarctata'

P. prostrata (E)

A small prostrate rambling shrub, much branched, only 2 cm. or so high but with a spread of 45 cm. or so when suited, branches stout, bark almost black glabrous; branchlets slender with dirty whitish hairs. Leaves crowded more or less sessile, deflexed ovate to elliptic oblong, concave, obtuse to sub-acute, coriaceous, grey-green, sometimes margined red. Flowers up to ten in axillary terminal clusters, white, silky daphne like, four oval lobes with a delightful perfume. May. These are followed by ovoid white glistening berries.

P. prostrata 'Coarctata' (E). (Syn. *P. coarctata*)

A form of *P. prostrata* which has for many years been grown under the

137

Pimelea Prostrata

name of *P. coarctata*, even at Wisley a plant is still labelled under this name, but its origin is a mystery for I can find no record of this plant and no New Zealand flora mentions it, but whatever its botanical standing it is a delightful plant. It makes a prostrate shrublet 2 cm. or so high and about 30 cm. across with congested interlaced stiff wiry greyish green not blackish branches and twigs. Leaves minute opposite, ovate, sessile, grey-green. Flowers in small axillary terminal clusters, four lobed daphne like covered with silky hairs, white, scented, May. Followed by glistening white berries.

138

Polygala chamaebuxus

POLYGALA (Polygalaceae)
A large genus of plants, the Milkworts have a wide geographical distribution over most parts of the world with the exception of the Arctic zone, Polynesia and New Zealand. There are a number that are suitable for the small garden and make attractive plants.
Cultivation. A good sandy loam with a fair proportion of leaf soil in a cool spot in half shade will suit these plants. In their native habitat they are, with the exception of *P. paucifolia* found primarily on calcareous soils but in cultivation all thrive just as well on a neutral or slightly acid formation. A light topdressing of equal parts of loam, leaf-mould and sand in early spring is desirable.
Propagation. Is by detaching runners with roots where possible, treating them as cuttings in late June, or green cuttings in June.
P. chamaebuxus (E)
A native of C. Europe, this is a dwarf shrub rarely above 15 cm. high and a spread of 30 cm. increasing by suckers when established. Stems, slender, erect. Leaves alternate, small oblong, glabrous, dull mid-green. Flowers borne on short scapes from the leaf axils of the terminal shoots, reminiscent of pea flowers sepals five and three petals forming a keel, white, mouth of keel bright yellow, fragrant. May.

P. chamaebuxus var. *grandiflora*, see *P. chamaebuxus* 'Purpurea'
P. chamaebuxus 'Purpurea' (E). (Syn. *P.c.* var. *grandiflora*)
A form that is identical with the species in form and habit but has
attractive flowers of purple-red, charmingly set off by the yellow mouth
of the keel. April.
P. paucifolia (E)
A native of N. America, this is a small prostrate shrublet rarely above 2
cm. or so high but spreading and increasing by underground stolons.
Leaves congested, ovate, slightly decurved, tapered to apex and base,
pale green, deep purple beneath. Flowers on short pedicels up to four
from terminal leaf axils light rich carmine, wing petals plain but the
keel fringed with bristly hairs. May. The R.H.S. *Dictionary of Gardening*
quotes this as a herbaceous perennial but it is definitely shrubby and
evergreen.

POTENTILLA (Rosaceae)
A large genus of plants containing up to 350 species mostly herbaceous
but with a few shrubs or sub-shrubs, natives of the northern
hemisphere. There are a number of the Cinquefoils which make good
plants for the small garden and of these the shrubby species and
varieties help to extend the flowering season into late summer.
Cultivation. A light, well-drained, sandy loam in sun is ideal although
some will tolerate a certain amount of shade, they are indifferent to
lime and do well on that or a neutral medium.
Propagation. This is by seed sown in March, cuttings or offsets in late
July, rooting these in the propagating frame.
P. curviseta (E)
A native of the Himalayas, this is a charming mat-forming plant only 2
cm. or so high and a spread of 20 cm. Leaves palmate, small, crowded,
leaflets trifid, dentate, bright green. Flowers solitary on short scapes,
rounded, golden-yellow. May-June.
P. 'Davurica' (D). (*P. glabra* × *P. parvifolia*)
This hybrid is a small much branched very slow growing shrub, less
than 30 cm. high and as much across with pendant stems. Leaves
palmate, sessile; leaflets five long oval, obtuse, glabrous, mid-green;
three central joined at base. Flowers solitary on small hairy pedicels,
five roundish petals white with green bracts. June to August.
P. 'Davurica Purdomii' (D)
Another from the result of the same cross but with flowers of a clear
light yellow. June to August.
P. frigida (H)
A small semi-woody plant with congested stems making a mat about 5
cm. high and 15 cm. wide. Leaves tri-ternate; leaflets wide linear
dentate at apex, grey-green, often margined red in Autumn. Flowers on
non-existing scapes, five rounded lobes, yellow. June to July. A native
of Europe.
P. 'Friedrichsenii' (D). (*P. fruticosa* × *P. glabra*)
This is a small hybrid shrub up to 30 cm. high and as much across with
more or less erect stems. Leaves pinnate, petiolate; leaflets, linear-
narrow oblong, green. Flowers in terminal clusters five rounded lobes,
lemon-yellow. May to July.
P. fruticosa (D)
The species is a shrubby plant which varies considerably in height from
140

30 cm. to over 1 metre, but there are several dwarf varieties and these will retain their dwarf habit over a good number of years. The type plant is a compact roundish shrub with erect branches and twiggy brown stems. Leaves sessile, palmate with three, five or seven leaflets, linear to lanceolate, overlapping, acute, the three central united at base, glabrous, mid-green, minutely hairy below, margins recurved. Flowers on short hairy pedicels, five lobed, deep yellow petals, alternating with five greenish yellow bracts. July to September. A native of England, Ireland, Europe and America.

P. fruticosa var. *beesii* (D). (Syn. *P.f. nana argentea*)
A dwarf form less than 30 cm. high and about the same across from China, with the typical palmate leaves. Leaflets three to five silver-grey. Flowers large five lobed open goblets, golden-yellow. July.

P. fruticosa 'Longacre' (D)
One of the smallest of the varieties, less than 20 cm. high with prostrate branches and much cut leaves, bearing many soft yellow flowers in July.

P. fruticosa var. *mandschurica* (D)
This is a dwarf shrublet less than 30 cm. high and about as much across with erect purplish stems and five-foliate leaves of silver-grey,

Potentilla fruticosa var. mandshurica

the three terminal leaflets joined at base. Flowers on short terminal pedicels, large, five rounded lobes, white. July. A native of Manchuria.

P. fruticosa nana argentea, see *P. fruticosa* var. *beesii*

P. fruticosa 'Red Ace' (D)

A distinct colour break which occurred recently in a group of fruticosa cultivars as a chance seedling. It is about 20 cm. high with the usual much cut foliage of a light green, and to date has a spread of 45 cm. Flowers large, bright red with a boss of yellow stamens and deep yellow on reverse of petals. July to September.

PTILOTRICHUM (Cruciferae)

A small genus of plants closely allied to *Alyssum* and often listed under that heading in catalogues and books. There are a few shrubby species that are suitable for the small or rock garden where they give a fine display in their flowering season.

Cultivation. A hot dry spot in well drained poorish medium is ideal and all require ample sunshine for them to give of their best. They are admirably suited to a hot ledge in the rock garden and once established drought holds no terror for these species.

Propagation. By seed in March, or green cuttings taken in June.

P. cyclocarpum (E). (Syn. *P. rupestre*)

A native of central Italy and the Balkan Peninsula, this makes a crowded mass of unbranched stems up to 10 cm. high and 23 cm. across, covered with silvery grey scales. Leaves, basal radical in a small rosette lanceolate, silver-grey, stem leaves small linear. Flowers in a crowded terminal head four petalled, white. June.

P. pyrenaicum (E). (Syn. *Alyssum pyrenaicum*)

This is a small shrub rarely above 23 cm. high and as much across with many tufted stems. Leaves obovate, thick, tapered to base, silver-grey, due to intense covering of fine hairs. Flowers in dense spikes, the usual four petalled, crucifer type, white with deep brown anthers. June. A native of the eastern Pyrenees.

P. reverchonii (E)

A dwarf shrub of pleasing and charming habit. It makes a small bush up to 23 cm. high and as much through with erect stems. Leaves crowded in rosette formation, spatulate, sometimes bluntly pointed, light greyish green. Flowers in dense globular terminal heads of four large rounded petals, white with green eye, fragrant. April. A native of the Sierra Carjora, Spain, its only known station, from where it was introduced into cultivation by Messrs Heywood and Davis in 1948.

P. rupestre, see *P. cyclocarpum*

P. spinosum (E). (syn. *Alyssum spinosum*)

It makes a 23 cm. bushlet of erect branches and congested laterals with a spread of 30 cm. Leaves lanceolate, acute silvery grey; the adult wood becomes intensely spiny. Flowers in large corymbs, white, borne in great profusion, completely hiding the foliage. June. Even young plants have the hoary appearance of old age. A native of Spain.

P. spinosum 'Roseum' (E). (Syn. *Alyssum spinosum* var. *roseum*).

This is the delightful pink form of the type which in a good colour form is an ideal plant. June

RHODODENDRON (Ericaceae)

This genus is one of the largest of the flowering shrub genera, contain-

Ptilotrichum spinosum 'Roseum'

ing a great diversity of plants that will surely appeal to all who aspire to growing a representative collection. All shades, with the possible exception of a true blue, are obtainable, ranging from white through pale cream to yellow and brilliant orange; light pale pinks to rose and flaming scarlets to crimson, returning via startling magentas and violets to pale reddish blue; all colours are fully represented and only the avid blue lover should have any cause to complain. The shapes and construction of the flowers too are extremely varied, so much so that it is possible that in the not too distant future, botanists may have to divide the genus into new genera. They range from wide open saucer like blooms, borne singly on short pedicels, through clusters of flowers shaped like those of a *Daphne*, to terminal heads of open campanulate and long tubular bells.

Azalea too, is now included in *Rhododendron* and species and varieties listed here as *Rhododendron* may still have to be sought under *Azalea* in the majority of nurserymen's catalogues.

Even out of flower the foliage is in itself attractive, the diversity of shape and colour has to be seen to be believed and the beauty of their leaves is enhanced by the invariably contrasting hue of their lower surface. Some of the species are intensely aromatic and no other genus containing so many dwarf flowering shrubs can produce as much

143

pleasure as these plants give over the whole of the year. With all this praise there is but one word of warning, lime! If your soil contains lime I am afraid this genus is not for you. They are lime-haters of the first degree and although special beds can be built, sometimes an expensive practice, sooner or later there is a leaching of lime from the indigenous surrounding soil and the tell tale yellowing of the foliage is the first sign of an ultimate demise. There is a preparation on the market today called Sequestrene, an iron chelate compound, which is sometimes used when growing lime-hating plants in a limy medium but this is an expensive process; the material is not cheap and it has to be renewed annually.

The race has its main centre in the Asiatic zone, embracing parts of India, Tibet and China with the Himalayas as the hub. Here the number of species is prolific and on many of the higher alpine ranges mat-forming types take the place of heather found on high moors in the British Isles. Several species are found in Japan while America too has its quota but the genus is not well represented in Europe; only two dwarf species of any importance are found, *R. ferrugineum* and *R. hirsutum*. These are the beloved Alpenrose of the Alpine tourist guides. The latter too, is of doubtful specific rank often quoted as only a hairy lime tolerating variety of the former.

Cultivation. The culture of the dwarf species of *Rhododendron* suitable for rock or small gardens present no great difficulty, provided their few requirements are attended to. They should have an open, moist, lime free soil containing a large proportion of humus in the form of leaf-mould or peat; a soil that is neutral or just on the acid side is ideal, and the drainage must be perfect. Unlike the larger species and varieties, the dwarf species and varieties will tolerate more sunshine, always provided there is ample moisture in the soil. In the north of England and Scotland planting in full sunshine may be carried out but in the south of the country a position facing west is probably best. Where space allows, they all make good plants for the peat bed. In this position they do not receive the early morning sun which can do a great deal of damage to both new foliage and flowers after a cold frosty night. The loss of one season's flowers although disappointing, does no permanent damage but the loss of the new foliage is more serious. Not only does this mean the loss of next year's flowers but also a grave weakening of the plant. Cold winds, too, should be avoided if at all possible. A windbreak is advisable in the form of a small evergreen hedge or flowering shrubs on the windward side. Whatever the position a topdressing twice a year is essential. This should consist of half-rotted leaf-mould or peat placed in the form of a mulch up to 5 cm. deep, according to the size of the species. One application should be given in late spring but before the top surface of the soil has dried out. All *Rhododendrons* are surface rooters and it is absolutely essential that the top 15 cm. must at all times be kept in a moist, cool condition. The other application of the mulch is best given in early autumn; this will do much to protect the roots against frost damage during a very cold spell. To digress for a moment, it is my opinion that there are more evergreen plants killed through drought during a cold spell than from actual frost. These will transpire moisture from their leaves in a temperature well below freezing point. During a prolonged spell of cold weather where temperature remains below freezing both day and night in an unprotected bed of

144

evergreens the frost will penetrate the soil and the roots will freeze causing many of the fibrous roots to fracture. This means that the frozen roots are unable to replace the loss of moisture due to leaf transpiration, thus leading to the collapse of the plant.

If watering has to be resorted to during hot dry spells it is best given by applying a mist spray in the early morning and late evening after the sun has set. Provided there is no prolonged drought I have found that if the mains supply is from a chalk source, no harm seems to occur if this water is used, possibly due to the chalk being neutralised by the acid conditions under which these plants grow. Pruning: it will only be necessary to cut back to maintain a symmetrical shape and to remove all dead wood. Many species will often throw out long straggling shoots from a plant that would otherwise be of a good shape. These should be pinched back to retain uniformity.

Propagation. There are three methods of increase that can be employed when propagating dwarf Rhododendrons, these are; by seed, layering or cuttings. All these methods have been dealt with in the chapter on propagation. Seed is a ready but slow means of increase as the majority set a large amount of good viable seed, but where a large collection of *Rhododendrons* is grown they may not always breed true although there is also a chance of raising a new hybrid of merit when this method is adopted. The seed is best sown in February. Layering must be resorted to where there is no other way of propagating the plants and cuttings are best taken of the current year's growth; green cuttings with a heel of the old wood in July are advised.

The following list is fairly representative of the dwarf species and hybrids which can be cultivated in the rock or small garden. Only those which are in commerce have been listed but there should be enough to satisfy all but the specialist to whom the necessity to grow all and every one is essential. Following the specific or varietal name is the series or sub-series abbreviated to s. or s.s. to which the plant under review belongs. To avoid repetition it should be noted that all Rhododendrons have short petiolate, alternate, entire leaves.

R. aperantum (s. *Neriiflorum.* s.s. *Sanguineum*). (E)
This is a dwarf spreading mat-forming plant of much branched scale covered stems up to 23 cm. high and a spread of 60 cm. Leaves dark green, oval, tapered, glaucous, white below. Flowers in terminal clusters up to six, tubular, bell shaped and can be white, rose or yellow. Native of Burma at altitudes of between 4,000 m. and 5,000 m. May to June.

R, brachyanthum (E). (s. *Glaucophyllum* s.s. *Brachyanthum*)
A native of Yunnan, China this species makes a dwarf, stiff bush with procumbent bright reddish brown scaly branches up to 30 cm. high and a spread of 60 cm. Leaves oval, apex recurved, dark bright green above, glaucous below, terminating in a minute acuminate tooth and a pronounced reddish midrib; scales on both sides. The flowers borne in clusters of three to eight are bell shaped, yellow tinged with green. June.

R. brachyanthum var. *hypolepidotum* (E). (Syn. *R. charitostreptum*)
A variety with erect, much branched slender brownish green stems. Leaves oval to obovate, dark mid-green and heavily netted with veins above; light grey-green, scaly below. The flowers in small terminal clusters are bell shaped, pale yellow. May.

R. calciphilum (s. *Saluenense*). (E)
A prostrate shrub from Burma where it sheets the hill with colour at
3,500 m. Tight congested branchlets up to 15 cm. high and a spread of
45 cm. Leaves oval-oblong, grey-green turning to bronze in winter.
Flowers open saucer shaped, rosy purple. May. It is confined to
limestone in its native habitat but requires a neutral or slightly acid soil
in cultivation.

R. calostrotum (s. *Saluenense*). (E)
A delightful lax shrub up to 30 cm. high and as much across with
slender brown stems. Leaves oval to lanceolate, thin, mid-green above,
glaucous below, petioles short, margined with bristles, underneath
turning reddish brown in the adult stage due to the intense covering of
fine scales. The flowers borne in May on small terminal pedicels are
open and flat, pink to purple with deeper spots. A native of Upper
Burma.

R. campylogynum (s. *Campylogynum*). (E)
A delightful semi-erect shrub up to 45 cm. high and a spread of 50 cm.
with congested branchlets. Leaves oval to orbicular, apex rounded with
terminal minute acuminate teeth, dark green above, paler below,
margins recurved. Flowers on long pedicels terminal wide bell shaped,
ranging in colour from rose-purple to almost black-purple. May. A
native of Yunnan, China.

R. campylogynum var. *myrtilloides* (E). (Syn. *R. myrtilloides*)
This is about 25 cm. high and 45 cm. wide of erect stout, reddish brown
branches. Leaves obovate, arranged round the stems, minutely
toothed, dark glossy green above, glaucous below, sparsely dotted with
scales on both sides. Flowers small solitary on slender pedicels, bell
shaped, deep plum. May. A native of N.E. Burma.

R. camtschaticum (D). (s. *Camtschaticum*). (Syn. *Therorhodion camtschaticum*)
This is one of the more difficult species to cultivate successfully, especially in the south of the country where it seems to resent the normal
dry atmosphere of those parts. The finest plant I have seen is growing
and thriving in the Royal Botanical Gardens, Edinburgh, home of
many delightful dwarf *Rhododendrons* in cultivation. In the north and
midlands it will grow in full sun, but requires half shade at least in hot
southern gardens. A native of Kamchatka and other parts of N.E. Asia,
it makes a 10 cm. high plant and about 45 cm. across of congested
stems in tufts. Leaves oval, nearly sessile, thin, mid-green and quite
glabrous. Flowers on 2 cm. pedicels held well clear of the foliage are
rosy crimson. May.

R. cantabile, see *R. russatum*

R. 'Carmen' (*R. didymum* × *R. forrestii* var. *repens*). (E)
A small hybrid less than 60 cm. high with a similar spread and typical
R. forrestii var. *repens* foliage, light green below, and terminal clusters of
velvety bell shaped flowers of a deep ruby red. April to May.

R. charitopes (E). (s. *Glaucophyllum* s.s. *Charitopes*)
A dwarf shrub from Upper Burma near to 30 cm. high and a spread of
38 cm. with erect, light brown slender twigs. Leaves crowded at apex of
the shoots, ovate to obovate, deep glossy green above, glaucous
beneath, with a covering of scales on both sides, terminating in an
acuminate tooth. Flowers in terminal clusters on short slender pedicels
up to three open bell shaped, pinkish mauve, speckled with crimson.
May.

146

Rhododendron chryseum

R. charitostreptum, see *R. branchyanthum.* var. *hypolepidotum*

R. 'Chikor' (E). (*R. chryseum* × *ludlowii*)
An outstanding dwarf hybrid up to 60 cm. high of close compact habit
and terminal clusters of lemon-yellow flowers, in early May.

R. chryseum (E). (s. *Lapponicum*)
A small shrub up to 30 cm. in height and as much across with many
branched reddish stems. Leaves long, oblong with a dense covering of
brown scales on both sides, margins recurved, dull olive-green above,
brownish white beneath. Flowers slightly funnel shaped in terminal
clusters of from four to six, good deep yellow. April to May. A native of
W. China, this species is one of the best yellows for the small garden.

R. ciliatum (E). (Ludlow and Sherrif's dwarf form). (s. *Maddenii* s.s.
Ciliicalyx)
The typical plant is a medium tall rather straggly growing species up to
2 m. in maritime and western gardens, but the dwarf form after ten
years in the open rock garden is still only 45 cm. high and a spread of
60 cm. Branches firm, erect, compact. Flowers from each lateral in a
substantial truss. A native of Sikkim, it has erect branches of light
green juvenile wood ageing to a deep red-brown, the whole covered
with short brown bristles. Leaves long narrow, obovate, tapered to

each end, terminating in a reddish acuminate tooth; densely covered with brownish bristles on the upper surface and margins, scaly below, pronounced midrib, veining reticulate, dull deep green above, paler below. Flowers in terminal trusses five to seven large open funnel shaped; corolla five deeply notched obovate lobes, stamens ten, style protruding, calyx lobes ovate, light green, margined with white bristles. The buds are a delightful bright rose, opening to glistening white flushed pink. March. Being an early flowerer some shelter is advisable, so that the morning sun cannot reach the flowers after cold nights.

R. dasypetalum (E). (s. *Lapponicum*)
Makes a small shrub of stiff branches about 30 cm. high and a similar spread, with grey-green oval scaly leaves, brownish-grey below. Flowers in April, short funnel shaped, purple-rose. A native of Yunnan.

R. fastigiatum (E). (s. *Lapponicum*)
This is an erect shrublet 30 to 45 cm. high and as much across with thin twiggy, brownish scaly branches. Leaves clustered at apex of the stems, oval to obovate, dark olive-green above, grey beneath, scales on both sides, but most prominent on the midrib and short reddish petiole. Flowers funnel shaped, light purple in colour are borne in small terminal clusters. April and sometimes again in September. A native of Yunnan.

R. ferrugineum (E). (s. *Ferrugineum*)
This is the Alpenrose of Switzerland and makes a good subject for the small garden, for it is very slow growing only reaching a height of a metre with a similar spread after many years. It makes a compact bush with young shoots covered with rust coloured scales. Leaves oval, tapered to both base and apex, deep glossy green above, golden-brown below due to the intense covering of rust-coloured scales. Flowers in terminal clusters from six to twelve, deep rosy crimson. June.

R. flavidum (E). (s. *Lapponicum*)
A small dense rounded shrub up to 45 cm. high and a spread of 30 cm. with very scaly branches. Leaves oval-oblong, thick, deep green above, lighter below, with scales on both sides. Flowers in terminal clusters of up to three to six, short funnel shaped, a good primrose-yellow. March. A native of W. Szechwan, China.

R. forrestii (E). (s. *Neriiflorum* s.s. *Forrestii*)
A native of N.W. Yunnan and S.E. Tibet, this is a creeping shrub rarely up to 30 cm. high but with a much wider spread. Leaves oval, deep glossy green above, purple below and having conspicuously grooved veins. Flowers solitary, rarely in pairs, long narrow bell shaped, extremely large for size of plant, deep crimson-red. May. This species should be planted with its roots under a piece of sandstone and the soil must be well drained, but moist at all times. I have not found it a prolific flowerer, but was called to task by a critic of a previous book, by saying that there is a free flowering clone of this species in cultivation.

R. forrestii var. *repens* (E). (Syn. *R. repens*)
If satisfied this is one of the finest of all dwarf Rhododendrons for the small garden and was until recently given specific rank. It is quite prostrate, only a few centimetres high but with a spread of 60 cm. to 1 m., with creeping stout stems. Leaves oval, dark green, glossy, thick textured, deeply grooved veins above, light green below. The foliage is the key to the slight botanical difference between *R. forrestii* and its var.

148

repens, the colour in the former being purple below. Flowers large for size of plant are narrow bell shaped, waxy in texture, deep crimson, generally solitary, rarely in pairs. April to May. A native of Tibet. Requires similar culture as for the species.

R. hanceanum 'Nanum' (E). (s. *Triflorum* s.s. *Hanceanum*)
A native of W. China this dwarf form of *R. hanceanum* is about 15 cm. high with stiff light brown shiny stems covering a space of 30 cm. Leaves crowded, obovate to lanceolate deep glossy green above, lighter beneath, veining heavy and reticulated on both sides, only sparsely scaled. Flowers in terminal clusters, small tubular with spreading lobes. Pale yellow. April to May. Reputed to be a shy flowerer but this is only a question of obtaining a free flowering form, my own plants never fail to set buds and flower each year.

R. hirsutum (E). (s. *Ferrugineum*)
A native of high elevations in Europe on limestone, but desires a lime free medium in cultivation. Also called the Alpenrose, it is closely allied to *R. ferrugineum* but differs for garden purposes in being less scaly and very hairy. Leaves bright green above, oval, tapered to base and apex, slightly scaly below. Flowers borne in terminal clusters are from deep pink to crimson. May to June.

Rhododendron hanceanum 'Nanum'

Rhododendron impeditum

R. hirsutum 'Album' (E)
This is the rare white form of the type and worth a place in the garden if obtainable. May to June.

R. impeditum (E). (s. *Lapponicum*)
A native of W. China, it makes a very prostrate mat of horizontal growth about 15 cm. high and a spread of 45 cm. with greenish-brown wiry stems. Leaves oval to ovate, dark dull green above, glaucous below, thickly covered with scales on both sides, margins slightly recurved. The flowers are clustered at the terminals of the shoots in twos and threes, open, pale purple and slightly fragrant. April to May.

R. imperator (E). (s. *Uniflorum*)
A very dwarf prostrate plant only a few cm. high and a spread of 30 cm. with slender horizontal scaly branches. Leaves lanceolate with a short acuminate tooth at apex, tapered towards base, margins decurved, dark glossy green above, silver-grey below. Flowers terminal, solitary, open funnel shaped, deep rose-purple. May. A native of Upper Burma.

R. intricatum (E). (s. *Lapponicum*)
A native of Szechwan, W. China, it makes a neat rounded bush up to 30 cm. high and as much across with reddish brown, scaly shoots. The leaves are oval to orbicular, dark green above, lighter below, both sides covered with glistening scales. Flowers small, in terminal clusters,

150

mauve. April. An attractive plant that will cover itself with flowers even from a newly rooted cutting.

R. keiskei (E). (s. and s.s. *Triflorum*)
A low, compact shrublet about 23 cm. high and 30 cm. wide with brownish scaly branches. Leaves oval-oblong, deep green, scaly on both sides but more dense below. Flowers in terminal clusters of four, open bell shaped, lemon-yellow. April. A native of Japan.

R. keleticum (E). (s. *Saluenense*)
From Tibet this makes a dwarf shrublet of much branched, slender, light brown, scaly stems about 23 cm. high and 45 cm. wide. Leaves thin, oblong to obovate, dark glossy green above, light brownish green below, very sparsely scaled on underside; margins hairy and slightly decurved. Flowers open saucer shaped, purplish crimson spotted with deeper markings on slender hairy pedicels. May.

R. ledoides, see *R. trichostomum* var. *ledoides*.

R. lepidotum (E). (s. and s.s. *Lepidotum*)
A species from Nepal, Sikkim, Himalayas, this is up to 45 cm. high and as much across, young wood, leaves and pedicels thickly covered with minute scales. Leaves oblong, deep green above, paler beneath. Flowers from one to three terminal, open saucer shaped, range in colour from pink to purple. May to June.

R. leucaspis (E). (s. *Boothii*. s.s. *Megeratum*)
This species must be considered one of the best of all *Rhododendrons* in cultivation. Its only fault, if this can be called one, is that flowering in February and March there is a tendency for frosts to kill the flowers. It makes a low evergreen shrub up to 60 cm. in height and as much through with spreading semi-erect stout, mid-brown hairy stems. Leaves terminal, oval to obovate, dark olive-green above, glaucous below, scaly on upper surface, midrib and margins covered with fine hairs. Both stems and leaves are bristly. Flowers large, over 5 cm. across, terminal in small clusters open bell shaped, pure satiny white enhanced by dark brown, long protruding anthers. February to March. This plant will flower from layers or cuttings in two years. A native of Tibet.

R. macrosepalum 'Linearifolium' (E). (Syn. *Azalea linearifolia*) (s. *Azalea*. s.s. *Obtusum*)
A Japanese garden form, this makes a flattish bush up to 45 cm. in time and about 1 m. wide, but will take many years to reach this stature. It is a very distinctive plant with extra long linear, dull green hairy, tapered leaves. The flowers are borne in terminal clusters of two to three, consist of long narrow lobes, similar to the leaves, bright lilac and the whole plant when in flower has a very shaggy appearance. May.

R. microleucum (s. *Lapponicum*). (E)
This is a choice rare shrub up to 30 cm. high and about 45 cm. across with twiggy scaly branches, leaves crowded, narrow almost linear, pale green above, covered beneath with buff scales. Flowers in small terminal clusters, short funnel shaped, glistening white. May. A native of Asia and N. America.

R. myrtilloides, see *R. campylogynum* var. *myrtilloides*

R. nitens (E). (s. *Saluenense*)
A native of N.E. Burma, this charming dwarf, the latest of the series to flower, July, makes a compact prostrate shrub up to 15 cm. high and 30 cm. across. Branches slender, brownish green, scaly. Leaves long

Rhododendron leucaspis

narrow oval, rounded or blunt at apex, tapered to base, margins slightly ciliate, bright glossy green above with a covering of light scales, greyish green below. Flowers terminal, open saucer shaped, bright magenta.

R. obtusum 'Amoenum' (s.*Azalea* s.s. *Obtusum*). (E)
This is a tight bushy shrub up to 60 cm. or more in height and as much across, but taking many years to reach this size. Leaves oval, very deep glossy green with bristles on both sides. Flowers small, seldom 2 cm. across, rosy purple. May. A native of Japan.

R. obtusum 'Japonicum' (E)
A form that is smaller than the type but very dainty, making a superior plant with its charming rose-purple flowers which are not less in size in relation to the type plant. May.

R. obtusum 'Macrostemon' (E)
Another form from Japan which is about 30 cm. high and has large solitary flowers of a bright pink. April to May.

There are many forms and hybrids of *obtusum* of which the following are representative with a flowering period from April to June:
'Apple Blossom'. Pink stained white.
'Bassetts Beauty'. Bright red.

152

'Benigiri'. Almost double crimson.
'Blaauus Pink'. Salmon pink.
'Blue Danube'. Blue mauve.
'Christmas Cheer'. Double deep red.
'Hatsugiri'. Red-purple.
'Hino-Crimson'. Bright red.
'Hinomayo'. Salmon-pink.
'Hinodegiri'. Clear red.
'Kirishima'. Lilac-mauve.
'Kokin-shita'. Bright salmon-red.
'Kure-no-yuki'. White hose-in hose.
'Miyagino'. Clear light pink.
'Mother's Day'. Semi-double red.
'Princess Juliana'. Orange.
'Rasho-mon'. Clear salmon red.
'Rosebud'. Pink.
'Surprise'. Pale orange-red.
'Ukamuse'. Vermilion and salmon-rose.
'Vuyk's Scarlet'. Scarlet.
R. pemakoense. (E). (s. *Uniflorum*)
An erect dwarf shrub about 30 cm. high and up to 60 cm. across,

Rhododendron pemakoense

spreading by underground runners; stems light green. Leaves narrow obovate, dark glossy green above, greyish green below, petioles long, intensely aromatic. Flowers terminal generally solitary, sometimes in pairs, open tubular clear pinkish purple. April. A native of the province of Pemako, E. Tibet.

R. prostratum (E). (s.s. *Saluenense*)
As its specific name implies this is a prostrate plant only a few cm. high and a spread of 45 cm. making a trailing bush with prostrate horizontal branches, light pinkish brown, sparsely covered with hairs. Leaves elliptical-oval, apex decurved, rounded at base, sparsely margined with hairs, glabrous and glossy dark green above, rust coloured beneath due to the covering of scales. Flowers terminal, single, sometimes in pairs, open saucer shaped, rose-violet, spotted with red. April. A native of Yunnan, China.

R. pumilum (E). (s. *Uniflorum*)
A fine dwarf species up to 15 cm. high and about 30 cm. across making a close compact shrub. Leaves small, oval, dark glossy green above, lighter below. Flowers from one to three borne on short pedicels, bell shaped, rose-pink. April to May. A native of Burma and Assam.

R. racemosum (E). (s. *Scabrifolium*)
A shrub that will reach over a metre in time with a similar spread, but flowering as it does from one year old cuttings and owing to the ease with which it is possible to trim it into shape, it makes an ideal shrub for the small garden. It is a much branched semi-prostrate shrub with stout wiry stems, light brown and covered with scales. Leaves oval, apex recurved, tapered to base, deep dull green above, glaucous beneath, clothed with minute scales. Leaves oval, apex recurved, tapered to base, deep dull green above, glaucous beneath, clothed with minute scales. Flowers open bell shaped, borne in terminal and axillary clusters up to six; the colour ranges through pale pink to deep pink. April. The best form of this species is that which was introduced from Forrest's 1921–2 Expedition in N.W. Yunnan under number 19404, which is a good clear red-pink.

R. radicans (E). (s. *Saluenense*)
This is possibly the dwarfest of all the *Rhododendron* species less than 2 cm. in height, with quite prostrate and compact brownish red branches. Leaves minute, lanceolate, clustered at the end of the thin wiry twigs, deep glossy green above, light brownish green below and scaly. Flowers solitary on 2 cm. bristly pedicels, very large for size of plant, up to 3 cm. across, ranging in colour from a light mauve to a deep purple. May. A native of S.E. Tibet.

R. radinum, see *R. trichostomum* var. *radinum*

R. repens, see *R. forrestii* var. *repens*

R. rupicola (E). (s. *Lapponicum*)
Is one of the best of the *Lapponicum* series. It makes a compact shrub up to 45 cm. high and about 60 cm. across. Leaves crowded, oval to oblong, dull deep green, glabrous above, rusty coloured below, apex terminating in a short acuminate tooth. Flowers in terminal clusters up to five rich purple. May. A native of Yunnan, China.

R. russatum (E). (Syn. *R. cantabile*). (s. *Lapponicum*)
R. cantabile has until recently been regarded as a distinct species, but is now considered to be only a dwarf form of *R. russatum*. From personal experience it is to be preferred for its small compact habit. The type *R.*

154

russatum is a shrub which will attain 60 cm. after many years and a similar spread with congested yellowish brown branches. Leaves oval to ovate, dull green, rounded at apex, rusty yellow below; branches and foliage densely covered with brown scales. Flowers in terminal clusters of from five to ten, short tubular with spreading lobes, blue purplish with a white throat. April. A native of Yunnan. This plant can be kept dwarf by hard pruning, for it will readily break from the old wood.

R. saluenense (E). (s. *Saluenense*)
This, the type plant of the series, is all that a first rate dwarf shrub should be, and must be considered essential to a collection of dwarf *Rhododendrons*. A compact shrub up to 45 cm. high and about the same wide, with slender branches, erect, light brown, covered with scales. Leaves rough, oval to obovate, terminating in a minute acuminate tooth, dark green above, lightish green-brown beneath with pronounced reddish midrib. Flowers terminal in pairs on short bristly pedicels, wide open saucer shaped, deep purple with darker markings. May. A native of Yunnan.

R. sargentianum (E). (s. *Anthopogon*)
A dwarf compact, very aromatic shrub, with rigid branches up to 60 cm. in height and about 45 cm. wide. Leaves crowded, small, oval, deep glossy green, paler below. Flowers in terminal clusters up to twelve lobes, spreading, tube short, pedicels small, yellow. May. A native of W. Szechwan.

R. scintillans (E). (s. *Lapponicum*)
This dwarf species should be chosen when in flower, for at its best it can be almost a royal blue, but there are a large number of forms which are a poor lavender-blue. It is a more or less open shrublet, up to 60 cm. in height and the same across with much branched stems. Leaves lanceolate, deep green, grey beneath, pointed at apex, tapered to base. Flowers in terminal clusters from five to six open bell shaped with a short tube. April. A native of Yunnan.

R. sphaeranthum, see *R. trichostomum*

R. tapetiforme (E). (s. *Lapponicum*)
A native of Tibet, this is the smallest of the *Lapponicum* series, only a few centimetres high and about 23 cm. with prostrate, stiff branches. Leaves oval to ovate, dull green, paler below, densely covered with scales. Flowers in terminal clusters up to six small, pinky-mauve. April.

R. tephropeplum (E). (s. *Boothii* s.s. *Tephropeplum*)
This is a shrub that will after many years reach up to a metre in height and as much across but can be kept dwarf by hard pruning. It has been included as it is a very desirable plant, well able to hold its own amongst the other aristocrats of this diverse genus. Although a member of the *Boothii* series and not considered to be too trustworthy in inland gardens in the south, it has never suffered in any way in my garden during the last ten years in west Kent and can always be relied upon to produce a fine crop of flowers every year. It makes an open bush with stiff erect branches; leaves long, narrow-oblong, tapered to base, mid-green above, similar below but covered with scales. Flowers in terminal trusses up to five, long tubular, pink, darker at base. May. A native of Burma and S.E. Tibet.

R. trichostomum (E). (Syn. *R. sphaeranthum*; *R. ledoides*; *R. radinum*). (s. *Anthopogon*)
Until recently the three synonyms of this species were regarded as

distinct but now *R. sphaeranthum* has become *R. trichostomum* and the other two, varieties. The type plant is a much branched shrub eventually reaching 1 m. and as much across, with erect slender stems, densely covered with scales, deep brown in colour, striped white. Leaves long, narrow, oblong, very deep dull brownish green above, light brownish green below, completely covered with brown scales on both sides, margins slightly recurved and edged with scales and an occasional hair or so. Flowers in rounded terminal clusters up to twenty, daphne-like, good rose-pink; corolla scaly on exterior. April. A native of W. Szechwan.

R. trichostomum var. *ledoides* (E). (Syn. *R. ledoides*)
This is a smaller variety and differs from the type in having a glabrous corolla. April

R. trichostomum var. *radinum* (E). (Syn. *R. radinum*)
A close compact plant only about 45 cm. high and as much across with similar foliage and flowers and the corolla is densely scaly on exterior. April.

R. williamsianum (E). (s. *Thomsonii* s.s. *Williamsianum*)
This is an outstanding plant for the rock or small garden and when well established is a delightful sight with its unique foliage and large flowers. It is a shrub up to 1 m. in height in its natural habitat, but is more prostrate in cultivation, only about 30 cm. high, often less and a spread of 1 m. with wiry glossy reddish brown stems. Leaves terminal orbicular, smooth, dull mid-green above, light grey-green below, deeply reticulated veining, margins slightly decurved, apex terminating in a blunt acuminate tooth, petiole long, smooth reddish blue. The young foliage is a delightful shade of bronze. The flowers are borne in terminal pairs, large, bell shaped, wax like and of a beautiful shade of shell pink. April. A native of W. Szechwan, China.

ROSA (Rosaceae)
When one thinks of English gardens, the mind automatically turns to roses. Unfortunately these seem to be too stiff and formal for the rock garden. The miniatures however are ideal subjects for the small garden and create a pleasant picture if grown en masse.
Cultivation. A good rich loam but well drained, in sun, is desirable and a position not too high in the garden should be chosen for these dwarf forms.
Propagation. Green cuttings should be taken in June and rooted in the propagating frame.

R. chinensis 'Minima' (D). (Syns. *R. Lawranceana*; *R. roulettii*)
This is a dwarf China Rose, less than 15 cm. high and 10 cm. across with almost smooth branches. Leaflets three to five ovate, obtuse, reddish purple in colour. Flowers double rose-red. June. Presumed to be a sport from 'Pumila' which achieves greater height.

R. lawranceana, see *R. chinensis* 'Minima'

R. 'Peon' (D)
A dwarf bush of unknown parentage up to 15 cm. high with clusters of small crimson rambler type flowers. May.

R. roulettii, see *R. chinensis* 'Minima'
Miniature Roses.

There is on the market today a large collection of really miniature roses from 15 to 30 cm. high, which are very popular and sometimes seen on rock gardens, providing colour once the first flush of flowers is over. They are also ideal subjects for the small garden, or in sinks and troughs. The following list is not complete but many nurserymen's catalogues have a choice to suit all tastes:

Flowering from late May until the end of autumn.
'Baby Crimson'. 15 cm. compact, crimson.
'Baby Gold'. 15 cm. double gold and orange.
'Baby Masquerade'. 15 cm. gold and red.
'Baby Ophelia'. 15 cm. salmon-pink.
'Baby Virgo'. 15 cm. pure double white.
'Bo-Peep'. 15 cm. pale green leaves, flat pink flowers.
'Calibri'. 23 cm. orange.
'Carolim'. 23 cm. red turning to orange.
'Cinderella'. 25 cm. shell-pink with white margins.
'Eleanor'. 23 cm. coral-pink.
'Elf'. Only 10 cm. high with deep crimson flowers and golden stamens.
'Granata'. 23 cm. garnet-red.
'Humpty Dumpty'. 15 cm. double deep carmine-pink.
'Jackie'. 15 cm. pale yellow.
'Little Buckaroo'. 15 cm. clear red with a yellow eye, scented.
'Little Flirt'. 15 cm. red inside, yellow outside.
'Maid Marion'. 15 cm. double scarlet.
'Midget'. 25 cm. carmine-red, tinted white at base.
'Mr Bluebird'. 23 cm. lavender-blue.
'Pigmy Gold'. 15 cm. double golden-yellow.
'Pink Heather'. 15 cm. clear pink flushed white, scented.
'Pixie Rose'. 15 cm. deep pink, scented.
'Posy'. 23 cm. deep pink in a compact form.
'Pumila'. 24 cm. bright rich pink.
'Red Imp'. 15 cm. deep carmine-red.
'Scarlet Gem'. About 15 cm. high with scarlet and orange-red flowers.
'Simple Simon'. 15 cm. deep pink.
'Sunbeam'. 10 cm. clear yellow.
'Tinker Bell'. About 15 cm. high with flattish deep pink flowers.
'Tommy Tucker'. 15 cm. high salmon-pink.
'Yellow Doll'. 23 cm. clear yellow.

SALIX (Salicaceae)
The Willows are a large and mighty race numbering up to 300 species and ranging from fine erect and pendant trees, through tall shrubs in exposed positions at high altitudes. These prostrate species in company with the creeping Azalea, *Loiseleuria procumbens,* are the last of the hard wooded plants found almost to the edge of the eternal snows. With few exceptions the willows are dioecious, that is male and female flowers are borne on different plants. The catkins of the male plants are generally more decorative than the female and these are to be preferred for this reason. They have a wide geographical distribution over most parts of the northern hemisphere, generally from higher altitudes.
Cultivation. In cultivation these plants prefer a more lowly aspect, liking nothing better than to be placed in a moist but well-drained position in the garden or at the base of the rock garden in full sun. The key to success is an ample supply of moisture at the roots during the growing

Salix x boydii

season and they will replay with an attractive display of beautiful foliage and, in due season, either yellow or golden catkins. Topdress in early spring with equal parts of leaf-mould, loam and sand, working the mixture well down in between the branches.

Propagation. Presents no difficulty. Cuttings taken in November and placed round the edge of individual small pots, plunged in a cold frame and kept moist until rooted will soon be ready for planting out. All willows are intolerant of root disturbance and should be planted in their permanent quarters while still young.

158

S. apoda (male form). (D)

A charming, desirable and extremely attractive prostrate shrublet. The male form is smaller and more procumbent than the female, rarely exceeding 2 cm. in height with a spread of 23 cm. It is best planted against a rock ledge so that it can mould itself to the contours of the rock face. A native of the Caucasus it makes a creeping mass of bronze-green branches. Leaves tufted, small oval, tapered to base, margins minutely serrate, texture thin, veining not pronounced, a bright apple green in colour. The catkins, large for the size of the plant, are long narrow, oval, emerging dark woolly grey, turning rose-pink and finally orange due to the colour of the pollen; bracts black tipped. April.

S. arbuscula (D)

A very variable plant ranging from 23 cm. to 60 cm. in height and about 38 cm. across but rarely reaching the latter size in cultivation. A much branched, slender, semi-erect shrublet with smooth stems. Leaves crowded, alternate, oval to oblong, tapered to base and apex, generally entire dark green, glabrous above, grey beneath. Catkins produced at the apex of small leafy stems in May. Female larger than the male. A native of Europe including Scotland and Siberia.

S. arbuscula 'Humilis' (D)

This is a prostrate form of the above rarely up to 15 cm. high and 23 cm. across with densely clothed congested branches, typical foliage, reduced in proportion to the size of the plant. Catkins similar. May.

S. × *boydii* (D)

One of the finest of all the dwarf *Salix* and still a rare plant, due in some measure to its slow growth, although it was discovered over seventy years ago. It is a natural hybrid found only once, by the late Dr Wm Boyd while plant-hunting in Forfarshire, and is considered to be a cross between *S. reticulata* and *S. lapponum*. The original plant is still in the garden of Miss Boyd at Melrose and is only about 1 m. in height after seventy years. A small erect, stout dwarf tree with a distinct bole, rounded smooth and gnarled, giving the appearance of being age old. Leaves alternate, wide, obovate, cordate, obtuse, deeply veined, entire grey-white due to covering of fine down above and thickly covered below. The upright, oval, sessile catkins are silky and light yellow. May.

S. herbacea (D)

A prostrate ground hugging species, branches often touching the ground and rooting as they creep along the surface, also increasing slowly by underground runners. Rarely above 5 cm. high and a spread of 30 cm. with rounded smooth stems, sparsely clothed with small, alternate, oval, cordate at base leaves, each having a small notch at apex; margins obscurely dentate, dark glossy green, veining reticulate. Catkins oblong, yellow on short stems. April. A native of Europe including Britain, Scotland and Ireland.

S. × *morrei* (D)

This is a natural hybrid between *S. herbacea* and *S. phylicifolia* discovered in Ireland. A low, semi-erect dwarf shrub with smooth rounded stems up to 30 cm. high and 23 cm. across. Leaves oval-oblong, rounded or tapered at base, notched at apex, obscurely dentate, dark glossy green. Catkins on small stems, erect cylindrical, reddish yellow. April.

S. myrsinites (D)

A semi-erect shrublet of slender hairy stems about 30 cm. high and as

much wide. Leaves alternate, oval, pointed at apex and base, lightly
toothed, pale green, heavily veined. Catkins upright on small leafy
stems, long oval reddish yellow. May. A native of Europe, including
Scotland and Ireland.

S. myrsinites var. *jacquiniana* (D)
This is a geographical variant of the above from the Tyrol. The leaves
are entire and the catkins are deep orange-red.

S. polaris (D)
A true arctic species from high altitudes in the Polar regions. It is near
to *S. herbacea*, quite prostrate, only 2 cm. high and a spread of about 23
cm. ground hugging; the leaves are smaller and entire. May.

S. repens (D)
A note of warning is included here in connection with species. The
specific name refers only to the underground stems which creep along
just under the surface of the soil and at intervals produce erect
branches which, although in nature are only about 30 cm. high, will in
cultivation reach over 2 m. This is a plant to be avoided in a small
garden.

S. repens 'Compacta' (D)
A garden form which unlike the species does not tend to spread far and
wide but makes a compact plant up to 23 cm. high, spreading to 36 cm.
of ascending and prostrate, silky branches. Leaves oval, oblong-
lanceolate, greyish green underneath covered with glistening silky
hairs. Catkins large, oval, bright yellow. April to May.

S. reticulata (D)
This is one of the gems of the race making a dwarf, procumbent shrub
only 2 cm. or so high and a spread of 15 cm. with congested, angled,
smooth brownish branches. Leaves sparse, alternate, oval to orbicular,
petiolate; irregular margins, occasionally tapered at apex, crinkled,
deep green on upper surface, greyish white with deep reticulated veins
beneath. Catkins on lax stems at the apex of the laterals, oval to
globular, yellow. May. A native of England and Scotland. The more
exposed position that this plant can be given, the more compact it will
remain.

S. retusa (D)
A much branched prostrate creeping shrublet only about 10 cm. high
and about 20 cm. across, with greenish brown, smooth stems. Leaves
alternate, entire, long oval, roundish or obtuse, tapered at base, smooth
deep glossy green. Catkins terminal on small leafy stems, oval. May. A
native of Europe.

S. retusa var. *pyrenaica* (D)
This differs from the species in having reddish brown branches and
narrow oval or elliptic, grey-green foliage. The catkins also reddish or
violet in colour. May. A native of the Pyrenees. Now given specific
status.

S. serpyllifolia (D)
A smaller edition of *S. retusa* and often quoted as only a variety of that
species. Quite prostrate, forming a dense congested mat only 2 cm. in
height and a spread of 15 cm. with smooth wiry stems. Leaves small,
oval to orbicular, tapered or obtuse, margins slightly indentated, dark
glossy green on both sides. Catkins on short leafy stems, cylindrical,
yellow. May. A native of Europe, often found in exposed positions at
high altitudes as a tiny mass of congested twigs not more than 1 cm.

high, only a few centimetres wide, but when introduced into cultivation soon reverts to type.

SANTOLINA (Compositae)

A small genus of shrubs which add interest to the garden with their dainty, sometimes silvery foliage and heads of yellow flowers. All are intensely aromatic and natives of the Mediterranean region.
Cultivation. Any good but not too rich soil in an open, well drained sunny position. They are all avid sun lovers and if touched or bruised on hot summer days their fragrance will pervade the air over a large area.
Propagation. Is by cuttings taken with a heel in June and rooted in the propagating frame.
S. chamaecyparissus (E)
This is a much branched shrublet up to 45 cm. high and 60 cm. across, commonly known as Lavender Cotton or Cotton Lavender, with more or less erect stems clothed with a thick white wool. Leaves pinnatisect, dense on short twigs, alternate, segments in two to four rows, short, obtuse, dentate, covered with a thick white wool, aromatic. Flowers in great profusion, on long slender stems, rounded mop heads without rayflorets, golden-yellow. June to July. A native of the Mediterranean region.
S. chamaecyparissus var. *corsica* (E). (Syn. *S. chamaecyparissus* 'Nana')
A much smaller and desirable variety suitable for the small garden with intensely silvered foliage, less than 20 cm. high and a spread of 30 cm. Flowers on short slender stems, golden 'half suns'. July. A native of Corsica.
S. leucantha, see *S. pinnata*
S. chamaecyparissus 'Nana', see *S. chamaecyparissus* var. *corsica*
S. pinnata (E). (Syn. *S. leucantha*)
Not so showy as the other species, it makes an erect shrub about 45 cm. high and as much across with slender bushy twigs, quite devoid of wool. Leaves on short petioles, crowded, pinnate, segments small narrow in rows of four, glabrous, mid-green. Flowers on erect stems up to three on short pedicels, rounded, creamy white. July. A native of Italy. Now *S. chamaecyparissus* sub. species *tomentosa*.

SATUREJA (Labiatae)

This genus contains about fourteen species all with the exception of one from the Mediterranean region and the one species, a dwarf form noted here, is worth a place in the small garden for its scent alone, as the whole plant is aromatic and after hot days it will fill the air with its delightful fragrance.
Cultivation. An open well-drained light soil in full sun is required; a medium, not too rich is ideal.
Propagation. Green cuttings should be taken in June.
S. montana (D)
A close compact bush with slender stems covered with a fine down up to 45 cm. high and as much across. Leaves opposite, long narrow, nearly linear, sessile, entire, pointed mid-green above, greyish green below with ciliate margins. Flowers in densely crowded, axillary

whorls from near the apex of the shoots, white to lilac, in colour. July. A native of S. Europe.

S. montana 'Pygmaea' (D)
This is a small form of the type only about 15 cm. high and as much through, otherwise similar in all respects. July. Garden origin.

SCHIZOCODON (*Diapensiaceae*)

A genus closely related to *Shortia* and regarded by some authorities as being congeneric with it, of which there are four varieties of the single species in cultivation that make ideal plants for the small garden where the necessary conditions can be provided.

Cultivation. A cool lime-free, open but moist soil well enriched with humus in the form of rotted leaf-mould will suit these plants. Shelter from cold searing winds, with protection from early morning and midday sun is also necessary for their health. Less shade is permissible in the north of England and Scottish gardens and a position facing south west is ideal. They are very suitable plants for the peat or woodland gardens. In April a topdressing of leaf-mould or peat should be worked in amongst the prostrate wiry stems and a further mulch is advisable in autumn.

Propagation. By careful division with roots attached and placing these in a cool shady frame until established, or seed sown in March.

S. macrophyllus, see *S. soldanelloides* var. *magnus*

S. soldanelloides (E)
This is a small procumbent tufted herb rarely above 5 cm. high and 38 cm. across with thin wiry stems. Leaves coriaceous, crowded in tufts, orbicular to cordate, unevenly dentate, bright green above, paler beneath, turning to red and bronze in autumn. Flowers up to four in a raceme on a short stem and almost erect pedicels, open campanulate, margins deeply fringed, rich rose. April to May. A native of Japan.

S. soldanelloides var. *alpinus* (E)
A smaller variety rarely above 2 cm. high and about 20 cm. across with proportionate stems and leaves. Flowers large, almost pendant in terminal clusters, campanulate open fringed bells, deep rose. May. A native of Japan.

S. soldanelloides var. *ilicifolius* (E)
This is a rare Japanese variety, making a dwarf prostrate mat only 2 cm. or so high and about 15 cm. wide with short slender stems. Leaves crowded, cordate, deeply cut, teeth irregular, dark glossy green above, paler below. Flowers congested on a 10 cm. scape, pendant, campanulate, fringed, deep pink in colour. May.

S. soldanelloides var. *ilicifolius albus* (E)
A rare, extremely dainty, white variety which is worthy of every attention if obtainable. May. A native of Japan.

S. soldanelloides var. *magnus* (E). (Syn. *S. macrophyllus*)
A prostrate herb which until recently had specific rank but is now regarded as only a large variety. It is up to 5 cm. high and 23 cm. wide with thin wiry stems, increasing by runners when satisfied. Leaves in tufts, large, cordate, unevenly serrated, dark glossy green above, paler below, veining pronounced, reticulate. The leaves turn to delightful shades of red and bronze with exposure. Flowers congested on 2 cm. erect stems, pendant, campanulate, deeply fringed, rich pink. A native of Japan.

SENECIO (*Compositae*)

This genus of plants is one of the largest in the world with a wide distribution over many parts of the globe. The Groundsels are in the main weeds or plants of poor merit but there are two which can be admitted to the small garden.

Cultivation. They require a light well-drained soil in sun or at most half shade and present very few cultural problems.

Propagation. By green cuttings in May or seed sown when ripe.

S. abrotanifolius (E)

This is a prostrate sub-shrub up to 23 cm. high and a spread of 45 cm. with radiating, horizontal, light green, smooth rounded branches. Leaves alternate, crowded, arranged in whorls on the last few centimetres of the branches; five parts each segment with protruding teeth, thick fleshy, pointed, margins recurved, petiole appressed and furnished with up to six fine pointed teeth; deep glossy green. Flowers on 15 cm. stems, arranged in groups of two or three ray florets, deep orange-red with fiery orange disks. June. A native of S. and E. Europe.

S. adonidifolius (E)

Makes a more or less erect shrub up to 30 cm. high and as much through with simple, rounded, glabrous stems. Leaves pinnatisect, petiolate, segments linear, acute, dark green. Flowers in compound corymb on 30 cm. stems, ray florets bright orange deeper disks. July. A native of S. France and Spain.

SHORTIA (*Diapensiaceae*)

A small genus of perennial herbs closely related to *Schizocodon* and having much in common, but whereas the latter is confined to Japan, *Shortia* has one species there and another native to North Carolina.

Cultivation. A well-drained medium with a high humus content in the form of leaf-mould or peat; amongst other choice ericaceous plants in half shade is necessary in the southern half of the country. A more open and less shady position can be given in the cooler and more humid counties. Protection from cold east winds is desirable and avoid planting in a frost trap for although indestructibly hardy they resent dry winds and late spring frosts once active growth has begun. Topdress in late autumn and early spring with a mulch of well rotted leaf-mould.

Propagation. By careful division in late March, planting the divisions in a cool shady frame until re-established. Seed if available in March.

S. galacifolia (E)

A native of N. Carolina, this makes a congested mat of wiry slender stems, rarely above 10 cm. high and a spread of 30 cm. Leaves tufted on short stems, rounded to cordate, dentate, heavily veined, wavy, deep shiny green above, lighter beneath turning to shades of crimson in late autumn. Flowers solitary on 8 cm. stems, broad tubular, five to six lobed, joined near base, margins deeply crenate, white. April.

S. 'Intertexta' (E)

A garden hybrid between *S. galacifolia* and *S. uniflora* 'Grandiflora', this is intermediate between the two species with the foliage and habit of the former and large pale pink lightly fringed flowers. April.

S. uniflora (E)

A native of Japan, it is a prostrate plant, rarely above 2 cm. high and a spread of 30 cm. with tight widely spaced congested tufts. Leaves rounded on long petioles with facing groove; margined with irregular blunt serrations, more pronounced at apex, recurved at base, veins reticulated and outstanding, bright glossy green above, paler beneath, both petiole and leaf turning a brilliant red in autumn. Flowers solitary on short scapes, large open campanulate, five to six lobes, joined at base, margins deeply serrated, bright pink, stamens white. April.

S. uniflora 'Alba' (E)

This is a rare white form, with outstanding flowers of a crystalline texture. April.

S. uniflora 'Grandiflora' (E)

A fine form which is much larger in all its parts, more tufted and compact with typical foliage and flowers in proportion. April. A native of Japan.

S. uniflora 'Rosea' (E)

Another outstanding variety with similar habits but deep rose-pink flowers in early spring. This plant is often in flower at the end of February in sheltered gardens. A native of Japan.

SKIMMIA (Rutaceae)

A small genus of slow-growing shrubs, there is one species that is suitable with delightful fragrant flowers, followed by outstanding coloured fruits which are retained throughout the winter.

Cultivation. A position in half shade in a humus enriched soil is suitable; not at their best on shallow chalky soils.

Propagation. This is by cuttings taken in June, seed for the species which will often self sow, and layering.

S. reevesiana (E)

A native of China, this is a small roundish compact shrub, less than 60 cm. high with narrow, oval, bright green leaves. Flowers in terminal panicles, white, intensely fragrant. Fruit large, crimson, persistent. This species is bi-sexual, so that individual plants can be grown which will flower and fruit well.

SORBUS (Rosaceae)

A genus of trees and shrubs allied to *Pyrus*, with a wide distribution over Europe, N. America and N. Asia, the Mountain Ash has provided us with one dwarf species which is suitable for the small garden.

Cultivation. A good open light soil in full sun suits this species and is not particular as to its position in the small garden.

Propagation. By detaching the rooted runners thrown out by this plant and potting them up in early June; keep them close until re-established. Seed in March.

S. reducta (D)

Of recent introduction from W. China and N. Burma, making a dwarf slow growing shrub but spreading freely by suckers up to 30 cm. high and 45 cm. across in time with smooth reddish grey, stout, semi-erect branches, laterals having a few bristles. Leaves alternate, pinnate, leaflets sessile, nine to thirteen, narrow ovate, tapered to apex, coarsely serrate, serrations ending in a mucronate tip, deep glossy green above

164

Skimmia reevesiana

with a few appressed white hairs, veining reticulate. Flowers in terminal clusters small five petalled, white, slightly downy on inner surface. April to May. Berries globose, crimson. Foliage has a good autumn colouring.

SPIRAEA (*Rosaceae*)

A large and varied genus of plants containing about eighty species, with tall herbaceous perennials and shrubs of which there are a few that make good plants for the small garden. The genus has a wide geographical distribution over the northern hemisphere and this has helped to make the nomenclature rather involved.

Cultivation. Any good well-drained, open medium in full sun will suit these plants, at the same time ample moisture is essential for their well being. The very dwarf species are best planted in a sunny raised scree bed.

Propagation. By division in March, suckers which can be removed with roots attached, or by rooting detached rosettes in early June in the propagating frame.

S. bullata (D). (Syn. *S. crispifolia*)

A tight congested ball of erect stiff branches rarely up to 30 cm. high and as much across with reddish brown stems, due to intense covering of hairs. Leaves crowded, wide ovate, almost orbicular, dentate, margins recurved, dull deep green. Flowers in profusion, wide flattish corymbs from the apex of the current year's growth, rose. July. A native of Japan. Now considered to be a form of *S. japonica*.

S. bullata 'Nana' (D)
A dwarf form only 15 cm. high and across with rich deep rose flowers in July.

S. caespitosa, see *Petrophytum caespitosum*
S. crispifolia, see *S. bullata*
S. decumbens (D). (Syn *S. procumbens*)
A native of the Austrian Tyrol, it makes a small prostrate shrublet with slender branches, open and lax, rarely above 15 cm. high and 30 cm. across. Leaves oval, tapering to apex, serrate on upper third, dull mid-green. Flowers, small in tight corymbs on erect wiry stems, white. July.
S. hendersonii, see *Petrophytum hendersonii*
S. japonica 'Bumalda' (D)
The type plant is too large for the small garden but it has produced one or two smaller forms that are suitable, although this form is doubtfully named as it is only considered to be of hybrid parentage. It makes a bushy plant about 30 cm. high and as much across with erect stems.

Spiraea bullata 'Nana'

Leaves lanceolate to ovate-oblong, dentate, glabrous, glaucous below. Flowers from terminal axils in flat corymbs, crowded, small, carmine. June to July.

S. japonica 'Bumalda Nana' (D)
This form is only about 10 cm. high and 20 cm. across of semi-erect stems, oval, acute, light green leaves, dentate. Flowers in a close corymb, bright rose. June to July.

S. japonica 'Bumalda Nyewoods' var. (D)
An even smaller form about 8 cm. high, narrow oval leaves on semi-erect stems and congested clusters of cherry-red flowers. June to July.

S. procumbens, see *S. decumbens*

SYRINGA (Oleaceae)
It is with great diffidence that I have included the following two species for the small garden, for both of these lilacs will in course of time outgrow their allotted space, although in their favour it must be stated that it will take a number of years before this happens. They can be kept to a reasonable size for quite a period by planting them in their pots in the garden, as this method will help to restrict growth. Both are extremely floriferous, and to flower in six months from a rooted cutting is not unknown, and a shapely plant can be built up in a matter of two years or so.

Cultivation. Any good, open, well drained but not too rich soil is suitable for these plants, but care must be taken as to where these species are planted for their removal will become imperative after a period of approximately ten years when the specimens have filled their allotted space.

Propagation. Green cuttings taken in June and rooted in the propagating frame.

S. microphylla (D)
A small shrub with slender, downy, greenish shoots eventually 2 m. in height and 60 cm. across. Leaves ovate to orbicular, 1 to 3 cm. in length, 1 to 1½ cm. in width, dark green above, greyish green beneath with a light covering of down on both sides, margins ciliate. Flowers on 8 cm. panicles, fragrant, narrow, tubular with four wide open, round ended lobes, bright lilac in colour. May. A native of N. and W. China.

S. palibiniana, see *S. velutina*
S. velutina (Syn. *S. palibiniana*). (D)
This is an erect, much branched shrub growing up to 3 m. in time and 1 m. across, with smooth, rarely downy shoots, reddish purple in the juvenile state. Leaves oval to lanceolate, 3 to 5 cm. long, 1 to 1½ cm. wide, pointed, tapered to base, dull dark green, glabrous, lighter and downy below. Flowers in pairs in terminal panicles up to 10 cm. long, sparsely set with tubular, very narrow four roundish lobes, deep lilac outside, white within, fragrant. May. A native of Korea.

TEUCRIUM (Labiatae)
This is a large genus of mostly shrubby or semi-shrubby plants some being quite aromatic and although not showy, except in a quiet way, they have a charm of their own and flowering in late summer help to prolong the floral display. All are natives of the temperate and warmer climates but the species noted here are reasonably hardy except in the coldest of gardens.

Cultivation. Any good, open, light rich soil in full sun will suit these species, but they should not be planted in a frost trap.

Propagation. Is by green cuttings taken in July or seed in March.

T. ackermanni (E)

A native of Asia Minor, it is a sub-shrubby plant up to 10 cm. high and about 20 cm. wide, forming a close compact clump. Leaves narrow, oval to wide linear, grey-green. Flowers in a terminal cluster, two lipped of light plum-purple. July.

T. chamaedrys (E)

A small semi-prostrate sub-shrub up to 23 cm. high and 30 cm. across with slender stems, densely covered with down. Leaves opposite, oval to ovate, deeply toothed, petiole winged, light mid-green, covered with fine hairs. Flowers in whorls from the leaf axils up to six long tubular, two lipped, five lobed, calyx purplish red, lips bright rose. July to August. A native of S. Europe.

T. marum (E)

The Cat Thyme is a sub-shrub up to 15 cm. high and with a spread of 20 cm. Leaves oval to lanceolate, green, hairy, covered with a white woolly tomentum below, petiole small. Flowers from the upper leaf axils in pairs, tubular two lipped, basal lobes rounded, bright red. July to August.

T. montanum (E)

This makes a small tufted procumbent sub-shrub rarely above 5 cm. high and a spread of 15 cm. with hairy semi-erect, thin slender branches. Leaves opposite, crowded on stem, linear, tapered to base and apex, mid-green, slightly downy, silver-grey below due to the thick downy covering. Flowers in congested terminal clusters, tubular two lipped, five lobed calyx, yellow, upper lip has reddish streaks. July to August. A native of S. Europe.

T. pyrenaicum (E)

This is a small semi-prostrate shrublet up to 5 cm. high and 20 cm. wide, with slender wiry, hairy branches. Leaves crowded, opposite, small, long narrow rounded, scalloped, covered with hairs on both sides, bright green above, lighter beneath. Flowers crowded in terminal clusters, tubular, two lipped, cream coloured calyx; five lobed, soft lilac corolla. July to August. A native of S.E. Europe.

T. pyrenaicum 'Roseum' (E)

A native of Spain, this variety differs from the type in that the lips are tinged purple. July to August.

T. sandrasicum (E)

A native of Turkey, it makes a densely branched dwarf sub-shrub about 23 cm. high and 30 cm. across. Leaves entire, small, linear, grey-green above, white beneath, densely covered with soft hairs. Flowers in small cymes from the leaf axils, lavender-blue. June.

T. subspinosum (E)

This is a small woody shrub, or rather, shrublet with congested branches up to 30 cm. high and as much across, very twiggy, often ending in a silver-grey spine. Leaves congested, fleshy, opposite, small, linear, rounded at base, tapered to apex, dark glossy green above, silver-grey beneath, margins decurved. The whole sparsely furnished with bristly hairs, twice the length of the foliage. Flowers in terminal clusters, two lipped, pale lilac; five narrow calyx lobes of a deeper hue. July to August. A native of S. Europe.

THYMUS (Labiatae)
A large genus of plants containing about one hundred species mostly shrubs or sub-shrubs, natives of the temperate zone of the Old World. There are a number which make fine specimens in the garden and all have the added attraction of being aromatic.

Cultivation. For the easy species and varieties any light well-drained soil is suitable and a sunny place should be chosen for they are avid sun lovers and rarely get enough in this country. The few temperamental species are best in a loose, sunny raised scree bed where the drainage is perfect, they will rarely be successful in cold gardens. All appreciate a topdressing well worked in among the prostrate stems in early spring, consisting of equal parts of leaf-mould, loam and coarse sand.

Propagation. Despatch rooted runners, or green cuttings in early June, and root these in the propagating frame.

T. caespititius (E)
This forms a prostrate mat of interwoven, lax, woody stems less than 5 cm. high and a spread of 38 cm. Leaves opposite, crowded in tufts, linear, margins covered with grey hairs, grey-green. Flowers on 2 cm. erect hairy stems from the leaf axils, light lilac-blue. July. A native of S.E. Europe.

T. carnosus (E)
A native of Portugal, it is an erect small shrub about 15 cm. high and as much across with firm, hairy almost parallel branches. Leaves in tiers, clustered at the nodes, small, thick, elliptic, sessile, margins revolute, sparsely covered with hairs. Flowers in hemispherical heads of pink. June.

T. cilicicus (E)
A recently introduced species from Asia Minor, making a close upright much branched shrub about 10 cm. high and 20 cm. wide of erect hairy four angled branches. Leaves sessile, linear, hard, bristly, veined, grey-green, margins ciliate, downy below. Flowers in globular heads, surrounded by small hairy green bracts, pale mauve. June.

T. comosus. (E). (Syn *T. transsilvanicus*)
This species forms a procumbent straggly shrublet up to 10 cm. high and about 20 cm. across of hairy branches with a strong smell of turpentine. Leaves wide ovate, obtuse, base orbicular on long petioles, grey-green, hairy with thick marginal veins. Flowers in open globular heads with roundish bracts and light purple flowers. June. A native of E. Europe.

T. herba-barona (E)
A dwarf, often procumbent, woody sub-shrub only a few centimetres high but has a spread of 45 cm. very aromatic, reminiscent of caraway seeds. Stems sprawling, thick, clothed with fine hairs. Leaves small lanceolate, mid-green, glabrous above, hairy beneath, ciliate, petiole small. Flowers in loose globular heads, deep pink. June. A native of Corsica. Rather tender.

T. longiflorus (E). (Syn. *T. moroderi*)
A fine small rare Thyme, recently introduced from Spain. It is aromatic and forms a shrubby bush up to 23 cm. high and wide with erect, crowded twiggy woody, finely downy branches. Leaves borne near the apex of the branches and laterals, small, opposite, linear, tapered to apex, mid-green, greyish green beneath, covered with a fine down, margins revolute. Flowers in terminal clusters, from purple,

Thymus membranaceus

ovate, veined bracts; tubular, labiate, lilac-purple with a white lip.
July. Requires care in cultivation and demands full sun for it to
succeed.

T. membranaceus (E)
An upright rounded aromatic bushlet rarely above 20 cm. high and a
spread of 30 cm. with erect wiry branches, very twiggy, brown,
glabrous. Leaves crowded, small, stiff, linear, rounded at base, tapered
to apex, obtuse, greyish green, lighter below, margins recurved.
Flowers on short leafy stems in terminal clusters, white, narrow,
tubular, two lipped, arising from large pink flushed papery bracts.
June. Spain. Sunshine is essential for this species to produce a good
crop of flowers.

T. membranaceus var. *murcicus* (E). (Syn. *T. murcicus*)
A small compact aromatic, much branched shrublet up to 23 cm. high.
Leaves crowded, rhomboid-ovate, pointed, grey-green. Flowers long
narrow tubular, white from large white papery bracts which are more
attractive than the actual flowers. July. Spain. Requires same conditions as the species.

T. moroderi, see *T. longiflorus*
T. murcicus, see *T. membranaceus* var. *murcicus*

170

T. richardii var. *nitidus* (E)
A small shrublet with lax, wiry stems up to 15 cm. high and a spread of 30 cm. and ascending hairy laterals. Leaves thick, small ovate-rhomboid, deep glossy green, lighter below, margins ciliate. Flowers in loose terminal clusters, two lipped, lower broad, three roundish lobes, lilac-pink, backed by ovate bracts. June-July. A native of Marettimo near Sicily. Only suitable for really warm gardens.

T. serpyllum (E)
The wild thyme has a wide distribution over Europe including Britain and is a well known plant which has produced a great number of varieties and forms suitable as cover for bulbs. It makes a creeping, rambling, woody plant of interwoven hairy stems, only 2 cm. high and a spread of 45 cm. Leaves small, narrow elliptic to ovate-obtuse, glabrous, margins ciliate towards the short petiole, glossy green. Flowers in a hemispherical cluster, bracts obovate, purple hairy calyx and two lipped purple corolla. June to July.

T. serpyllum 'Albus' (E)
This form has brighter green glossy leaves and heads of pure white flowers. June to July. A native of Europe.

T. serpyllum 'Annie Hall' (E)
A form which originated in the wild, has smaller foliage and bright colourful heads of clear pink. June to July. A native of Europe.

T. serpyllum ''Aureus' (E)
This has foliage of green which turns gold in winter and deep lilac flowers. June to July. A native of Europe.

T. serpyllum 'Citriodorus' (E)
A garden form about 15 cm. high with lemon scented foliage and lilac flowers. June to July.

T. serpyllum 'Citriodorus Argenteus' (E)
This is similar but with variegated green and white leaves.

T. serpyllum 'Citriodorus Aureus' (E)
Another lemon scented form with green variegated gold foliage.

T. serpyllum 'Carmineus' (E)
A colour form with carmine flowers. July to August. A native of Europe.

T. serpyllum 'Coccineus' (E)
This form has bright crimson flowers. June to July. A native of Europe.

T. serpyllum 'Lanuginosus' (E)
A form with grey leaves covered with a woolly tomentum topped with lilac flowers. June to July. A native of Europe.

T. serpyllum 'Lanuginosus Floribundus' (E)
A charming form with silver-grey foliage and flowers of deep lilac, purple in bud. June to July.

T. serpyllum 'Major' (E)
This is a more lax form up to 8 cm. high with green leaves and larger flowers of a bright crimson. June to July. A native of Europe.

T. serpyllum 'Minor' (E)
A very small form less than 2 cm. in height with minute green leaves and countless flower heads of bright lilac. June to July. A native of Europe.

T. serpyllum 'Nummularius' (E)
This form is up to 15 cm. high and a spread of 45 cm. more open with grey-green scented foliage and large sprays of rose-lilac flowers, later

than some of the other forms. July to September. A native of Europe.

T. serpyllum 'Pink Chintz' (E)
A garden form with large rich rose flowers. June to July.

T. serpyllum 'Silver Queen' (E)
A garden form about 2 cm. high with small variegated leaves of silver and green and bright lilac flowers. June to July.

T. transsilvanisus, see *T. comosus*

T. villosus (E)
This makes a small conical shrublet with upright branches about 10 cm. high and 30 cm. wide, densely clothed with minute hairs. Leaves clustered at internodes formed along the shoots, linear, sessile, grey-green, margins revolute, covered with long white hairs. Flowers in globular heads, deep rose emerging from green bracts. July. A native of Portugal.

TSUSIOPHYLLUM (Ericaceae)
A rare dwarf monotypic shrublet from Japan, the country of many fine and beautiful plants. It is unfortunately not too easy of culture here, requiring skilful care to grow successfully.
Cultivation. A cool spot among dwarf ericaceous plants, sheltered from cold parching winds is suitable, in a position facing west so that the foliage is protected from the early morning sun. A topdressing of 5 cm. of well rotted leaf-mould should be applied in late spring.
Propagation. By cutting of half ripened wood in July.

T. tanakae (E)
It forms a semi-erect shrublet, much branched, about 30 cm. high and 23 cm. across, the juvenile wood covered with appressed hairs. Leaves alternate, small oval to oblanceolate, covered with fine flat hairs, grey-green, margins slightly recurved. Flowers small, in pairs, rarely in threes, below a terminal rosette of leaves, tubular, five rounded open lobes, wiry, white. June.

TUBERARIA (Cistaceae)
A small genus of plants of which there is one suitable for the small garden and this until recently was included in *Helianthemum*.
Cultivation. A warm moist but well-drained spot is suitable and a rich soil should be avoided.
Propagation. By seed sown in March.

T. lignosa (E). (Syn. *Helianthemum tuberaria*)
A small prostrate plant with much branched decumbent stems spreading over an area of 20 cm. square, and when in flower about 15 cm. high. Leaves plantain like in rosettes, oblong-ovate, obtuse, wedge shaped to base, three nerved, shiny green, white below with a dense covering of down, petiolate. Flowers on a 15 cm. slender scape in a three to seven terminal cluster, clear yellow. June to July. A native of S. Europe.

VACCINIUM (Ericaceae)
A large genus of shrubs containing over 130 species, natives of most parts of the northern hemisphere including Britain, but more prominent in the New World where there is abundant material to choose from. Some of these species are suitable for the rock or small garden, providing a quiet but attractive display of flowers in spring, followed

172

later by beautiful fruits and in many instances a glorious display of autumn tints from the foliage.

Cultivation. The Cranberries, like their cousins the Heaths, are found in nature on open pastures of the hills and moorlands, but in captivity, at least in the southern part of the country, a modicum of shade is necessary for their well being. In northern and Scottish counties, where there are moister atmospheric conditions, these plants desire more sun and a good selection can be seen in this position in the Royal Botanic Gardens, Edinburgh. Coupled with sun or half shade, according to where these species are being grown, moisture is essential. This must be constant during the growing and flowering season, but once the new wood has begun to harden, drought holds no fears.

For general purposes a good light lime-free loam, well enriched with humus in the form of peat or leaf-mould, in a cool airy spot is ideal. Topdress with leaf-mould in early spring to a depth of 5 cm. working this well down among the branches. A further similar mulch should be applied in late autumn. A watch should be kept for strong vigorous suckers which often spring from the rootstock just below the surface of the soil. These should be pinched back when young to retain a dwarf symmetrical plant.

Propagation. By seed sown in March, or half ripened cuttings taken in July and rooted in the propagating frame.

V. brachycerum, see *Gaylussacia brachycera*

V. caespitosum (D)
A native of N. America, it is a small shrublet making tufts rarely above 15 cm. high and 60 cm. across with smooth, rounded, sometimes hairy branches. Leaves alternate, obovate, tapered to base, bright glossy green, margins dentate. Flowers solitary from the leaf axils on decurved, slender pedicels, urn-shaped, five semi-pointed lobes, pale rose-pink. May. Berries black with a silvery blue bloom.

V. caespitosum 'Major' (D)
This form is similar to the type but more erect, up to 30 cm. high with larger flowers and fruit. May.

V. canadense, see *V. myrtilloides*

V. delavayi (E)
A shrub up to 60 cm. in time and as much through but taking a long time to reach this stature. If forms a close compact, semi-erect plant increasing by suckers, branches slim, sturdy, brown with a thin covering of hairs. Leaves alternate, thick, crowded, oval to ovate, slightly tapering to base with a small petiole, notched at apex, bright glossy green, paler below, margins decurved. Flowers in terminal and axillary racemes on bristly pedicels, urn shaped, lobes five pointed, white, flushed pale pink. May. Berries globular, black with a grey bloom. A well flowered specimen of this was given an Award of Merit at Chelsea in 1951, after I had received a Cultural Commendation the previous year. A native of Yunnan, China.

V. deliciosum (D)
A dwarf tufted shrublet about 23 cm. high and 45 cm. across with rounded glabrous stems. Leaves opposite, thick, obovate, pointed at apex, tapered to base, slightly crenate, bright green, glaucous below. Flowers pendant from the leaf axils, solitary, roundish urn shaped, five lobed, pink. Berries black with a grey bloom. A native of the Olympic Mountains, N.W. America.

V. fragile (E) (Syn. *V. setosum*)
This makes a small shrub less than 45 cm. high and a spread of 60 cm. with rounded branches, densely clothed with reddish brown bristles. Leaves alternate, oval to ovate, tapering to base and apex, acute, margins serrulate, glabrous bright green, covered with down below. Flowers in crowded pubescent racemes from the terminal leaf axils with red bracts, corolla urn shaped, five pointed, reflexed lobes, rose-pink. May. Berries globular, black. A native of W. China.
V. hirtellum, see *Gaylussacia dumosa*
V. modestum (E)
A native of W. Yunnan, this makes a dwarf shrublet less than 15 cm. high and a spread of 30 cm. with slender procumbent stems and ascending laterals. Leaves at apex of shoots, ovate to obovate, tapered to base, smooth glossy green, glaucous below. Flowers solitary from terminal leaf axils, flattish roundish, five reflexed lobes, deep rose. Fruit globose, glaucous violet. May.
V. moupinense (E)
A small compact shrublet, eventually reaching 45 cm. high and a spread of 60 cm. with congested, woolly, grooved branches. Leaves crowded, alternate, entire, obovate to oval, apex obtuse, tapered to base, deep glossy green. Flowers in terminal axillary racemes, crowded, pendulous on bright reddish pedicels, urn shaped, five narrow, tooth like lobes, reddish brown. May. Berries globular, deep purple. A native of W. Szechwan, China.
V. myrsinites (E). (Syn. *V. nitidum*)
A small prostrate plant spreading by suckers, rarely above 30 cm. high and up to 60 cm. across with slender, angled, hairy branches. Leaves alternate, oval, pointed at apex, tapered to base, margins minutely dentate, smooth, deep green, paler beneath with deeply marked veins, bristly. Flowers in small terminal clusters, pitcher shaped, five tooth like lobes, white flushed pink. May. Berries globular, black with grey bloom. A native of the S.E. United States.
V. myrtilloides (D). (Syn. *V. canadense*)
This forms a procumbent, twiggy, bristly shrublet up to 30 cm. high and 60 cm. wide. Leaves alternate, entire, long, oval, tapered to base and apex, mid green, covered with fine hairs on both sides. Flowers in small axillary clusters, five lobed, bell shaped, white tinged rose. May. Berries deep bluish black. A native of Eastern N. America.
V. myrtilloides var. *leucocarpum* (E)
This variety is similar to the type but with white berries.
V. myrtilloides var. *microphyllum* (E)
A dwarf edition of the species, smaller in all its parts scarcely above 15 cm. in height, with flowers and fruit as in the species. A native of western N. America.
V. nitidum, see *V. myrsinites*
V. nummularia (E)
An outstanding dwarf shrub which may need protection in cold bleak gardens. It makes a compact much branched plant, spreading by runners over 60 cm. across and rather less than 45 cm. high when mature. Branches stout, erect, reddish brown, densely clothed with stiff brown bristles. Leaves alternate, thick, leathery, orbicular with pronounced net veining on upper surface, margins ciliate, petiole small; dull mid green, glaucous below. Flowers in terminal and axillary

crowded racemes, narrow, pitcher shaped, five lobed, pinkish. May. Fruit a black round berry. A native of N. India.

V. praestans (D)

A small procumbent shrublet less than 10 cm. high and a spread of 38 cm. with solitary stems from a creeping rootstock. Leaves alternate, obovate, rounded at apex with a small spine, tapered to base, minutely serrulate, glabrous mid green, slightly hairy below. Brilliant autumn coloration of the foliage. Flowers solitary or rarely a small cluster on short pedicels, each having two narrow leaf bracts, bell shaped, five erect lobes, white flushed pink. June. Berries globular, bright red. A native of Japan.

V. retusum (E)

A small dwarf shrub rarely above 23 cm. high and a spread of 45 cm. with semi-erect downy shoots. Leaves thick, entire, obovate, obtuse, notched at apex, tapered to base, margins recurved, glabrous bright green. Flowers generally solitary from the terminal shoots, rounded, urn shaped, five lobed, white striped red. May. Fruits not seen. A rare and far from easy species which so far does not tend to flower freely even under protected conditions. A native of the Himalayas.

V. setosum, see *V. fragile*

V. vitis-idaea (E)

A small shrub up to 23 cm. high and a spread of 60 cm. with procumbent wiry stems, clothed with minute black hairs. Leaves alternate, small, ovate, notched at apex, deep bright green above, paler beneath with a few black dots. Flowers in dense terminal racemes, bell shaped, well-marked four lobed, white flushed pink. May. Berries rounded, deep red. A native of America, Asia and Britain.

V. vitis-idaea var. *minus* (E)

This is a much smaller edition of the species, only a few centimetres high, but with just as large clusters of pink flowers and globose deep red berries. May. A native of N. America.

VERBASCUM (Scrophulariaceae)

A genus containing over 300 species of plants of which the majority are far and away too large for the small garden, but there are a few that can be used and these make ideal plants.

Cultivation. A hot, dry spot in the garden should be chosen where the soil is light, open and well drained, or a position in a sunny raised scree is suitable.

Propagation. Is by seed sown in February, or cuttings taken with a heel in May and rooted in the propagating frame.

V. dumulosum (E)

A small sub-shrubby species from S.W. Anatolia, making an erect plant up to 30 cm. high and about 20 cm. across. Leaves in whorls, dense, arranged the whole length of the stems, ovate, tapering to a thick, appressed petiole, greyish white in colour due to the intense covering of wool. Flowers in small terminal racemes of up to twelve, open saucer shaped, bright yellow with deep basal crimson blotch, stamens completely surrounded with violet wool. May to June.

V. 'Letitia' (E)

A hybrid between *V. dumulosum* and *V. spinosum*, making a crowded woody sub-shrub about 20 cm. high and 30 cm. wide Leaves in rosettes, lanceolate with small lobes narrowed to a small petiole, blue-

175

grey, covered with a fine woolly down. Flowers in large racemes at apex of stems, open saucer shaped, bright yellow, brown at base, anthers orange. May to July. Originated in the R.H.S. Gardens at Wisley.
V. pestalozzae (E)
A much smaller and more compact species about 23 cm. high and 20 cm. wide with dense woolly stems. Leaves crowded in whorls, ovate to narrow oval, tapered to base and short petiole, not so appressed as in *V. dumulosum*; apex obtuse, sometimes acute, coarse irregular minute marginal serrations, greyish white due to intense covering of wool. Midrib pronounced on underside, veining reticulate. Flowers in small terminal racemes on woolly 23 cm. stems, sparsely clad with the typical foliage, open saucer shaped, clear yellow, stamens covered with orange wool. May. A native of Asia Minor.
V. spinosum (E)
This forms a compact globular mass of congested branches and spines, silver-grey in colour, up to 30 cm. high and as much across. Leaves oblong to narrow oblanceolate, covered with a grey tomentum. Flowers small, solitary from the leaf axils in a much branched panicle, open saucer shaped, yellow with orange filaments. August. Endemic to Crete. Requires a sheltered sunny spot in a well-drained scree.

VINCA (Apocynaceae)
A small genus of plants, the Periwinkle provides species and a number of varieties useful in filling bare patches in the small garden, normally where little else will grow, either in shade or full sun, the latter position for preference and a more generous display of flowers.
Cultivation. A good, sandy, well-drained loam in either sun or semi-shade where the species and varieties will quickly become acclimatised. A topdressing of equal parts of leaf-mould, loam and sand worked in amongst the trailing stems in early spring will be appreciated. All old growth should be cut back at the same time.
Propagation. Is by rooted runners, as the species root where the tips of the shoots come into contact with the soil. These should be severed from the parent plant in early June, lifted and placed in a cool frame until established.
V. minor (E)
A small compact mat of wiry smooth branches, up to 15 cm. high and 60 cm. across with small erect flowering stems. Leaves opposite, entire, elliptic-ovate, tapered to a rounded base, and apex, petiole small, deep shiny green on both sides. Flowers solitary on short slender pedicels from the leaf axils, bright blue, open campanulate, five lobed. May to September. A native of Europe and Asia Minor.
V. minor 'Alba' (E)
This is a charming white form which acts as a good foil to the type. May to September.
V. minor 'Alboplena' (E)
A double white flowered garden form. May to September.
V. minor 'Argenteo-Variegata' (E)
This form has leaves of white and green and pale blue flowers. May to September.
V. minor 'Atropurpurea' (E)
A garden form with large flowers of deep purple. May to September.
V. minor 'Bowles Var' (E)

A good form of garden origin with smaller habit and large blue-purple flowers. June to September.
V. minor 'Elizabeth Cran' (E)
Another garden form with large purple flowers. June to September.
V. minor 'La Grave' (E)
A form with outstanding large lavender-blue flowers. June to September.
V. minor 'Multiplex' (E)
This has large double purple flowers. May to September.
V. minor 'Punicea' (E)
A garden form with flowers of a deep red-purple. May to September.
V. minor 'Roseoplena' (E)
Another form with double flowers of a good red-purple. May to September.
V. minor 'Variegata' (E)
Similar to the type but with variegated leaves of yellow and green, flowers light lavender-blue. May to September.

ZAUSCHNERIA (Onagraceae)
A small genus of plants, containing about four species of sub-shrubs, natives of Western N. America of which there are two species and one variety suitable for the small garden. Flowering as they do in the late summer and early autumn they do much to provide a late display of vivid coloration at a normally dull period of the year.
Cultivation. All require a hot dry position in full sun in a light well-drained soil and they need ample room, to accommodate them with their spreading habit.
Propagation. This is by green cuttings taken in June.
Z. californica (D)
This is the 'Californian Fuchsia' a bushy sub-shrub up to 30 cm. high and a spread of 45 cm. Leaves sessile, dense, linear-lanceolate, sometimes obscurely dentate, hairy, grey-green. Flowers in loose spikes from the upper leaf axils of the stems, erect, funnel shaped with inflated calyx, then four spreading lobes, notched at apex and eight exserted stamens, scarlet. September to October. A native of California and Mexico.
Z. californica var. *angustifolia* (D)
This variant is more compact and with smaller narrower leaves having an intense covering of grey hairs. Flowers similar to the type. September to October.
Z. cana (Syn. *Z. microphylla*) (D)
A larger species up to 38 cm. high and a spread of 45 cm. with long woody stems. Leaves very narrow linear, crowded, sessile, silver-grey. Flowers in a loose raceme from the upper leaf axils, similar to *Z. californica* but more brilliant in colour. September to October. A native of California.
Z. microphylla, see *Z. cana*.

Glossary of Botanical Terms

Acuminate, long pointed, generally applied to the extension of the midrib past the apex of the leaves.

Adventitious, generally applied to plants whose stems root where they come in contact with the soil.

Anther, the tip of the stamen bearing pollen.

Apex, the tip as applied to leaf, flower and stem.

Apical, end of an organ, terminal point.

Apiculate, having a point, leaves, petals.

Appressed, lying close to or flat for its whole length.

Awned, stiff or bristle like projection.

Axil, the angle formed by the junction of the leaf stalk and stem.

Berry, a fruit in which the seed is enclosed in a soft succulent mass.

Bifarious, arranged in two opposite rows.

Bifid, twice cleft, divided into two.

Binate, generally of a leaf, divided into two parts.

Bipinnatifid, twice cut in pinnate manner.

Biserrate, double toothed, each tooth divided again.

Biternate, in two clusters of three, generally leaves.

Bracteate, provided with bracts, often much-reduced leaf.

Bracts, modified leaves at the base of the flower.

Calyx, outer covering of the flower, outside the petals.

Campanulate, bell shaped.

Capitate, flowers growing in a head.

Cartilaginous, gristly, tough.

Cauline, belonging to the stem.

Ciliate, margined with hairs.

Cleistogamous, flowers which fertilise themselves without opening.

Concave, hollowed out, saucer like.

Connate, united in pairs at base.

Convex, domed with rounded surface, like an overturned saucer.

Cordate, heart shaped as base of a leaf.

Coriaceous, thick, leathery.

Corolla, the inner envelope of the flowers, the petals.

Corona, an appendage between the petals and stamens, for example the cup of the daffodil.

Corymb, A flat or slightly dome-shaped head of flowers, opening from the outside.

Corymbose, arranged in flattish heads, flowers.

Crenate, having a scalloped-toothed or notched edge generally leaves.

Crenulate, notched with roundish teeth.

Cuneate, wedge shaped, narrow to base.

Cyme, a flat or slightly dome-shaped head of flowers opening from the inside first.

Decurved, turned down.

Deltoid, broad triangular.

Dentate, with outward pointed teeth.

Denticulate, minutely toothed.

Dioecious, having male and female flowers on different plants.

Drupe, a fruit in which the seed is covered by a stone which in turn has an outer covering of a succulent nature.

Ebracteate, without bracts.

Elliptic, shaped like an ellipse, rounded at both ends, widest in the middle.

Emarginate, with a shallow notch at apex.

Endemic, native confined to one locality.

Ensiform, sword like, generally applied to leaves.

Erecto-patent, erect and standing away from stem; applied to leaves.

Exserted, protruding; stamens beyond corolla.

Fastigiate, with parallel erect branches.

Filiformis, slender, thread like.

Flabelliformis, fan shaped.

Glabrous, hairless, smooth.

Glandular, covered with hairs having glands at their tips.

Glaucous, covered with a white or greyish bloom.

Hastate, shaped like an arrowhead, basal lobes generally pointed widening abruptly.

Hirsute, rough, hairy.

Imbricated, covered with overlapping scales like tiles on roof.

Imparipinnate, feathered, but having the terminal section unequally so, generally of leaves.

Indumentum, the hairy substance which sometimes covers parts of the plant.

Involucre, a ring of bracts surrounding several flowers.

Labellum, lip, here specifically applied to the structure of one of the floral lobes of orchids.

Lamellae, in thin plates or scales.

Lanceolate, with lancet like leaves.

Linear, narrow with sides almost parallel.

Lingulate, with small tongues or tongue like membranes.

Median, central, having a middle channel, line etc.

Membranacous, thin, having the texture of membranes.

Monocarpic, dies after fruiting once.

Monoecious, having male and female flowers separate on the same plant.

Monotypic, a genus with only one species.

Mucronate, terminating with a straight, stiff, sharp point.

Mucronulate, with a diminutive sharp point.

Obconic, of conical form and attached at the point.

Obcordate, reversed heart shaped.

Obovoid, inversely solid egg shaped.

Oblong, longer than broad with almost parallel sides.

Obtuse, blunt.

Obovate, inversely ovate.

Ovate, wider below the middle, shaped like an egg.

Palmate, radiately lobed or divided, like shape of a hand.
Panicle, flowers in branching racemes.
Partite, cleft but not quite to base.
Pectinate, comb shaped.
Pedicel, the stalk supporting a solitary flower.
Peduncle, the stalk of a solitary flower or main stalk of a compound inflorescence.
Peltate, shield like, stalk joined well within the margin.
Pendulous, hanging down.
Perfoliate, having the stem as it were passing through a leaf.
Perianth, the floral envelope consisting of sepals, petals or both.
Petiolate, having a leaf stalk.
Petiole, the leaf stalk.
Pilose, covered with long soft hairs.
Pinnate, feathered, generally applied to leaves.
Pinnatisect, pinnately divided.
Plicate, folded into pleats.
Pruinose, having a waxy or powdery bloom.
Puberulous, somewhat downy.
Pubescent, covered with soft hair or down.
Raceme, a simple inflorescence, like a bunch of grapes.
Radically, in the form of a ray from a common axil.
Radical, rising from the root at or below soil level.
Recurved, bent down.
Reniform, kidney shape, generally of a leaf.
Reticulate, in the shape of a net, generally applied to the leaf veins.
Revolute, rolled back from margin or apex, generally of leaf.
Rhomboid, diamond shape, an equilateral oblique figure.
Rosulate, making small rosettes.
Rotate, wheel shaped, circular and flat.
Rugose, wrinkled.
Scapes, the flowering stem bearing one or more flowers.
Serrate, with saw like teeth.
Serrulate, toothed with minute teeth.
Sessile, without stalk or stem.
Simple, a leaf which is not compound.
Sinuate, with shallow broad waves to the margin.
Spadix, a spicate inflorescence with thick fleshy axis.
Spatulate, spoon shaped.
Spike, a long narrow, crowded head of stalkless flowers.
Stellate, minutely star shaped.
Stipules, small appendages to the base of the leaf stalk.
Stoloniferous, having suckers or runners.
Striated, notched with vertical grooves, generally of a distinctive colour.
Subulate, awl shaped.
Ternate, divided into threes.
Ternatisect, ternately divided.
Tetragonus, four sided.
Thryse, a crowded more or less cone shaped panicle.
Tomentum, dense covering of short soft hairs.
Triangularis, three angled or sided.
Tridentate, thrice toothed or pronged.

Trifid, with three parts, the division at least half way.
Triternate, divided into three.
Truncate, ending abruptly, as if cut off.
Umbel, having the flowers arranged in the form of an umbrella.
Whorl, flowers or foliage arranged in a circle round the stalk or branches.